Praise for *Generative Trance*

Generative Trance: The Experience of Creative Flow, Stephen Gilligan's newest book, is not only exciting to read, it gives new ways of looking at already-known information and adds whole new dimensions of different perspectives. Firmly built on his mentoring by Milton Erickson, Gilligan did what Erickson urged all his students to do - he took ideas from Erikson and made them applicable to new and different circumstances.

Beginning with understandable definitions, Gilligan lays out his own framework. The reader is captured with new ideas for hypnosis – an "up-dating", so to speak, of what hypnosis is. Generative trance is the "real" communication. It is not a place where the therapist provides answers and techniques for change, but where the client can have experiential learning, a reconfiguration of his own unconscious or forgotten resources. This, as evidenced by Erickson's work, is how lasting and sometimes remarkable and quick changes are achieved.

Under this umbrella of generative trance, he breaks his ideas into separate pieces. He discusses the familiar situation of a client "frozen" and seemingly unable to act, explaining how this is part of what he refers to as neuromuscular lock and literally takes apart what is happening. Then he provides clear methods of using generative trance, how client resources can be accessed and how different, more productive responses, can be learned and practiced. His approach is convincing, intriguing and eminently do-able.

His idea of centering is inclusive of what most people understand this term to mean. But typical of all of his writing, he uses words so precisely and carefully, that the reader stops to absorb his more expansive definition fully. Some of his phrases are immediately transferable to any therapeutic session – "you (can) feel both a part of and apart from an experience ... be with something without becoming it ...". He points out that when people learn to be centered, they can be vulnerable. Then with generative trance states, they can provide new and safe places within themselves and new learning and the transformation of dysfunctions can occur more easily.

Gilligan believes, as Erickson did, that people's realities and fixed meanings have to be broadened. A change in perspective allows people to respond differently; each person can create a different sense of self – a different "identity" – as all of us have done since childhood. Generative trance allows this easily and naturally.

He goes into detail with some of the ideas – for example, "Creative Acceptance" which red   Wir   curiosity about what

9

D1145583

something might be if it were accepted. This counter-intuitive idea – accept something to change it – is detailed in one of Erickson's cases – the girl with the gap between her two front teeth. Gilligan connects this to the first part of his book seamlessly.

Part of the book holds case examples in script form. This clarifies and demonstrates the uses of generative trance states. He gives explanations of what he was doing and even little, easy-for-all to do ideas, such as various phrases to insert in any hypnotic work –"trance is a learning place" and the words Erickson used so often, "trust your unconscious". Each script is primarily aimed at one of the points Gilligan has made earlier in the book, and the how – and why – is explained. Additionally, as he points out, shorter versions of the scripts are useful to all in everyday life – we all need to be able to become more centered, to be in touch with our bodies and relax comfortably while maintaining alertness.

One of the "bonuses" always present in Gilligan's writing is his use of meaningful, often beautifully poetic, quotations from a huge variety of sources to begin every chapter. And it's in this book too.

Generative Trance is an extraordinary book ... filled with different and new perspectives, captivating, and most important – valuable. My father would be so proud!

Betty Alice Erickson, M.S.

Steve Gilligan is the closest I've experienced to being with Milton Erickson since Erickson's death in 1980. His new book, *Generative Trance,* delivers a tour-de-force of the latest thinking of third-generation hypnosis in a charming and organized way. This is the definitive overview of a new approach in psychotherapy and change work. I continue to learn from Gilligan and look forward to returning to this book, again and again, to gain even deeper insights.

Bill O'Hanlon, author of *Taproots, An Uncommon Casebook, A Guide to Trance Land* and *Solution-Oriented Hypnosis*

Steve Gilligan says we are on a journey – a journey of infinite possibilities – but only if we are open and aware. Generative Trance is not another cognitive change process. It is about using trance to learn how to love and access the wisdom of your deeper mind, so that new awareness and choice can emerge. Whether you read this exceptional book for your personal development, or you facilitate others in theirs, you will discover that Generative Trance leads to a kind of sacred sight, after which your world will never look quite the same again. What a journey!

Penny Tompkins and James Lawley, authors of *Metaphors in Mind: Transformation through Symbolic Modelling*

There is a revolution taking place in psychotherapy that sheds the limitations of naïve models of therapy and change. Stephen Gilligan is one of the most important leaders in this transformation of practice, particularly as it applies to hypnosis. His "generative trance" marks a major advance in helping us resourcefully relate to all that clients and therapists bring to a session. We enthusiastically recommend it to both your conscious and unconscious mind!

Bradford Keeney, Ph.D. & Hillary Keeney, Ph.D., authors,
Circular Therapeutics: Giving Therapy a Healing Heart **and** *A Master Class in the Art of Performing Change*

This latest book by Steve Gilligan puts into practice the Ericksonian principles he has taught brilliantly for decades. He extends his self-relations model in several important ways, especially in the memorable sections on welcoming and weaving the identity parts into generative trance in order to allow new parts of the self to be born through generative transformation.

Though not a simple book, *Generative Trance* provides several easy-to-follow frameworks, including the four steps of generative trance and the five key generative methods presented in the book's second section. Specific scripts are offered to help the reader learn to vocalize hypnotic suggestions so that their receivers connect with positive intentions, with the five somatic dimensions of generative trance, and can explore and engage with generative fields where creative acceptance and transformation can take place.

If you want to learn deeply from a true hypnotic artist, do not miss this book!

Maggie Phillips, Ph.D.,
Co-author of *Healing the Divided Self* **and**
Finding Freedom From Pain

This important new book by Stephen Gilligan goes far beyond the generally accepted concept of trance and of its value as a means of improving lives. Generative trance stresses the efficacy and benefits experienced when the conscious and unconscious mind are encouraged to work together in a creative way.

The contents of the book will be of great value to individuals wishing to improve their own lives as well as to professional therapists wishing to help others to do the same. It deserves a place on every bookshelf.

Ursula Markham, Founder and Principal of The Hypnothink Foundation

Generative
Trance

Generative Trance

The Experience of Creative Flow

Stephen Gilligan

Crown House Publishing Limited
www.crownhouse.co.uk
www.crownhousepublishing.com

First published by

Crown House Publishing Ltd
Crown Buildings, Bancyfelin, Carmarthen, Wales, SA33 5ND, UK
www.crownhouse.co.uk

and

Crown House Publishing Company LLC
PO Box 2223, Williston, VT 05495, USA
www.crownhousepublishing.com

British Library of Cataloguing-in-Publication Data
A catalogue entry for this book is available from the British Library.

Paperback ISBN 978-178583388-5
Hardback ISBN 978-184590781-5
Mobi ISBN 978-184590782-2
ePub ISBN 978-184590783-9

LCCN 2011940616

Acknowledgments

Creativity is not an isolated act, but rather a magical process that occurs when individual self-awareness joins with a greater field of consciousness. In this regard, the writing of this book and development of this work owes much to the support, participations, and contributions of many people. I want to thank all my teachers, students, sponsors, clients, friends and family who have been such an integral part of this development. I have truly been blessed to have such extraordinary positive resources in my life.

A special thank you to Abbe Miller, who created the cover art and all the illustrations in the book.

With each breath of belonging,

the light in all things

cherishes the light in you.

With each smile of belonging,

the light in you communes

with the light in all things.

The heart, the hands, the tree,

the stars; consciousness in light,

in stone, cosmic and ordinary,

comfortable and divine.

Light breathing light,

breathing you –

This perfect, precious light.

Dvorah Simon

(inspired by Abbe Miller's cover art)

Contents

Preface

The goal of all our living is to become transparent to the transcendent.

Karlfried Graf Durckheim

This is a book about how to live life as a great journey of consciousness. It emphasizes reality and identity as constructed, and trance as a major means to create new realities. This view of trance differs markedly from traditional ideas of a person losing control, instead focusing on its potential to elevate consciousness to higher levels of creativity.

My own experience with trance has been a long and winding road. I spent much of my childhood in trance. Part of it was in the wonderment of watching the many unspoken connections between people, most notably my family. I loved to absorb in the magical qualities that seemed to be everywhere – in my grandfather's twinkling eyes, my mother's loving stories, my dog's blissful playfulness, even the "dancing dots" that swirled in the darkness after my mother turned out the lights at bedtime. This happy world had its counterpart: another part of my childhood trance experiences was in the dissociational escape from family alcoholism and violence. I learned trance as a sanctuary, a safe place to get away from the dehumanizing parts of life, to be alone and not confused and lied to by words.

I entered adolescence in the late 1960s in San Francisco, where traditional consciousness was being shaken to the core by a myriad of movements: hippies, Black Panthers, gay pride, the women's movement, and anti-war activism, to name a few. In my all-boys, Jesuit high school, a counselor introduced me to my first group therapy, where it was possible to talk about experiences I had previously only witnessed and silently experienced. I also found my way to meditation during this time, an important balance to the "sex, drugs and rock n' roll" ethos of the time.

At 19, I met the great psychiatrist healer, Milton Erickson, who changed my life forever. He showed me that trance could be used to come *into* the world, not just to leave it, and illuminated the uniqueness of each moment, each person, and each experience. It set me on my adult path as a psychotherapist using trance therapeutically to help others creatively deal with the many ego-disruptive challenges that touch each human life – births, deaths, traumas, marriages, divorces, and so on. The trance work was not just for my clients, but myself as well. I am grateful that Erickson modeled and emphasized the need for each person to continue to learn and develop and change throughout life.

All of this has taught me to appreciate the deep creative consciousness that lives within human beings, and how it may be tapped into through trance. I am continually amazed how trance can help people realize their dreams, heal wounds, transform problems, and live their life callings. Not artificial trance, not trance where somebody is manipulating somebody else, but a natural state where it is possible to take a step back from having to perform some fixed role and open a creative space where new reality may be created.

This is what I'd like to share with you in this book. How to develop higher states of consciousness that can help you live beyond fears, limits, and negative beliefs. I want to describe a type of trance that requires a cooperative relationship of mutual respect between the conscious and creative unconscious minds. In other words, you don't go to sleep in generative trance, you awaken to a deeper type of creative consciousness.

This central emphasis on creative trance as a conversation between different levels of a person decouples it from the outdated assumptions of hypnosis. It sees trance as a natural experience arising whenever identity is destabilized, and hypnosis as but one of many possible social rituals for unfolding trance. Given that traditional hypnosis seeks to bypass or "knock out" the conscious mind of a person, I believe it has limited value in promoting self-mastery and creative transformation. The work here is presented as an alternative method, whereby a person can experience an integrated self-wholeness that can guide and experience creative change.

I wrote the book for individuals who want to live life as a creative journey, as well as for people-helping professionals working with clients in such ventures. It needs to be emphasized that the work is not a substitute for essential medical or psychological care, nor should unqualified professionals use it to treat serious maladies. What it can do is help reawaken the wonderment of being alive, and allow realization of a happy, fulfilling life.

We live in challenging times. The longing for deep transformational change often clashes with rigid ideological "fundamentalisms," resulting in a "betwixt and between" state, suspended between old realities that no longer work and new ones that have not fully ripened. Such times present great opportunities for growth and transformation. May this work help you to make creative use of each moment of your life, no matter who or where you are.

Introduction

Let your mind start a journey through a strange new world. Leave all thoughts of the world you knew before. Let your soul take you where you long to be ... Close your eyes, let your spirit start to soar, and you'll live as you've never lived before.

Erich Fromm

The journey of life has infinite potential. At each step of the way possibilities open, each moment bringing a wholly new beginning. But to realize these possibilities, we must live in a way that is creative and meaningful. It is easy to go on unconsciously acting and reacting in predictable, tiresome ways. This book is about how to move into more creative states of consciousness using a process that I've developed called *generative trance*. *Generative* here means *to create something new* – a new future, a new state of health, a new relationship to self and the world. As we will see, generative trance is not a traditional hypnosis where one gives up control or consciousness, but a creative art in which conscious and unconscious minds are woven into a higher consciousness capable of creativity and transformation.

The experience of generative trance is grounded in the notion of *life as a journey of consciousness*. This idea was formalized by the mythologist Joseph Campbell (1949), who noted how every culture features myths about a hero living life as a great path of transformation. (Interestingly, the *Star Wars* movies were directly based on Campbell's work.) Such a life is not primarily about fame or fortune, but about bringing a greater healing and wholeness into the world. This might be done through any of a number of domains – art, science, social justice, family, business, and so on. Most important, especially in these challenging times, is the awareness that each of us can live such a life. This book is an exploration of how to help yourself and others to do so.

There are many examples of living life as a great journey. One of my main inspirations was Milton Erickson, the renowned psychiatrist who revolutionized ideas about how trance could be used for creative healing and transformation. I studied with Erickson during the last six years of his life. He was a classic Yoda-like character by then, a wizened old healer with twinkling eyes and amazing skills. His skills in no small part arose from his personal journey, as life gave him so many significant challenges. He was tone deaf, dyslexic (including not knowing the dictionary was alphabetized until he was an adolescent!), and color blind (purple was the only color he could "enjoy"). He was severely paralyzed with polio at 17, and suffered a related setback at mid-life. He met each challenge in courageous, creative ways, and then helped his psychiatric patients to do the same. This book looks to honor and extend that work in various ways.

To live life as a journey, we must consciously choose to do so. There are, of course, other possibilities. Campbell suggests three available paths: (1) *the village life*, where we play out the routines of the ego ideal; (2) *the wasteland*, where we sink into the shadow world of cynicism and despair; and (3) *the journey*, where we live life as a great call to adventure.

The village life

This is the conventional path of the ego ideal, where you live a "normal" life within the roles and social strictures of mainstream society. Here "the good life" moves through a clear sequence. For example, in the "American dream" (if it still exists), you are born into a happy family, obey your parents, do well at school, graduate and get a job, marry and have kids, buy a house and make a lot of money, then retire and die. This is the village life, and as Campbell points out, there is nothing wrong with it. For some people it is their main path.

Others, however, cannot or will not live in the village. Membership may be denied by virtue of having the "wrong" skin color, sexual orientation, religion, gender, or socioeconomic status. You may be exiled by something like a trauma, which shatters the "ego trance" and drags a person into the underworld. Or you may voluntarily leave the village, unwilling or unable to work within its orthodoxies or hypocrisies. Whatever the case, it raises the question of what lies outside the village.

The wasteland

The dark alternative to the ego ideal is the shadow world of what T. S. Eliot called *the wasteland*. Its inhabitants reject (or are rejected by) the shallow "happy face" of the village. Based on negation, the predominant experiences are cynicism, apathy, and destructiveness. You drop out of the mainstream and live alone or with some isolated subculture. The wasteland could be the despair of depression, the numbed glaze of television, the hatred of gossip and prejudice, or the toxic worlds of drugs, alcohol, and other addictions. Self-awareness and human dignity disappear, and consciousness descends into disconnected despair.

When people seek help, they are typically mired in the wasteland, unwilling or unable to participate in normal village life. Often the request, explicitly or implicitly, is to get them back to the village, so they can just be "normal". It is important to realize that this may or may not be possible. In generative trance, we see that the experiences that led to the "village exile" may be a "soul signal" that some deep transformation is needed – that a person can no longer continue in the restrictive role assigned to them. Luckily, a third alternative exists.

The (hero's) journey of consciousness

The ego ideal of the village and the shadow world of the wasteland are polar opposites, each containing what the other rejects. The *journey of consciousness* is a third path that integrates and transcends these dualities. Here you are neither blindly following the established rules and roles, nor cynically rejecting them. Instead, you "go where no man (or woman) has gone before," in the words of the old *Star Trek* series. On the journey, life is a great mystery unfolding daily deeper into greater awareness and possibilities. Many great people have spoken about this living of life as a great adventure:

> *Some men see things as they are and ask why. Others dream things that never were and ask why not.*

> George Bernard Shaw

> *Do not go where the path may lead, go instead where there is no path and leave a trail.*

> Ralph Waldo Emerson

> *Seek out that particular mental attribute which makes you feel most deeply and vitally alive, along with which comes the inner voice which says, "This is the real me," and when you have found that attitude, follow it.*

> William James

The journey is often initiated by what Campbell termed "the call". Something touches a deep place in your soul. A sense of magic or amazement awakens, and an awareness dawns of what you are in the world to do. When I first met Milton Erickson at the ripe age of 19, a fire ignited in my soul, and a quiet voice said, "This is why you are here". I often ask clients if they can remember similar moments of "soul awakening" or magical mystery in their lives, especially as children. Interestingly, most initially say no, but as we continue they begin recalling such moments. Maybe it was when reading poetry, or playing with animals, or drawing or painting, or becoming absorbed in science and technology, or feeling deep connections flowing between people.

Some hear the call and don't look back, their lives coalescing around it. Campbell called this "following your bliss". While often misunderstood as an irresponsible encouragement of hedonism and debauchery, he was actually inviting people to notice when they are touched by wonderment or passion. This "bliss" tells you what you're in the world to do.

Others hear the call and turn away from it. You might be hypnotized by the suggestions that "it's not realistic" or "you should be doing something else," and then try to lead a village life to make others happy. Campbell observed that sometimes we climb the ladder all the way to the top, only to discover that we've placed it against the (wrong) wall of other people's expectations. You can live away from your soul force and then die, "not with a bang, but a whimper".

But for many there comes a wake-up call: at some point (often in mid-life), symptoms begin to appear – health problems, relationship failures, depression or addiction, you name it. In generative trance work, we see such symptoms as "calls to return" to soul resonance, to reconnect one's outer self with the callings of the inner self. In this way, we see problems as openings to deep transformation, if met with positive and skillful human presence.

I start with these three life paths to emphasize generative trance as a tool for living the third path of life as a journey. It is not primarily to "fix abnormalities" so one can live within a sanitized village world, nor to get "lost in trance". Rather, it is a set of practices for living life at its highest levels, replete with many creative possibilities: joy, transformation, great accomplishments, and good health.

The book explores the approach in two main parts. The first part over-views a framework for generative trance work. Chapter 1 presents the key premise that reality and identity are constructed (through reality filters) and may be deconstructed and reconstructed when needed. The principle of *creative flow* is central to this skill, while the process of *neuromuscular lock* prohibits it. Chapter 2 examines trance as a process of creative flow that is naturalistic, necessary, and capable of many forms and values (both positive and negative), depending on its context. We will touch upon generative trance as a high level state based on the creative interplay between the conscious and creative unconscious minds.

Chapter 3 outlines the basic model of generative trance. Three minds are distinguished: *somatic, cognitive,* and *field* – along with the three levels of consciousness at which they can operate: *primitive, ego,* and *generative.* The general goal of the work is to move each mind to a generative level, thereby awakening new dimensions of consciousness capable of signifi-cant creative transformation. Chapter 4 outlines how this can be done in four steps: (1) *preparation* (developing the generative state); (2) *weaving the identity parts into a generative trance;* (3) *transformation and integration;* and (4) *the return into the ordinary world.*

The second part of the book focuses on how to implement the model. Chapter 5 explores somatic methods for developing generative trance, emphasizing *mind–body centering* as the central principle, along with how to optimize the five somatic dimensions of a generative trance: *relaxa-tion, absorption, openness, (musical) flow,* and *groundedness.* Chapter 6 explores *generative fields* as subtle spaces of mindfulness that can hold and transform their contents. For example, we will see how trance can be used to develop an "energy ball" that contains and allows creative engage-ment with difficult experiences; or a "second skin" that opens around the physical body; or an interpersonal relational field within which generative trance work can occur.

Chapter 7 identifies the *creative acceptance* of experiences and behaviors as a major way to develop trance and transformation. Chapter 8 explores the principle of *complementarity*, showing how holding opposites is one of the most succinct methods for popping the binds of the conscious mind and opening the gateways to the creative unconscious. Chapter 9 describes the principle of *infinite possibilities*, which holds that every experience and behavior can be experienced and expressed in many ways, as another major means for activating the creative unconscious.

Underlying the entire work is a *two-level theory of experiential construction*, which posits that (1) at the primary (quantum) level, experience has infinite possible forms and meanings, until (2) at the secondary (classical) level, an observing consciousness creates one actual form and meaning from all the potential possibilities. Integrating these two worlds of action and potential is at the heart of creative consciousness. Unfortunately, it is easy to get trapped within the fixed realities of the conscious mind, walled off from creative consciousness. This self-contained world is maintained by a *state dependency effect* that constructs reality to affirm its own position. Generative trance loosens these binds so consciousness can drop back into a generative field, then invites the conscious mind to move within this field with aesthetic intelligence. As we will see, musicality and resonance are primary languages of this creative consciousness, allowing the systemic parts to fluidly create ever changing mandalas of creative wholeness.

This great journey of uniting the two worlds was beautifully described by T. S. Eliot:

The point of intersection of the timeless

With time, is an occupation for the saint –

No occupation either, but something given

And taken, in a lifetime's death in love,

... you are the music

While the music lasts.

"The Dry Salvages" from *Four Quartets*

May the words on these pages help us to hear this music and find this intersection point.

Part I

The Framework of Generative Trance

Chapter 1

Consciousness and the Construction of Reality

Imagination is the beginning of creation. You imagine what you desire, you will what you imagine and at last you create what you will.

George Bernard Shaw

Mary[1] led a charmed life. She was smart, socially poised, and attractive. She had lived on the "fast track" to success: drawing the praises of adults and excelling in school as a child, earning a doctoral degree in science from a major university, marrying a wonderful man, and giving birth to two wonderful daughters. She was a superstar at work, happy in her family, and secure economically. So when she received a major lifetime achievement award at mid-life, she was understandably bewildered to find herself depressed and unhappy. Something was missing from her life.

Mary began a series of deep life explorations using trance work. She found tears and fears, as well as amazing and delightful awakenings of consciousness. Most important, she realized that she had been living away from her soul dreams. She hadn't even realized she *had* soul dreams, longings deeper than external achievement or social pleasantries. She discovered a desire for spiritual development, as well as for mentoring young female scientists in her high-stress professional world. In addition, she and her husband began a series of interesting journeys through different psycho-spiritual processes.

In all of this, her old world wasn't abandoned, just deepened to allow a more complete and fulfilling life. She was especially delighted to realize that she was responsible for, and capable of, creating her own life. The journey that became her life was a joy to behold.

---

1 All the names and identifying details of the case examples have been changed to honor the privacy of those cited. The core parts of their stories have been preserved.

The longing to live a deeply meaningful life is, of course, quite common. Many people feel a calling to go beyond the village life, to allow their light to shine brightly and uniquely into the world. If such callings are accepted and supported, beautiful miracles can happen. Generative trance is a great process for supporting such a journey.

The experience of generative trance begins with the appreciation that reality is constructed, and that each of us is responsible for creating our own lives in a meaningful way. To navigate such a journey, it is helpful to have some sense of this creative process. So in this first chapter, I want to offer a general map by which reality construction occurs, so that you can support yourself and others in such a venture.

I start by noting three different worlds that creative consciousness moves through: (1) a "pure consciousness" world of creative love and light; (2) a "quantum world" of the creative unconscious, with infinite possibilities and pure imagination; and (3) the classical world of the conscious mind, with its consciousness of time-space, matter, and other "reality" elements. Creativity requires flow between these three worlds of creative light, infinite imagination, and practical realities.

Accordingly, I next focus on how information/energy moves between these worlds. I suggest that there are "consciousness filters" that transduce one world into another. These gateways are akin to stained glass windows through which coherent light flows, creating a patterned world on the other side. A crucial idea for the entire book concerns whether these filters are open (in *creative flow*) or closed (in *neuromuscular lock*). Neuromuscular lock traps consciousness in a fixed and disconnected reality, giving rise to tremendous suffering and problems. Generative trance activates the *creative flow* that allows transformation, healing, and a great journey.

The three worlds of consciousness

How do you create a life that has purpose and growth? When your life isn't working, how do you let go in order to reconnect with wholeness and peace? And from that place of wholeness, how do you create new realities that heal brokenness and generate new possibilities? These are core questions regarding generative trance, and to answer them we distinguish three worlds:

1. Consciousness itself ("original mind")

2. Quantum world ("creative unconscious")

3. Classical world ("conscious mind")

The "original mind" of pure consciousness

Now, all the medical rituals we have been examining aim at return to origins. We get the impression that for archaic societies life cannot be repaired, it can only be re-created by a return to sources. And the "source of sources" is the prodigious outpouring of energy, life, and fecundity that occurred at the Creation of the World.

Mircea Elaide, *Myth and Reality*

Be a light unto yourself.

Buddha

We start our creative journey in "the middle of nowhere". Milton Erickson used to playfully use this term when inviting people in trance to experience a safe place where one could detach from all content. This trance field served as a sort of transitional space where old identities could be released and new realities born.

The Buddhists use the term *original mind* to refer to this empty space of pure consciousness from which everything comes and goes. Experientially, it is a non-dual awareness, empty of all forms and qualities, but luminescent. In other words, consciousness at its source is pure creative light.

Lest this sound too far-fetched, note the metaphors used across different cultures and languages to describe creative consciousness. New ideas *flash* from *out of nowhere* or *out of the blue*. A person is *brilliant, beaming, shining, light-hearted, radiant,* or *enlightened. The light went on,* and it was like being *hit by lightning.* Heightened awareness may be *free of thought, unclouded,* or *wide open*. Taken together, these common expressions intuitively point to a consciousness *before and beyond* form that carries wisdom and bliss.

The practical relevance is that when we are connected to this creative consciousness, we are at our best – happy, healthy, healing, and helpful to others. Countless poems, songs, and stories sing its praises. Philosophical traditions give it different names: *spirit, élan vital, life force, shakti, chi, divine consciousness,* and *prajna*. It appears at moments of great success, or beholding aesthetic beauty, or in the presence of deep love. Suddenly an indescribable space opens beyond all thought and form, and a euphoric bliss fills you, if only for a few lovely moments.

For consciousness to be creative, connection to this first realm is vital. Without it, we feel disconnected and trapped in compulsive doing and thinking. Ironically, it is at such times that we are often most afraid of letting go, fearing a drop into an abyss of no return. Thus, one of the first goals in generative trance is to become comfortable with letting go of all content, surrendering to the creative source. T. S. Eliot spoke to this beautifully in writing:

> I said to my soul, be still, and wait without hope
>
> For hope would be hope for the wrong thing; wait without love
>
> For love would be love of the wrong thing; there is yet faith
>
> But the faith and the love and the hope are all in the waiting.
>
> Wait without thought, for you are not ready for thought:
>
> So the darkness shall be the light, and the stillness the dancing.
>
> "East Coker" from *Four Quartets*

Appreciating this as our first base – *the light of "all that is" is within each of us* – allows a great creative energy to guide our path. Martha Graham, the late great luminary of the American modern dance field, expressed it in the following way:

> *There is a vitality, a life force, an energy, a quickening that is translated through you into action, and because there is only one of you in all of time, this expression is unique. And if you block it, it will never exist through any other medium and it will be lost. The world will not have it. It is not your business to determine how*

*good it is nor how valuable nor how it compares with other expres-
sions. It is your business to keep it yours clearly and directly, to
keep the channel open. You do not even have to believe in yourself
or your work. You have to keep yourself open and aware to the
urges that motivate you. Keep the channel open.* (Quoted in de
Mille, 1991: 264)

Generative transformation is possible when we keep the channel open to
this creative light source. We will see how this can be done skillfully. If
you are confident that you can let go of your mental thinking and allow
something underneath to safely catch and support you, a great freedom is
achieved. Generative trance work looks to develop the conditions where a
person can sense the immense goodness and intrinsic wholeness of this
source level, so that it can be skillfully accessed again and again.

When we work in generative trance, we "follow the light" in various ways.
For example, close attention is paid to to somatic resonance and subtle
energies, such as when a person's "light brightens" in a conversation. Such
signals suggest that what is being communicated is deeply connected to
creative consciousness, and encouragement is often given to slow down,
take note, and attune to the resonant connection.

As a final note, this content-free, subtle field of awareness is the basis of
what is called *mindfulness*. We will see how mindfulness supports the generative skill of *being with something* – a thought, feeling, behavior, person
– *without becoming it*, thereby allowing creative engagement and transformational relationships. So we want to make friends with the great void,
and discover that it is imbued with a subtle light of love, wisdom, even
bliss.

The quantum world of the creative unconscious

The fundamental process of Nature lies outside space-time but generates events that can be located in space-time.

Henry Stapp

From the world of creative light we move to the quantum world of pure imagination. This is the creative unconscious mind, a field of infinite possibilities from which new realities are created. It is before and beyond classical time or space, empty of real (material) forms but pregnant with infinite potential ones.

As the source of all possibilities, it is to the creative unconscious that we turn when we need new visions, identities, ideas, or experiences. It is a sort of visionary consciousness that can see beyond the limitations of a given situation. It can create new possibilities "out of nowhere" and show many possible ways to proceed in a given situation. A journey of consciousness cannot proceed without such a presence.

One of the most interesting properties of a quantum field is *superposition*, which is a virtual wave field that contains all possible states of something simultaneously.[2] Applied to psychological identity, this means that the creative unconscious holds all possible states of a given individual, in terms of identities, futures, pasts, relationship fields, and so on. So whatever state or identity you may be in at a conscious level, your creative unconscious is carrying many other possible states at the same time. The trick is how to connect to the creative unconscious when your present state isn't satisfactory.

For example, let's say a fellow named Dave complains that he is depressed. We would accept and welcome this as his present identity state, while

---

2   This is not to say that all possibilities are equally likely. Indeed, each possibility carries a probability of its likelihood to move from the quantum reality to the classical reality. In psychological terms, the past is one of the best predictors of the future. That is, the more that one possible reality is actualized, the more likely it is to occur again; this is the basic idea of conditioned learning. One of the things that we can do in generative trance is loosen the conditioning on an experiential field, and thereby allow new possibilities to emerge.

also appreciating that there are many other identity states resting in his creative unconscious – some playful, some young, some old, some wise, some wounded, etc. The challenge becomes how to make room for the conscious identity – the "depressed Dave" – while also inviting and welcoming other (complementary) ones.

This is what we can do in generative trance: *connect an isolated problem state to a creative (trance) field that contains many resourceful states, and skillfully weave them into a new mandala of identity.* For example, when a "depressed" part connects with "playful" and "affectionate" parts, many helpful transformations can occur. *The isolation of one part of a system creates problems, while the skillful activation of many complementary parts into a creative field allows solutions.* As we will see, this is a major characteristic of trance: the capacity to simultaneously hold (and creatively weave) multiple contradictory truths or realities without conflict. Many significant transformations can be created in this "trance soup".

The view of the unconscious as holding multiple possible forms of a given state is closely related to the idea of *archetypes*. The concept was proposed by philosophers such as Plato and Kant and later developed more fully by Jung. It assumes that core life challenges are not unique. Luckily, we don't have to reinvent the wheel every time we face a challenge – for example, finding love with another person. Our ancestors have dealt with this challenge since time immemorial.

The theory of archetypes posits that each time such an experience occurs, a trace of it drops into a collective field of consciousness. For example, each time someone experiences love, the pattern of that experience drops into the quantum field. From thousands upon thousands of such drops, a general abstract pattern slowly develops. This is what an archetype is: *an abstract, deep structure than can be experienced and expressed in many possible ways.* The creative unconscious contains general archetypal patterns plus infinite numbers of possible ways that they can be expressed. Thus, the human need to protect identity may be represented by the archetypal pattern of the *warrior*. This warrior archetype can be experienced or expressed in many ways, some negative and some positive. As we will see, *in the conscious world we identify with one of those forms, while in the creative unconscious countless other possible forms are simultaneously present.*

So when a specific experience isn't working, don't despair. Your unconscious carries many other possible ways to do or view this challenge, and trance is the means by which you can activate them. In trance you can safely let go of your old patterns and discover ones that work better.

For example, Martin grew up with a violent, alcoholic father, so his first examples of "warrior energy" were dark and destructive. Like many, he vowed to never be like his father, which translated into always trying to be a "nice guy". His inability to speak his own needs created many relational problems, and he found himself lonely and bitter. He used trance to find that he was carrying a negative map of assertiveness – namely, images of his violent father making endless demands. Trance then allowed him to discover and implement more positive images of assertiveness. Throughout the book I will emphasize this central use of trance: when you need to let go of what's not working and find new possibilities, trance is a great way to do it.

In applying the ideas of quantum superposition and archetypes to the nature of the unconscious, one additional point is worth making: there is no single unconscious mind, there is an infinite number. The unconscious mind is a construction (usually involving many people, over many years) and it can be constructed in a variety of different ways. To be sure, traditions ensure that certain versions are much more probable than others, but in principle there are no fixed or innate structures. Thus, Freud looked into the unconscious and saw sex, violence, and repressed emotions. Similarly, fundamentalist Christians see a dark seething cauldron of satanic evil and hell fire. Alternately, Jung "discovered" a pantheon of archetypal figures, and Erickson observed a vast storehouse of experiential learnings that could be used as resources for creating a happy, fulfilling life. In the quantum view, all are possible, but none exists in actuality until an observing (human) consciousness makes it real.

When generative trance work looks into the unconscious, it sees a creative field of infinite potential for human being and becoming. It sees a creative consciousness that can generate new possibilities "out of nowhere" and show many possible ways to proceed in a given situation. Of course, it is not a complete system. Contrary to some popular misconceptions, the unconscious is not independently intelligent. It is one part of a multi-level system. We need the creative life force of the original mind as the source and then, on the other side, the skillfull presence of the conscious mind to set intentions, create filters and meanings, and make creative use of whatever comes from the unconscious. It is to this third world that we now turn.

The classical world of the conscious mind

The classical world is the conventional reality of time–space: matter, physical energy, Newtonian physics, stuff *really* there. This physical universe has been unfolding for almost 14 billion years, the planetary consciousness for about 4 billion years. As biological and then psychological consciousness has evolved, the classical world has developed many levels. From a traditional Western view, we typically regard it as the empirical world of single values: something is true or not; if you're here, you're not there. Causal logic abides: that which is born must also die; things are as they are. The classical world includes a history and many traditions and patterns.

In creative consciousness, something isn't real until it exists in classical reality. So while there may be infinite possibilities in the quantum field, none of them "really matter" until they appear in the classical world. You're merely a dreamer until you practically realize your dreams; then you're a creative genius. So you need a decent grounding in the classical world to be "really creative". This can mean many things: a healthy body, good social connections and skills, emotional intelligence, education, perseverance, behavioral plans and commitments, and so on.

When we go into trance, we usually take a step back from the classical world, to let go of our restrictive "performance selves". We then open to the creative unconscious to generate new reality maps for navigating the world. While the trance may be an extraordinary experience, it has no "real" value until it translates in ordinary life. For this reason, we need both a creative unconscious mind and a conscious mind for generative work. The creative unconscious generates new possibilities, and the conscious mind translates and implements them into classical reality.

Unfortunately, trance can often be associated with the fantasy that somehow if you just "trust your unconscious," eternal happiness will result. (Or similarly, if you just let an external hypnotist "program" you to change your behavior, it will work.) In strongly emphasizing both the conscious and creative unconscious minds, generative trance work is a bridge between the two worlds of infinite possibility and specific reality. Transformation is born on this bridge.

Given this emphasis, we should have some understanding of how the conscious mind of classical reality can work in partnership with the creative unconscious of the quantum world. As the organizing consciousness of classical reality, the conscious mind is most often constructed in terms of managerial control. It uses what McGilchrist (2009) calls the "3 Ls" of the left hemisphere: language, logic, and linearity. It sets goals, sequences actions, creates order, and focuses on control and predictability. As such, it is an essential tool for living, allowing us to make sense of the day-to-day world and to reliably repeat what we've done in the past. When we make a cup of coffee, we don't need to be in visionary mode. But if we can't make a cup of coffee (and related routines), the visionary world is of no use to us. Creative living requires each world of consciousness to support the others.

But the conscious mind can be more than managerial. Just as there is no fixed structure to the unconscious mind, there are many possible conscious minds. While the traditional Western conscious mind too often operates as a disembodied intellect bent on controlling or consuming whatever it encounters, there are many other possibilities. For example, Milton Erickson modeled an exceptional conscious mind that was curious, cooperative, relationally connected, and eminently creative. As we will see, a conscious mind patterned in this way is an integral and necessary part of generative trance.

Relationship between worlds: creative flow vs. neuromuscular lock

In viewing the three worlds of consciousness, we can see how each is integral to creative experience. The primary world gives the pure, luminous consciousness that pervades everything, experienced as presence, spirit, and light. The secondary world of the creative unconscious holds the visionary, non-linear imagination of infinite possibilities. The tertiary classical world of the conscious mind carries the managerial competence and self-awareness to translate a possibility into an actuality.

Creative flow between and within these levels is at the heart of generative living. Echoing Martha Graham, we must "keep the channel open". At the primary level, this means staying connected with the creative source that energizes, illuminates, and sparks our thinking and acting. This light of creative consciousness informs, guides, and brings genuine love for ourselves and the world, without which we are reduced to empty egos trying to survive or get ahead. The practices of centering and opening to resource fields are ways that we will explore to support this connection to the creative source.

With this source connection, we can see the patterning of the creative process as an interplay between the conscious and creative unconscious worlds. Knowing how and when to shift between these two worlds is one of the most important skills in creativity. Figure 1.1 shows their complementary nature. While the creative unconscious holds infinite possibilities, the conscious mind makes them real. The conscious mind breaks the wholeness of the creative unconscious into the classical consciousness of many parts. The shifting relationships between the different parts of the whole are what allows time, space, self-awareness, and existence to emerge. The creative interplay between the worlds is what moves consciousness to its highest levels.

Figure 1.1. Two worlds of consciousness: quantum and classical

Quantum	Classical
Infinite possibility	Specific actuality
Visionary ("dreamer")	Managerial ("critic", "realist")
Creative unconscious	Conscious mind
Superposition (quantum wave field)	Position (specific actuality)
Virtual	Real
Subtle	Material ("hard reality")
Timeless	"In time"
Multiple values	Single value
Quantum logic	Classical logic
Wholeness (implicate order)	Parts (explicate order)
Ideal (unwounded/ unwoundable)	Actual (broken and wounded)
Translucent	Opaque
N-dimensional, un-imageable	4-dimensional, imageable

Filters: gateways between the worlds

We thus come to the question of how consciousness moves between these two worlds. In generative trance work, we say that information/energy flows between the different realms through *reality filters* that function as gateways. The nervous system is a prime example of such a filter. For example, neuropsychologist Karl Pribram (1971) proposed a holographic model of consciousness in which sensory systems are filters or lenses that convert the swirling patterns of the quantum world into the (classical) languages of the human being. Thus, what we experience as reality is not "out there," but rather is created by our filters. Our filters transduce the waves of the quantum world into the realities of the classical world. This means that we are ultimately responsible for our reality; the good news being that with this responsibility comes the possibility for transformation.

This process of moving from infinite potential to specific realities is a central dimension of quantum theories. In the quantum view, an observing consciousness is needed to "collapse the superpositional wave" of the quantum field into one specific reality. Without the observing consciousness, no reality exists. And the reality that does come into being is a function of the filter of the observing consciousness. A filter is thus like a stained glass window through which the quantum waves of the creative unconscious flow, with the world as a result.

Reality filters are central to generative trance work, the premise being that how they are set determines the reality we experience. This may be described in terms of a *two-stage process of human experience*, illustrated in Figure 1.2. In the quantum world of the creative unconscious, there are many possible forms and meanings for any experiential pattern. For example, sexuality can be experienced and expressed in many ways. *All are present as virtual possibilities in the creative unconscious.* When the patterns of the creative unconscious pass through the gateway filters (represented by the middle circle), they are transformed by human presence into a specific classical value and form (represented by the inner circle). The same core sexual energy could be either positive or negative, depending on how it is humanly engaged. Thus, your reality is a function of the setting of these filters. So if you don't like your reality, change your filters. Simple in principle yet challenging in practice, this is a central focus of generative trance.

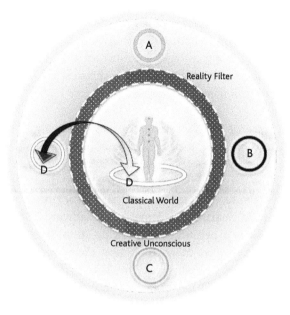

Figure 1.2. A reality is constructed

There are many types of reality filters: neurological, cultural, familial, personal, social, and so on. The body is a filter, family is a filter, educational background is a filter, the social context is a filter. All are gateways through which consciousness flows, translating information/energy into classical and human form. Each filter has multiple dimensions – for example, a specific filter may carry beliefs, histories, images, verbal languages, rules, images, defining narratives – and each dimension can be set in many ways. For example, in your intimacy map you may believe that you're unlovable, or that you can enjoy intimacy, or that intimacy is never fulfilling. As the "observing consciousness," your belief becomes a filter setting that "collapses" the quantum wave of the creative unconscious in accord with the belief. In other words, your belief significantly influences what you end up experiencing.

Of course, there are many filters operating at many levels, so we don't want to fall into the solipsistic trap of assuming that your conscious thoughts singularly create the whole universe. You belong to a culture, a family, a gender, social groups, and so forth. All these different levels of identities are in play, each with their own filters, so the process is complex. That said, trance can help you sense and then change the reality-determining filters that you're holding. One person really can make a great difference.

Filters also explain how in a world of infinite possibilities, we keep experiencing the same old reality again and again. When a filter is locked in a relatively invariant (static) structure, it becomes a *state of consciousness*, such that *the specific reality that emerges is a function of the state of the observing consciousness*. In generative trance work, we express this central idea as *the principle of state dependency*:

> The state of an observing consciousness significantly constrains what it is able to experience and create.

There is much evidence in support of this state-dependency idea. For example, my graduate research showed that emotional mood state significantly influences learning and memory (Gilligan, 1983; Gilligan and Bower, 1984). When a person is in a happy state, they remember more happy experiences, orient more to happy characters, and make more optimistic predictions. But when in a sad state, their cognitive processes shunt in that direction. Other state dependent effects have been found with physical location, linguistic context, drug states, and social groups. Related research shows how our experienced reality is significantly shaped by our expectations, ideas about the future, stereotypes, family and cultural beliefs, and social setting.

While a static filter can result in the same reality being continually created, it is possible to change our relationship to the filters so they operate more fluidly and creatively. This is a main focus of generative trance: we unbind (deconstruct) fixed identity states to allow new ones to be created. It is to this question of how we hold reality filters that we now turn.

Creative flow: when the gateways are open

> *The sun shines not on us but in us. The rivers flow not past, but through us, thrilling, tingling, vibrating every fiber and cell of the substance of our bodies, making them glide and sing.*

> John Muir

The quality of consciousness is a function of the quality of the underlying state. Informally speaking, *you're only as good as your state*. For example, if you're tense and shut down, not much good will happen for you. Optimal states feature what we will call *creative flow*, a state studied extensively by Mihály Csíkszentmihályi (1991). In such states, it feels like life is moving *through* you, its subtle currents bringing a sense of deep connection, presence, and intuitive awareness. Thoughts, feelings, and behaviors feel unified in the service of a greater purpose.

Figure 1.3. The generative state of creative flow

In creative flow, filters are held fluidly, not set in stone. Figure 1.3 suggests how in creative flow, you connect with the deeper world of the creative unconscious (represented by the outer "Quantum Field of Infinite Possibilities"), as well as with the ongoing reality of the classical consciousness (represented by the inner circle of the "real" world). The movement between the worlds occurs through the reality filters shown in the figure.

The figure also shows how in creative flow, energy flows from a human center into the quantum field, establishing resonant links with the creative unconscious. The flow connects the classical and quantum worlds in a creative dance. Think here of any extraordinary performer – an artist, a political leader, an executive, or a great healer. Such individuals need the conscious mind skills of holding a positive intention, having a general plan, and being attuned and responsive to what's happening in each moment. But they also need a connection with creative intuition, linked to wisdom and intelligence beyond the local context. Connecting to the two worlds puts them in a creative flow state which is changing in every moment. Sometimes the changes are minor; at others a major shift occurs. To know how or when to make these changes, filters need to be flexible and fluidly attuned, both with the external world and some "X factor" beyond. This is the creative state that allows you to live at the highest levels, and this is a primary goal of generative trance.

Neuromuscular lock: when the gateways are closed

When creative flow between the levels is blocked, suffering and problems result. In generative trance work, this is called *neuromuscular lock*:

> When consciousness locks inside a state, learning and change become impossible, and problems inevitably develop.

Neuromuscular lock involves both (1) a fixed brain map and (2) the muscular tension (and breathing inhibition) to lock it in place. As Figure 1.4 shows, this tension makes the filter rigid and opaque, so you can't see or feel beyond your limited reality. You are locked in the contents of your fixed state, believing your map is the whole territory, while feeling isolated in a static world of disconnection.

Neuromuscular lock is extraordinarily pervasive in contemporary life. An extreme example of how it develops is trauma. Researchers such as Peter Levine (1997, 2010) and Robert Sapolsky (1998) have described how virtually all mammals respond to severe life threats with what I call a *trauma trance*, a paradoxical state of body immobilization accompanied by high internal arousal. While such a trauma trance lasts only a short period in most mammals, releasing once the threat recedes, humans (and animals conditioned by humans) can stay in it indefinitely – years, decades, even generations. In such states of neuromuscular lock, consciousness is restricted to recreating the same experience over and over again.

Figure 1.4. Neuromuscular lock. Filter is opaque, isolation in ego constructions, dissociation from creative unconscious

A lucid example comes from the work of Vilayanur Ramachandran (2011), a neuroscientist who emphasizes that the only reality we really know is what our brain is imaging. That is, we don't know the world directly, only indirectly through our maps (filters). (These brain maps are more than visual images, carrying many different representational forms.) His research with phantom limb pain illuminates this idea beautifully. Many individuals who lose an arm or leg end up with excruciating pain in the area of the missing limb, as if it were still there. For some, it feels like they can move their phantom limb, while for others the limb feels paralyzed, often in a cramped position of extreme pain. Ramachandran suggests that when a limb is lost, the brain image of the traumatic loss locks in place, so it feels like the painful severation is still occurring. And because there is no physical arm to move, no new images develop to replace the old.

Based on this hypothesis, Ramachandran devised a simple but ingenious "mirror box method" to relieve the pain (see Ramachandran and Blakeslee, 1999). Patients sit at a table with arm sleeves on either side and place their physical arm through one sleeve, while imagining placing the phantom limb through the other. Several mirrors are then situated to produce a reversed image of the arms, creating the illusion that the phantom limb is physically there. Patients then move the physical arm in a happy and carefree way, which in the mirror appears as if the phantom limb is moving. As this occurs, the pain is relieved.

This fascinating demonstration of how brain images determine experience represents a central principle of generative trance. The irony is that we are typically not aware of how our (multi-level and multi-dimensional) state is creating our reality. Instead, we assume that reality is "out there"; that we are passive recipients of, not active participants in, reality creation. It certainly feels like that, as in most cases reality is being created from unconscious filters that have been in place for some time. Once set, they automatically function as default values until disrupted or transcended. Transcending or transforming these fixed filters is no small feat, but it is precisely the goal of generative trance work: to identify, release, and reorganize the underlying identity maps that are being used to create our realities.

The 4Fs of neuromuscular lock

Neuromuscular lock is the main obstacle to creative consciousness, so it is important to appreciate its central place in contemporary consciousness. Generally speaking, neuromuscular lock occurs via any of *the 4 Fs of stressful reactive responses* shown in Figure 1.5: fight, flight, freeze, or fold.

Figure 1. 5. *The four types of neuromuscular lock*

1. Fight	3. Freeze
2. Flight	4. Fold

Each of these four relational strategies has many versions. For example, *fight* may be experienced and expressed as aggression, anger, hatred, domination, or resentment. *Flight* can take the form of fear, avoidance, withdrawal, or anxiety. *Freeze* might show up as immobilization, dissociation, disembodied thinking, or paralysis. *Fold* might manifest as falling asleep, numbing, collapsing, depression, apathy, or torpor.

These responses are considered in Tibetan Buddhism to be the main poisons of the "original mind," which might be visualized as a deep pool of clear wisdom and joy. *In other words, they block us from the creative life source.* When we live in anger, fear, separateness, or numbness, it is like pouring toxic chemicals into this pool, thereby poisoning our primary source of happiness, health, healing, and creative living. Held in place by muscular tension, these contaminated states can easily become our base identity, so that we live in chronic states of resentment, fear, and disconnection. Furthermore, the practices we may use to try to get out of these states – television, consumerism, drugs and alcohol, blaming others – may actually deepen them. Generative trance is a set of practices for releasing the neuromuscular lock that binds these states, to restore connection with the unconditioned waters of creative consciousness.

Most chronic states of neuromuscular lock develop and operate outside of conscious awareness, beginning early in life. As a child in school, you may be taught that "paying attention" means sitting up straight and rigid, not moving. You may model parents or other adults in how they rigidly or mindlessly respond to certain challenges. You can easily get caught up in anxiety, loneliness, resentment, fear, and so on. Neuromuscular lock underlies all these stress-based reactive responses, and generative trance can release the lock.

Once developed, neuromuscular lock may become a pervasive underlying state. For example, a person might become fixed in a slumped posture that implicitly feeds depression. Other stress-locked states are situational, becoming triggered by a certain person, place, or topic. Perhaps most insidiously, *what we usually call "thinking" is a core state of neuromuscular lock, evidenced by muscular tension and inhibited breathing.* I sometimes joke that thinking and constipation are, for most people, basically the same muscular patterns, with lots of effort and not much to show for it. The more serious point is that when we think and act with tense muscles and inhibited breathing, we pretty much doom ourselves to repeating the past. We become trapped in a self-enclosed prison without access to anything beyond our state.

The central point in all this is that neuromuscular lock prohibits creative consciousness. The trauma research by Levine and Sapolsky (cited above), for example, shows that healing (e.g., tissue damage from an attack) occurs only when an organism releases from trauma trance and moves back into a resting position, whereupon accelerated healing immediately begins. The same can be said about any creative consciousness – coming up with a new idea, transforming a relationship, healing a past hurt, performing at the highest levels, and so on. At such times, we need to *include but transcend* the past, to think outside the box, to create something totally new. Neuromuscular lock is the enemy of such creativity, while creative flow is its closest ally. This is the purpose of generative trance, a topic to which we turn in Chapter 2.

Summary

Generative trance work takes the view that consciousness is the underlying creative force in the construction of reality. To do the work, we find it helpful to distinguish three different realms of consciousness: (1) the original mind of consciousness itself, empty but luminescent; (2) the quantum field of the creative unconscious, with infinite possibilities and pure imagination; and (3) the classical world of the conscious mind, with its existential, evolutionary world of time-space, matter, and many more "real" elements.

Creative consciousness may be seen to move between these realms, each an integral part in the process. The gateways between the worlds are *reality filters* akin to stained glass windows through which the coherent light of consciousness flows, thereby creating an experiential reality. When these filters are held "not too tight, not too loose," they become translucent gateways that allow *creative flow* between the worlds. When they are held too rigidly, the filter becomes opaque so that you can't feel or see beyond your limiting reality. This is caused and maintained by a *neuromuscular lock* that results in stagnation and not being able to change or grow. Generative trance is helpful when change or new realities are needed and desired, with a main goal being to relax the neuromuscular locking of the reality filters to enable a creative flow of new possibilities.

Chapter 2
The Many Faces of Trance

Above all, be alone with it all

a hiving off, a corner of silence

amidst the noise, refuse to talk,

even to yourself, and stay in this place

until the current of the story

is strong enough to float you out.

Excerpt from "Coleman's Bed" © 2007, David Whyte

Trance work is a creative art of soul expression. Like other art forms, it should not be thought of in the singular, but rather in terms of its plethora of possible forms and experiences. Only then can we intelligently sense how it might be best used in a given situation. This chapter explores different dimensions of this view, emphasizing how trance unbinds fixed realities in classical consciousness and re-opens the gateways to the creative unconscious.

This approach sees trance as natural and integral to consciousness, not artificial. In this naturalistic view, trance occurs whenever identity is destabilized, as a means by which identity can be deconstructed and reconstructed. Its specific form and meaning arises from the human context in which it occurs. Hypnosis is one of many such contexts, one unfortunately associated with one person controlling another person. Generative trance is a third generation approach that rejects this old-fashioned view of hypnosis, emphasizing instead a creative consciousness that emerges from a cooperative relationship of mutual influence and respect between the conscious and unconscious minds, one that can either occur intra- or inter-personally.

"Just let it happen": trance as creative flow

We saw in the last chapter how creative consciousness flows between the quantum world of the creative unconscious and the classical world of the conscious mind. The former is the source of visionary possibilities and creative wholeness, while the latter is the base for order, sequence, and control. Generally speaking, the reality filters of the conscious mind allow us to reliably repeat the past – and there are many times when this is desired – while the creative unconscious is best when we need to generate something new or different. Trance is a means of accessing the creative unconscious, and can generally be defined as follows:

> Trance is (1) a temporary suspension of the reality filters of the conscious mind, and (2) an experiential absorption into the quantum world of the creative unconscious.

As adults, we live mostly in the conscious mind. This virtual reality is one step removed from direct experience, a world enclosed within the "reality maps" we implicitly carry. It is easy to get stuck in this box of identity, succumbing to what Henry David Thoreau called "lives of quiet desperation".

When you attune to trance, the ego-box releases. You drop from the disembodied intellect of analytical thinking into the experiential world of unbounded images, feelings, symbols, movements, and energies. Like in dreams or play, in trance you can go anywhere from anywhere; the normal classical reality gives way to a more subtle quantum field of creative possibility. All the ordinary structures of identity that are usually fixed – time, embodiment, memory, logic, identity – become variable, free to generate new patterns and identities.

In various traditions, the core "mantra" to access the creative unconscious is "just let it happen". When you can do this in a secure and centered way, tremendous benefits occur.

In creative work this "letting it happen" is not a passive capitulation, but rather a "disciplined flow" that allows a deeper intelligence to join the conscious mind. As we will see, the discipline involves maintaining resonant connections with intention, embodied centering, and the positive resources needed to develop and sustain a high quality state. As the creative consciousness is allowed to flow through such a state, new realities are possible.

Not all trances are created equal

That trance *can* generate new possibilities doesn't mean it automatically *will*. It depends on how human presence engages with it. Some trances are low quality – spacing out, television trances, numbing out – that may give a break from active ego processing, but don't refresh or transform consciousness. Other trances are positive but non-transformative – you can relax, get a temporary feeling of security, but not really shift anything in your core patterns. They're "nice" experiences that don't really make a lasting difference.

Other trances are negative, such as depression and addiction. We'll see how these symptoms are *trances* in that a person deeply moves from classical reality into non-rational consciousness, but *negative trances* because of a neuromuscular lock reaction to the loss of ego control. (This is like pressing down the accelerator pedal on a car while simultaneously pulling the emergency brake, with the predictable consequence of ending up in a ditch or crash.) We'll also see how these negative trances can be transformed by developing a positive trance of conscious/unconscious harmony and then transferring the experiences from the old negative context to the new one.

The idea that trance has many forms and values became clear to me during my university years. I was studying with Milton Erickson (in Arizona) while also doing my graduate work in psychology at Stanford University, where the great experimental psychologist, Ernest Hilgard (1965), ran the largest hypnosis laboratory in the world. (This is where the most important hypnotizability tests were developed.)

Because my research used hypnosis, I worked under Hilgard's supervision. I had this interesting experience of running standardized hypnosis inductions in a research environment, then going to visit Erickson out in the desert and experiencing a vast range of extraordinary trance experiences. The trances could not have been more different. The ones in the lab were confined by an impersonal "one size fits all" suggestion script, while each trance with Erickson seemed to open a whole new dimension of consciousness. While the standardized trances may be appropriate in the research context – where you want to control extraneous variables – the creative trances are more suitable to personal development and transformation – where you want to utilize personal strengths and unique capacities.

In short, many types of trance exist. Generative trances are experiential states in which you are capable of extraordinary transformation. As we will see, this requires that both the conscious and the unconscious minds be in optimal states and in creative conversation, making it possible to create something totally new. Each of us is challenged to do this at certain points in our lives, and generative trance is a great tool in this regard.

Trance is natural

Trance is natural and fundamental to the fabric of consciousness. It is a state that humans must drop into periodically in order to renew, protect, recreate, and transform their identities. This idea, central to Erickson's work, is radically different from the traditional view, which regards trance as an artificial experience caused by and under the control of another person (i.e., the hypnotist).

The premise that someone else is responsible for your experience is the problem, not the solution. This is the main reason why I generally no longer use the word *hypnosis*: it carries too many connotations of one person's conscious mind controlling another person's unconscious mind. We are looking instead to open a creative, mutually respectful relationship between the conscious mind and creative unconscious, both between and within people.

In a naturalistic view, trance arises whenever the filters of the conscious mind are transcended or otherwise released. This could be in very positive circumstances, as in deep absorption in a book or beautiful experience; or it could be under negative circumstances, such as a trauma or being in a strange situation where none of your normal identity maps work. At such times, we drop back into the quantum waves of the creative unconscious. Whether this is a positive or negative experience depends on the kind of connections we make when in the trance. For example, if in trance we hold our breath and feel fear, it will turn out to be a negative trance; but if we can stay centered, relaxed, and curious, the same experience will unfold as a positive trance.

The natural view of trance was integral to Erickson's work. He did not arrive at his understanding of trance primarily from theoretical speculation, but from intense experiential explorations and hard-won learnings.

He was forever curious about how life, especially its challenges and difficulties, could be dealt with creatively. When he developed polio at 17, the doctors told him he would never move again. He thought that was "an interesting suggestion" and began a series of deep inner explorations about how he might regain movement. He found himself attuning to long-forgotten pleasurable experiences – for example, a childhood memory of playing ball with his brothers. He didn't know why he was remembering that, but some inner resonance seemed to encourage him to deeply immerse in that memory. After an extended period – sometimes months – of doing so, something amazing would happen: the muscles involved in that childhood memory began to reactivate in his present body. In other words, the natural memory of throwing a ball became a central resource and "reference structure" for re-activating the same pattern in his present life.

Generative trance is an exploration of how such deep creativity can occur in many ways. In the deeper and more fluid context of trance, reality filters and their fixed meanings are loosened, allowing an experience to be deconstructed and reconstructed in many new ways. As we will see, much of this potential is realized only in a high quality trance, the nature of which is the main focus of the book.

Trance is developed by releasing the orienting response

When we see trance as naturally occurring, the question arises as to how it develops. A major way is via the relaxation (or habituation) of the neuropsychological "orienting response" that keeps us in "busy" mode. The orienting response is a survival mechanism that automatically activates in the presence of unexpected or novel environmental stimuli – for example, a loud noise, a sudden movement, a break in a pattern. From an evolutionary view, this could be a lion suddenly towards leaping towards you, so you better immediately awaken from any reverie and check it out. Thus, the brain instantly drops what it's doing, increases arousal, orients (especially with the eyes) towards the stimulus, narrows attention, and organizes around the questions, *What's out there? What do I do?* In other words, we move from a "being" or "being with" response to a "doing" mode.

The orienting response is a central component of the neuromuscular lock pattern, a cross-species reaction to potential threat involving body immobilization, high arousal, and hypervigilance. It is designed to be short-acting. When it appears there is no danger, the relaxation response sets back in.

But we humans have the ability to stay stuck in the orienting response indefinitely. We can even activate it by *imagining* something bad is about to happen. This can become our normal mode: walking around with a tense body, always worrying, unable to stop thinking, unable to relax or deeply absorb. Activities such as internet surfing, computer games, and television exacerbate this tension state by repeatedly triggering the orienting response. Stress builds up, and creative performance and happiness go down. As Hans Selye (1956) pointed out, prolonged stress is the underlying mechanism causing many "dis-eases".

In trance terms, the orienting response locks in a hypervigilant conscious mind and locks out the creative unconscious. This stress mode is kept active by further repetitions of the orienting response. You can see this in how people sit in a lecture hall – shifting postures, looking away, suddenly scratching the face, flicking imaginary lint off pants, etc. They seem like fairly innocuous responses, but they are all ways to stay out of trance, and keep the disembodied conscious mind dominant. Of course, it becomes unconscious and automatic, an unwitting pattern of never relaxing, absorbing, or feeling a deeper connection with self and the world.

To develop trance, the orienting response needs to be relinquished. If you look across cultures and through time, you will find two common (complementary) trance induction principles used for this purpose. The first involves *absorbing attention in a singular focus*. This might involve visually focusing on a candle light, a symbolic image, a point in the environment, or an imaginary point. Sustained concentration blocks the orienting response, which would be hypervigilantly scanning a visual field, tense eyes moving in arrhythmic patterns. In the absence of the stress-creating orienting response, attention can widen and deepen into trance.

The second, and more common, trance development principle is to *entrain attention rhythmically on a repetitive pattern*. This could be the chanting of a mantra, the repeating of a body movement, the beating of a drum, repetition of a prayer, singing a song, movement around a circle, the attunement to breathing, long-distance running, and so forth. The rhythmic repetition signals the brain that there is no new environmental information, so it's safe to open deeper into the world of relaxation and inner absorption. Only at this point is it possible to rest, release problems, and open to new creative possibilities. These are all core dimensions of generative trance.

We should remember, of course, that not all trances are positive. Thus, some repetitive patterns can induce negative trances. For example, violence can be induced by war-based drummings or feverish rants by Hitler-like dictators. Depression trances can be developed by internal chants of "nobody loves me, nobody loves me, nobody loves me". And other negative trances develop from catatonic freezing, stressed body rocking, or compulsive behaviors.

So in addition to releasing the orienting response, positive trance development also includes a rhythmic presence of relaxation, positive messages of loving kindness, and limbic attunement. As we will see, the resulting trance will have profound value on many levels.

Trance is integral to identity creation

In understanding trance as (1) a release of the reality filters creating classical consciousness and (2) an amplification of the creative unconscious, we can see when and why this happens: *trance occurs whenever identity needs to be recreated, healed, or transcended.* Our identity filters are the main maps by which we know ourselves and the world. When they are working well, the managerial skills of the conscious mind predominate. But when they need to be renewed or changed, the reality-binding conscious mind must yield to the reality-generating intelligence of the creative unconscious. There are four general occasions for this shift.

1. *Rest and renewal.* Identity is organic and impermanent, and thus needs rest and renewal periods. An obvious example of this is biological rest, including dreaming; without it, the mind–body cannot regenerate and integrate. Similarly, we need breaks from the tension-based performance self – this might involve naps, walks, vacations, exercise, and so on. Such periods allow us to let go of neuromuscular lock and associated limitations, and return to our performance challenges with a renewed self.

The need to release the conscious mind in order to access creative consciousness is at the heart of numerous creativity theories, many of which are based on the pioneering work of Graham Wallas (1926), who proposed that the creative process moved through four steps. The first is *preparation*, where conscious effort defines and explores a problem or goal. At the point of an impasse or diminishing returns, a second step of *incubation* occurs, where rest is taken and attention shifts away from the problem. In the third step of *illumination*, an answer "flashes" out of the creative unconscious, often in symbolic language. (For example, the German chemist August Kekule realized the structure of the benzene ring through an intense dream image of a snake biting its own tail.) In the final step of *verification*, the conscious mind returns to test, elaborate, and apply the creative development.

Thus, the first and last steps feature the conscious mind, while the middle steps involve the trance-related processes of the creative unconscious. The incubation period refers to the rest and renewal needed to "clear the decks" and allow a creative answer to flow from the quantum field of the creative unconscious.

2. *Re-creating identity.* As part of a living system, identity must be periodically re-created. This is the function of birthdays, anniversaries, religious and secular holidays. Music, special ceremonies and clothes, and other ritual aspects of trance are primary languages in these events, signifying a shift into a collective trance field where an old identity is renewed.

   For example, the Togo tribe in West Africa has a tradition of creating a song for each newborn baby. This is done in a trance ritual where the women of the tribe hold the baby in a circle, sensing its deepest identity and life calling. As they do this, a unique song begins to unfold among the women, one that expresses the core essence of that child. The special song is sung to the person, in a ritual circle, at different life points – birthdays, times of illness or change, death. In this way, a trance field is evoked as a means to renew the core identity.

3. *Healing and transformation.* Identity must also periodically heal and transform, and trance naturally occurs at such times as well. For example, psychological and medical symptoms are more likely

to develop at times of significant life changes – the death of a loved one, an illness, a new marriage, a retirement, a job change, and so on (Holmes and Rahe, 1967; Rahe and Arthur, 1978). Such events precipitate change at the identity level; you are no longer the same person as a result. Thus, the old identity maps of the conscious mind start to release, and a person is drawn into the creative unconscious to create new ones. *Whether the natural trance produces a breakdown or breakthrough depends on the human connection to it.* If the experience is met with neuromuscular lock, the negative trances of symptoms will result (depression, addiction, panic, etc.). But if engaged positively and skillfully, then healing and transformation can result from such crises. Thus, whether a trance is positive or negative depends on the human connection with it, an important implication being that "negative trances" can be changed to positive ones via skillful human engagement with them.

4. *Creating new identity.* At different points on our life journeys, new identities need to be created. We may be starting a new business, ending a long-term relationship or opening a new phase in our lives. At these thresholds, our past history does not carry the requisite maps, so new ones need to be generated.

For example, Barbara was a 48-year-old woman who received a breast cancer diagnosis. Her mother had died from breast cancer, and Barbara couldn't shake the feeling that she would suffer her mother's fate. Trance allowed her to release these old identity maps and open to creating a new identity. She was surprised and delighted by the resonant soul images she received in trance – such as a woman with a burning sword and a long road leading into a bright future – which helped forge a healthy future.

In seeing trance as occurring whenever identity is disrupted, it is helpful to appreciate that this can happen spontaneously – for example, a trauma suddenly overwhelms the ordinary self, or intentionally – such as when a person deliberately moves beyond their usual limits or comfort zone for a "transcendent high". In both cases, the classical consciousness of the conscious mind is released and the quantum world of the creative unconscious is amplified. This allows identity to be deconstructed and then reconstructed. All of this depends, however, on the human presence that engages the trance.

The process of identity deconstruction means the fixed aspects of a reality filter are unbound and up for renegotiation. These aspects can include beliefs, experiences, memories, specific associated behaviors, family patterns, and so forth. Thus, an identity map of "trust" might prominently feature experiences of being lied to, beliefs that you can never trust another person, and behaviors such as clandestinely checking up on another person. In trance, all those specific settings loosen, thereby allowing a fluid space where new settings can develop.

Milton Erickson would emphasize trance as a space to reorganize identity, and note that this need occurs at least periodically throughout the life cycle. Thus, you had one map of "trust" when you were 4 years old but, no matter how good it was, you'd better not have the same understanding at mid-life. So it is natural that our identity must die and be reborn throughout life, and trance is a main means by which this occurs.

The human relationship to trance determines its form and value

To appreciate how the many forms and values of trance come into being, we return to the two-stage theory of reality construction. In the first stage, the quantum pattern of an experience undulates with many possible forms and values, which get collapsed by an observing consciousness into the specific form of the second stage. When we apply this to trance, we see that:

> The meaning, value, form, and function of a trance is created by the human connection(s) to it.

Culture is one reality filter that shapes trance. In Africa and Brazil, trances often involve wild shaking. In Bali, they are expressed as sensual trance dances in which the dancers channel Hindu deities. In Eastern Asia, they may be experienced as quiet, still "meditation experiences". In the West, a hypnotic trance is often expressed with closed eyes and relaxed body, under the verbal commands of an outside expert (hypnotist).

These radically different forms of trance require us to differentiate the core experience of trance (which involves the loosening of classical consciousness and the amplification of the creative unconscious) from the particular form that it takes. The former is essential to human consciousness, the latter is reflective of the contextual filters used to shape and guide it. From this we can see that trance can be negative or positive, depending on the human context in which it is held. One important application of this dual-level view is that symptoms can be seen as trance experiences held in negative contexts, which can be transformed by opening a positive context that absorbs and reorganizes the negative experiences into positive ones. This was the basis for Erickson's utilization approach (see Gilligan, 1987) and also for Tibetan tantric work (Yeshe, 1987; Wangyal, 2002).

Generative trance derives primarily from a hypnotic context, which has evolved significantly over the years. I distinguish three generations of Western trance work, with generative trance being the third generation. Because most people associate trance with the earlier generations of hypnosis, a few clarifying comments should be made.

The first generation is the authoritarian approach that still holds sway in most places. Here both the conscious mind and the unconscious mind of the client are considered to be, well, idiots. So trance work involves first "knocking out" the conscious mind and then talking to the unconscious mind like a 2-year-old that needs to be ordered around. Individuals who come to a hypnotist seeking change are told, in effect, to close their eyes and be quiet, while the hypnotist installs new operating instructions. Is it any wonder that many people are (rightfully) leery of trance and hypnosis, and also that too often the changes don't last very long?

Erickson created the second generation of trance work (see Rossi, 1980a, 1980b). He approached the unconscious as having creative wisdom and each person as extraordinarily unique. Thus, rather than trying to program the unconscious, Erickson saw trance as a special learning state where a person's own creative unconscious could generate healing and transformation. This radical idea of the unconscious as tremendously intelligent led to a very different type of trance work – for example, each trance was unique, the communications were primarily derived from the person's own patterns and ongoing experience, and the hypnotist–client relationship was cooperative rather than authoritarian (Gilligan, 1987).

At the same time, Erickson for the most part carried the same low opinion of a client's conscious mind, seeing it as more a nuisance than an integral part of self-transformation and healing. Thus, Ericksonian hypnosis looks to bypass the conscious mind with indirect suggestions and dissociation, and depotentiate it with confusion techniques. The idea is that once the conscious mind is out of the way, the creative unconscious can do its thing.

The third generation of trance work sees this negative attitude towards the conscious mind as unnecessary and unhelpful.[3] Figure 2.1 represents how generative trance is a conversation between a skillful conscious mind and the creative unconscious mind. While Erickson showed how *he* could do that with a person's unconscious mind, generative trance is primarily interested in how individuals can learn to do that for themselves.

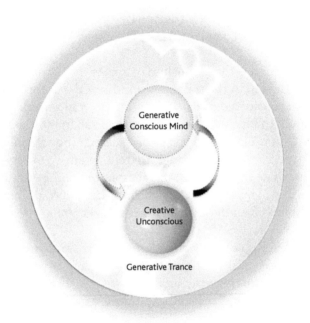

Figure 2.1. Generative trance

William James used to say that the unconscious mind is the horse and the conscious mind is the rider, and it is the relationship between the two that is of the greatest importance. Monty Roberts (1996), one of the original "horse whisperers," poignantly described different possible horse/rider relationships in his autobiography, *The Man Who Listens to Horses*. Growing

---

3   It should be said in Erickson's defence that in his time – the early and mid-20th century – the idea of a person having a generative conscious mind simply did not exist. It came of age in the 1960s, when the idea that each person could live with deep self-awareness was born.

up on a ranch where the standard relationship was to violently "break" horses into submission, Roberts knew in his heart that there had to be a better way. He spent years learning the relational language of horses in order to develop a skillful, non-violent way to "start a relationship" with them based on mutual respect and listening. Whereas it typically takes weeks to "break" a horse, Roberts forges a positive relationship with most horses within minutes.

In a parallel way, the old style hypnosis is generally based on the conscious mind being in a dominant/submissive relationship with the creative unconscious. Erickson, like Roberts, developed a "horse whisperer" method based on deep listening and relational attunement. Generative trance looks to extend this work by emphasizing that it is within each person's capacity to learn to communicate with their creative unconscious in a manner similar to Erickson. This requires reorganizing one's conscious mind to skillfully engage with the creative unconscious in a mutually influential and respectful way. In doing so, a person can "become their own Milton Erickson," internalizing the "hypnotist" and "client" roles in relational resonance. This allows one to "walk in two worlds," entraining the quantum world of the creative unconscious with the classical world of the conscious mind. *This unification of (1) the self-awareness of the localized conscious mind and (2) the collective wisdom and intelligence of the non-local deeper mind is the basis for generative consciousness.*

This does not mean that a person never needs help from others. We all "get by with a little help from our friends". Especially in those situations where a person is unwilling or unable to safely open to their experience, qualified guidance should be found. But such guidance should, in the present view, primarily focus on improving the intra-personal relationship, always keeping in mind that a person is their own best therapeutic presence. This emphasis allows each person to develop a generative self that can live a great journey of consciousness.

Summary

Trance is an experience of creative flow in which the bindings of classical consciousness are loosened and the quantum experience of the creative unconscious is amplified. It is both natural and integral to human consciousness, occurring whenever normal identity filters are destabilized or released. Trance unbinds the settings of reality filters, so that new identity maps can be created. It can take many forms and values, depending on the human relationship to it, and thus can be positive or negative. This allows us to see symptoms as forms of negative trance, and generative trance as a positive context for transforming problems into resources and also creating positive futures.

Chapter 3
Three Minds, Three Levels: The Generative Trance Model

I have thus far emphasized that reality is constructed, with trance serving as a natural means by which it can be deconstructed and reconstructed. Now I want to present a general model by which generative trance can be developed and creatively explored. The model distinguishes three types of consciousness filters – *somatic*, *cognitive*, and *field* minds. Each mind can be experienced through three different levels of consciousness; (1) the *primitive consciousness* of the right brain hemiphere; (2) the *ego consciousness* of the left hemisphere, or (3) the *generative consciousness* that integrates the two sides. We will see how at this generative level, new experiential dimensions emerge to enable a creative consciousness capable of transformational change.

The three minds of the generative self

Experiential knowing occurs through many mediums. Generative trance work distinguishes three different "minds" that interactively operate in human consciousness: the *somatic mind* of the body, the *field mind* of the larger contexts to which we belong, and the *cognitive mind* of the intellect (see Figure 3.1). Let's briefly consider each in turn.

Figure 3.1. The three minds of the generative self

1. Somatic mind

2. Field mind

3. Cognitive mind

The somatic mind

The *somatic mind* is the animal intelligence shared by all mammals. This embodied consciousness is about knowing yourself relationally in the world through feeling, action, nonverbal awareness, and emotion. The mammal mind carries a past and a present, but no future awareness. Like your pets and young children, it has the potential for amazing awareness, but no self-awareness: it can't think about itself or represent itself. It is attuned not only to personal history, but ancestral history as well. It carries instinct, archetypes, and intuitive knowing – all basic elements for transformational change. It also knows how to feel, heal, and maintain the extraordinary balance of human life, both within and around the body.

This is the first base of the unconscious mind, functioning as the embodied carrier of the history of consciousness. (The second base is the not-yet-lived quantum field possibilities.) So when we want to shift a state of consciousness, the somatic mind is a good starting point. It is the core platform for developing a generative trance. Chapter 5 is devoted to methods for moving the somatic mind to a relaxed, and resonant body state where the disciplined flow of creative process is possible.

The field mind

A second type of mental filter is the *field mind*. This is the non-local (systemic) intelligence all around us, the contexts that we live in. Many different fields operate at any given moment: cultural, family, personal history, political, and so on. You may work in the field of psychology, or be absorbed in the field of your "family trance," or sense a "negative field" in a business meeting. These contexts for our consciousness may be positive or negative, but are always influential.

A finding in social psychology called the "fundamental attribution error" (Ross, 1977) provides a good example of field influence. These studies found significant differences in how we explain other people's behavior versus our own. We generally use *trait explanations* regarding others ("He yelled because he's an angry person") but *situational attributions* for ourselves ("I yelled because that person was a jerk"). The best explanation of this effect is that we typically see most people in limited contexts, so we assume that they behave in the same way across all contexts. But we know ourselves much more extensively, appreciating that the way we are in one context is quite different than in another. We know that these fields strongly influence our behavior and experience, so that as the fields change, so do we. Thus, "the field made me do it" is not entirely a false statement.

The idea of fields can carry all sorts of meanings for people. The most basic meaning is that they are the many contexts – both internal and external – in which we live and know ourselves. In that we are usually not consciously aware of how much they influence us, they constitute another type of unconscious mind.

So a second major focus of generative trance is sensing the settings of the field filters and exploring how they can be shifted to creative patterns. Chapter 6 will describe how to develop trance fields that have positive resources and support to guide, encourage, and help you on your journey. It also explores how to develop mindfulness fields as safe contexts for transformational work.

The cognitive mind

The third filter we focus on in generative trance work is the *cognitve mind*. This is the conscious intellect "in the head". It uses verbal descriptions and symbols to "re-present" self and the world in terms of images, maps, plans, meanings, beliefs, and possibilities. It thinks in terms of narrative and story, sequences and values. It has the potential to see the world from many different perspectives and with many different values, even though it often gets locked in a tiny subset of these. In traditional hypnosis, it is the "conscious mind" that is usually targeted by a hypnotic induction to dissolve or at least relax for a while, so that the hypnotist's "conscious mind" can re-program the person's base somatic mind. As we will see, however, in generative trance the cognitive mind is shifted to a higher level of consciousness and invited to be an active part of the trance process, in reciprocal interaction with the other minds.

Chapters 7–9 describe the various methods we use to shift cognitive patterning to support generative trance. We move to thinking that is open, curious, creatively accepting, balancing, and capable of creating multiple solutions and possibilities at any point in time.

Each of these minds is a lens or filter through which experiential realities are constructed. They constitute the "states of mind" that guide who we are and what we can become in our lives. As such, life mastery requires an ability to set and adjust these settings in skillful ways. Practically speaking, developing a generative trance is a process of moving these three minds to a high level of creative flow. This leads us to the second set of core distinctions in the generative trance model.

Three levels of consciousness

I think there are three states of being. One is the innocent expression of Nature. Another is when you pause, analyze, think about it ... Then, having analyzed, there comes a state in which you're able to live as Nature again, but with more competence, more control, more flexibility.

Joseph Campbell

The three minds can take different forms, depending on the level of consciousness at which they are operating. As Figure 3.2 shows, we distinguish three levels of consciousness: primitive, ego, and generative.

Figure 3.2. The three levels of human consciousness

1. Primitive level: wholeness without self-awareness
2. Ego level: self-awareness without wholeness
3. Generative level: self-awareness within differentiated wholeness

The primitive level: wholeness without self-awareness

This base level is connected with the core energies and forms of the primordial world. It has "wholeness without self-awareness" – a great field of non-local consciousness without linear order or conscious control. Within it, time is cyclical rather than chronological. There is a rhythmic circulation of elements: night/day, exhalation/inhalation, active/passive, and so forth. It has virtually limitless energy and unbounded resources, as can be seen in the young. Everything is connected in primitive consciousness.

Nature is like this: everything is part of an ecological unity. The creative unconscious is another example: it is an unbroken pattern of innately poetic intelligence that guides the creation and balance of psychological life. The strength of this "dreamtime" consciousness lies in its wholeness: within it, "everything is connected to everything" as part of a deeper unity. Because it is the ocean from which our individual consciousness arises, we must connect to it for rest, integration, and healing. In this way, trance – whether it is developed through hypnosis, music, rituals, or symptoms – is a deep return to primitive consciousness, a psycho-biologically necessary state in which we can let go of our constructed separateness and return to our native wholeness and connection to non-local fields of consciousness.

However, primitive consciousness by itself is not especially generative; its evolutionary (or generative change) rate is slow. It recreates endless versions of itself, only very slowly growing beyond itself. In the ancient myth of the race between the tortoise and the hare, the tortoise is primitive consciousness.[4] (But as I tell my clients, always remember who wins that race!)

In a significant way, this primitive consciousness reflects the neuropsychological creations of the right brain hemisphere. That is, it is reality constructed through the filter of the right brain. As Ian McGilchrist notes:

> *The right hemisphere yields a world of individual, changing, evolving, interconnected, implicit, incarnate, living beings within the*

---

4 Interestingly, I have now asked in 17 different cultures whether they have this story, and all 17 have answered in the affirmative. Thus, it seems to be a universal myth of sorts, one that is relevant more than ever in contemporary times, where the "speed" of the conscious mind increases exponentially, while the slow soul growth of the creative unconscious goes unnurtured.

> *context of the lived world, but in the nature of things never fully graspa-*
> *ble, never perfectly known, and to this world it exists in a certain rela-*
> *tionship.* (2009: 174)

While the strengths of this primitive consciousness are its systemic wholeness and its unbounded energy and resources, its shortcoming is its lack of self-awareness. It cannot "stop time" and analyze a situation, or isolate one part of the system, or rapidly generate multiple different maps. It changes from the inside out, (very) slowly evolving a greater complexity.

Our identity at the primitive level is relational and *non-local*, a deeper wholeness of being without a fixed reference point. There is distinctive-ness at this level, but no isolated separateness. The separation of self, where non-local identity is replaced by local identity, occurs at the ego level.

The ego level: self-awareness without wholeness

One of the most astonishing evolutionary leaps in history is the emer-gence of self-awareness. This capacity for symbolic self-representation has given rise to a second level of consciousness, which we will call *the ego level*. At this level you can step out of time and create imaginary worlds in which symbols of all sorts are used to run endless simulations of possible realities. The historical fruits of this shift are stunning: verbal language, art, awareness of future possibilities, technology, cities, and other time-transcendent miracles.

There is also a dark side to this great evolutionary leap. Perhaps because self-awareness is still so relatively new in the history of consciousness, we only seem able to identity with (and thus have compassion for and con-nection with) a small part of consciousness at a time. Thus, I might end up identifying with the "me" of my physical body, or the "us" of my group, against the "it" or "them" of the rest of consciousness. In this selective identification, *the ego level has self-awareness at the cost of wholeness*. We end up dividing the unbroken wholeness of primitive consciousness into endless dichotomies – self vs. other, good vs. bad, us vs. them – *and then never integrating back together again.* Thus, whereas the primitive is distinguished by its unity, the ego is oriented around division (of the whole into parts).

To be clear, this capacity to divide and separate has considerable advantages. We can re-combine the parts in many novel ways, enabling the creation of new wholes. We can arrange linear sequences, which permits conscious plans, routines, and separate categories of thought, all of which allow change to take place at markedly increased levels.It is the way that we do it that spells trouble. First, we usually break our connection to the natural world to enter the symbolic world: conscious ego thinking is typically performed with the contracted muscles and inhibited breathing of *neuromuscular lock*, thereby causing a functional dissociation from the living world. Second, we identify with our ego position in a way that dis-identifies with other positions in the field. Third, we maintain these one-sided ego positions inflexibly and indefinitely, not allowing the rhythmic shifting among different positions that would enable a more integrated view. *In other words, we separate ourselves from the wholeness of life to achieve self-awareness.*

In the language of generative trance, this represents the dissociation of the conscious mind from the deeper wholeness of the creative unconscious. In neuropsychological terms, it is a fundamentalistic attempt by by the consciousness of the left hemisphere to impose its knowing as the only valid map.

McGilchrist (2009) details how the right hemisphere creates a "master plan" of systemic wholeness, which the left hemisphere can then make real with its impressive skills of language, linearity, and logic. When the two work in partnership, extraordinary creative wholeness is the result. Unfortunately, the left hemisphere can and too often does ignore the right and act as if its own maps are the only realities that exist. This can be disastrous, as the functionally isolated left hemisphere has glaring weaknesses. For example, it has only partial and indirect experience of the body (and thus the natural world), it represents only its own position (both visually and cognitively), and it prefers non-living things over living presences. Needless to say, this one-sided pattern is all too prevalent in today's world.

In summarizing the research, McGilchrist notes:

> The world of the left hemisphere, dependent on denotative language and abstraction, yields clarity and the power to manipulate

> *things that are known, fixed, static, isolated, decontextualized,*
> *explicit, general in nature, but ultimately lifeless. The knowledge*
> *that is mediated by the left hemisphere is, however, in a closed*
> *system. It has the advantage of perfection, but the perfection is*
> *bought ultimately at the price of emptiness.* (2009: 174)

The problem is in the practices that dissociate and isolate the ego consciousness from its deeper platform of systemic intelligence. These dissociated forms of self-awareness are unnecessary, though very seductive. Like an addict or a fundamentalist ideologue, once we get hooked it's difficult to let go. We no longer feel a part of a greater non-local consciousness, instead becoming isolated in a static, self-enclosed local position. Different views are cut off and evidence is ignored, resulting in an ever more limited and imbalanced reality. For many people, it is only when they "hit bottom" that new options become possible.

The generative level: self-awareness within differentiated wholeness

Whereas "mind–body" dissociation looms large at the ego level, the primitive and ego levels are reconciled into a deeper unity at the generative level. In neuropsychological terms, the two hemispheres cooperatively engage to open a higher level of creative consciousness that contains entirely new potentials. As we will see shortly, this means an integrated mind–body consciousness distinguished by centered mindfulness, relational connection, positive intention, and creative engagement. The somatic, field, and cognitive minds are patterned at a higher level, allowing transformational experience and action.

Let's take the somatic (body) mind as an example. Its patterning is instinctual at the primitive level, organizing around mammalian patterns of protection, food, sex, and belonging. While not self-aware, primitive somatic consciousness is ecologically intelligent and energetically alive. When hungry, an organism eats; when tired, it sleeps; when curious, it explores; when it needs connection, it seeks community. It organizes around balance, relational identity, and connection to the living world. While not much transformational change occurs, at the primitive level somatic consciousness is connected to the great "circle of life".

As consciousness moves to the ego level, an isolating self-awareness appears in its many forms: intention can be held, goals can be pursued, separate local identities can become primary, and symbols can be used to reveal or conceal. In this representational world, the body often becomes more isolated and abstractly regarded (e.g., as a "thing" or "dumb animal"). This allows behavior to be more tightly controlled, repeated, and reorganized to meet specific goals. We can consistently act in certain ways, and change our behavior when needed or desired, thereby allowing a conscious life to be forged.

But as we all know, ego control can lead to a disembodied experience of alienation and neuromuscular lock. Negative ego values such as hatred or greed can imprison the body into dark states of prejudice, bitterness, depression, or fear. Thus, it becomes crucial to skillfully integrate the ego awareness with a direct connection to the integrated wholeness of the world, making it a servant to a deeper intelligence.

This integration is possible at the generative level. Here consciousness is embodied, open, positively intentioned, able to fluidly hold and engage multiple truths and positions, and connected to creative consciousness. For example, imagine a great leader engaged in a daunting challenge. You would want him or her to be connected both to self and others; to have both courage and compassion; to think in many creative ways; and to communicate a unifiying vision, and ensure its implementation. Somatic consciousness at this generative level is centered, connected to larger fields, energetic and subtle, and deeply creative. You can see a sort of "aura" emanate from such leaders, a subtle energy that calms, inspires, and encourages others. When we witness an extraordinary performer – whatever field it may be in – we see such a generative state.

This shift to a generative level can occur only when the primitive and ego levels harmoniously connect. When they don't, a process Wilber (2001) calls "transcend yet disconnect" occurs. An example is the "mind over body" battles, where the disembodied intellect tries to force its will on the somatic mind. (This "mind over body" attitude is the basis for traditional hypnosis processes, as well as most "positive thinking" approaches.) Such relational patterns are based on neuromuscular lock rather than creative flow, and are thus incapable of creative consciousness.

When the three levels (and minds) operate in reciprocal flow, generative trance is possible. This integrated state balances intention with spontaneity, self-awareness ("I") with primitive consciousness ("we"), and receptive (*yin*) and active (*yang*) processes. The integrated wholeness of the field is present in each of its many differentiated parts. It is especially useful at those times when we want or need to be creative. While the isolated ego position is essentially conservative, looking to re-generate versions of the past, the generative state allows fundamentally new realities to emerge.

Much of this creative consciousness comes from the subtle field of mindfulness that opens at this generative level. The meta-intelligence of this non-reactive, content-free awareness can skillfully hold and unify the different parts of an identity field. Chapter 5 describes how at the somatic level, this mindfulness field is experienced as a subtle "body of bodies" that holds all the different states and patterns of the physical body. We feel this when in creative flow: an expanded field of subtle awareness moves through and around the body. Chapter 6 describes the "field of fields" that opens at a generative level, such that it can absorb the problem in a creative field connected to many resources. Chapters 7–9 describe the generative "mind of minds" that can creatively absorb and engage with experiential patterns. Examples of this are Milton Erickson's amazing skills of utilization, wherein a person's patterns were creatively accepted and transformed, as well as the aikido approach to martial arts that blends and redirects attacks without clashing with them.

In each instance, a non-dualistic state of creative awareness develops, allowing each experience to be met with curiosity, creativity, and optimal performance. Subject and object blend into a deeper unity, allowing the different parts of a field to integrate into creative wholeness.

The COSMIC consciousness of generative trance

The emergent properties of a creative consciousness are at the core of a generative trance. The most important ones can be described with the acronym, *COSMIC*, shown in Figure 3.4. Let us briefly consider each in turn.

Figure 3.3. COSMIC consciousness: dimensions of a generative state

---

Centered

Open (and mindful)

Subtle awareness

Musicality

Intentional (positive)

Creative engagement

Centered

Centered refers to a felt sense of mind–body unity, an integration of the somatic and cognitive minds that opens to a field beyond. Centering is a key experiential distinction in performance arts and martial arts, as well as other high performance endeavors. It unifies the different mind–body energies and movements around and through a "one point" focused in the body. As we will see, the center can be in different places on the mid-line – for example, the belly, the solar plexus, or the heart. By centering awareness, one can move and think in a creative, mindful fashion.

In any significant challenge, it is easy to get caught up in the problem. Centering allows you to "drop down" underneath all the drama and feel a simple, deep presence and connection. This allows you to think, act, and feel with a calm, non-reactive awareness. When you feel grounded and secure in your center, you can creatively flow without neuromuscular lock. Thus, centering is a basic precondition for generative trance work.

Open (and mindful)

In a generative state, an expanded sense of a non-dual awareness opens up, creating a feeling of being "at one" with the world. This is not some strange esoteric experience, but a meaningful part of each person's life. For example, think of a time when you really felt connected to yourself and the world – perhaps in nature, with a loved one, or experiencing art.

As you tune into that memory, notice where your sense of self ends. Most people report that it does not stop anywhere, it opens infinitely outward. This doesn't mean you are an undifferentiated blob of consciousness; rather, you feel a part of something bigger, beyond your individual or ego boundaries. This is a prime example of what we call a generative field awareness.

In Buddhist traditions, this state is talked about as *mindfulness*, which I define here as *a non-reactive and content-free field of subtle awareness*. That is, you can be with something without the neuromuscular patterns of "fight, flight, freeze, or fold" that distort and degrade consciousness. You can witness negative thoughts or feelings without being disturbed by them. You can become aware of different ego parts playing out their automatic games, and sympathetically analyze a particular conditioned pattern. Being mindful allows you to feel both *a part of* and *apart from* an experience. That is, you can *be with something without becoming it*, an observer and participant at the same time. This is a very generative combination indeed.

Subtle awareness

Opening to mindfulness, we become attuned to *subtle energy and awareness*. At the ego level, awareness is muscle-bound and relatively coarse; that is, most conscious mind thinking involves neuromuscular lock. At the generative level, experience flows with more grace and skillful sensing. This is apparent in aesthetic experiences – for example, reading a good book, cooking, playing a sport well, listening or playing music, being in nature. Awareness becomes more subtle, less rigid, more differentiated and intelligent.

I was once talking about this phenomenon in a Berlin workshop, and a participant raised his hand. He said that as a brain surgeon, he often performed 10 or 12 hour operations with his team. They typically listened to classical music and discussed philosophy while operating, and he had just realized why: such aesthetic practices created the subtle awareness that a brain surgeon needs to perform intricate, delicate work. (You probably should get pretty worried if you find your brain surgeon listening to heavy metal music in the operating room!) Subtle awareness is similarly needed for the challenging work of transformation and creativity.

One way to develop subtle awareness is through *limbic attunement and resonance*. The limbic system is the part of the old mammalian brain that creates a feeling of belonging. We experience limbic resonance in dancing, team sports, music, or deep relational connection. At such times, a felt sense flows between participants. Limbic attunement enhances both performance quality and well-being: not only do we perform better, but it feels great to do it! This experience of limbic resonance is a type of subtle awareness.

Limbic resonance can be shared with any living presence – people, animals, trees, and so on. As we will see, it can also be extended to inner experiences – for example, a feeling of anxiety – in ways that provide safety and transformation. Awareness of subtle energy and information gives quantum glimpses of the luminous and numinous nature of the world.

Musicality

> *Music is communication – it speaks to us, not about things. It does not refer (to a third party): it has an "I–thou" existence, not an "I–it" existence.*

Ian McGilchrist

> *The primal role of music is to some extent lost today, when we have a special class of composers and performers, and the rest of us are often reduced to passive listening. One has to go to a concert, or a church or a musical festival, to recapture the collective excitement and bonding of music. In such a situation, there seems to be an actual binding of nervous systems.*

Oliver Sachs

A core premise in generative trance work is that *musicality is the first language of human beings*; it is especially important at times when we want to access a non-local field of creative consciousness. Musicality is evident in most cultural (trance) rituals – for example, through singing, chanting, praying, drumming, dancing, or speaking in ancient languages.

Musicality is also primary in the bonding conversations between mothers and their young children (Malloch and Travarthen, 2009). For example, a mother points to a toy animal and says in a loving, musical voice, "Horse!" The child delights in gesturing similarly and repeating in kind, "Horse!" The mother smiles, praises the child again with an exaggerated musical voice, then adds something new. This musical "call and return" is the basic limbic dance by which a child enters the human realm.

Musicality is similarly central in bonding communications between intimate partners, people with their pets, or members of a cultural group. All these "intimacy fields" require sensitive use of nonverbal patterns that resonantly touch the body, create a relational bond, and open the inner self to a sense of belonging.

There is much evidence indicating that in human evolution, music was the first language (see Dunbar, 2004). As McGilchrist notes:

> [T]he evolution of literary skill progresses, if that is the correct word, from right-hemisphere music (words that are sung), to right-hemisphere language (the metaphorical language of poetry), to left-hemisphere language (the referential language of prose).
>
> Music is likely to be the ancestor of language and it arose largely in the right hemisphere, where one would expect a means of communication with others, promoting social cohesion, to arise. (2009: 105)

Thus, when the primary function of communication is to create integrative wholeness, musicality is of central importance. While this was basic to traditional cultures, the movement towards language to control and manipulate (a left hemisphere activity) became dominant in modern societies, thereby dissociating us from the musicality of creative consciousness. Musicality regains a central place in the language of generative trance, a means to generate the communal trance field wherein new identity can be created. In generative trance, words and behavior are connected with breath, rhythm, and resonance. Nonverbal patterning – both within and between people – is regarded as more important than the actual words. In this way, the creative unconscious is awakened and words once again become "magic".

Without musicality, what emerges from the creative unconscious is usually negative. *The underlying core of symptoms – aggression, fear, dissociation, giving up – share a general pattern of neuromuscular lock, non-musicality, and mindlessness.* As we will see, bringing such experiences into a generative space of musical resonance opens the door to positive transformation. Can you imagine waltzing with your anxiety or singing your depression? Musicality may not be sufficient for positive change, but is probably necessary. As the great Duke Ellington observed:

> It don't mean a thing if it ain't got that swing.

As a final note, musicality does not require instruments or formal expression to be present. We are talking here about the basic resonance, rhythm, and presence of living consciousness that is in each moment of time. This is present in silence as well as in sound. Attuning to this deeper musicality returns us to the basic creative flow of life.

Intentional (positive)

In his study of optimal flow experiences, Csíkszentmihályi (1991) found that to enter such states, you need to have future-oriented, positive goals. Not only an ultimate goal, but a series of testable sub-goals as stepping stones. Paradoxically, being "in flow" takes a lot of goal-setting, planning, and practice! This makes sense, as intentions are the drivers and organizers of consciousness. If you have a clear and resonant intention, held in a centered way, your creative unconscious will begin to organize around it. If not, you will likely get lost in the low-level drift of trance images or, worse yet, perhaps caught in some negative energies present in the field.

As we will see in Chapter 4, developing and sustaining a positive intention that is succinct and resonant is essential to generative trance work. This simple task is often not easy; many people start with either a negative goal ("I want to get rid of X") or not knowing what they want. Thus, we will explore how to develop positive intentions and make "trusting the unconscious" contingent upon holding them and other positive connections as the base.

Creative engagement

The two-stage theory of reality construction emphasizes that the meaning, form, and subsequent unfolding of an experience come from the human relationship with it. It therefore behooves us to understand how this process occurs. We have been emphasizing how the neuromuscular lock relationships of "fight, flight, freeze, or fold" will result in negative outcomes. The generative alternatives are what we call *creative engagement patterns*.

One such pattern is *creative acceptance*, the focus of Chapter 7. The idea is that struggling against something, trying to change it, typically produces agitation and resistance. By welcoming it in a centered and curious way, new possibilities can naturally emerge. Milton Erickson provided countless ingenious examples of this principle. For example, one psychiatric patient in a locked ward believed he was Jesus Christ. Erickson introduced himself, affirmed that Jesus was indeed a carpenter and someone who liked to help people, and then invited "Jesus" to join the carpentry crew engaged in a building project on the hospital grounds. The patient got very involved in that work, so much so that, as Erickson observed, he became too busy connecting with others to worry about being Jesus. As we will see, creative acceptance is not a process of passive resignation but an active curiosity about all the different ways that a pattern can positively unfold.

A second pattern of creative engagement is what we will explore in Chapter 8 as *the principle of complementarity*, a process of *both/and* thinking that weaves opposites together in creative integrations. For example, implicit in every problem is a conflict that might be expressed as,

> I want X, but Y happens instead.

In generative trance, we explore how a rhythmic shifting between the opposites opens a space beyond them. Say, for example, you would like to go out on a date but are too afraid to ask someone. In generative trance you can shift to one side and find its positive intention and form, then to the other, then hold "both at the same time". As we will see, this produces very interesting new possibilities.

A third creative engagement pattern, explored in Chapter 9, is *the principle of infinite possibilities*, which holds that there are virtually unlimited numbers of ways that an experiential pattern can be understood, experienced, and expressed. So if you're locked into a negative pattern, you can shift into trance, let go of the content to feel the underlying energy and pattern, and then become curious about all the different ways that it might be experienced.

All these generative properties are part of the integral consciousness of generative trance: being centered, open and mindful, attuned to subtle awareness, musicality, positively intentioned, and creatively engaged. When you take the time to first develop a generative state before engaging in a challenging experience, positive results are likely to follow.

Breakdowns vs. breakthroughs: how problems and solutions develop

Generative states are especially relevant at the inevitable crisis points of life. At these times, our ego filters fail us, and we totter on a threshold that could lead either to a breakdown or a breakthrough, depending on how we meet them. Figure 3.4 shows the general sequence involved.

We start by assuming that most of the time we move through life at the ego level – a "business as usual" identity of social roles, ordinary routines, and the soap operas of everyday life. But at some point, this ego identity destabilizes. Trauma may strike, long-term stress may build, or perhaps you realize that you just can't continue the same way in your job or personal life. The destabilizing event could also be a happy one – becoming a parent, completing a long-term goal, or going on an African trek.

In all these situations, you're in new territory. Your old identity maps don't work, and so you lose your "normal" orientation and drop into primitive consciousness. This makes sense, since this is where all the energy and resources are for healing or creating new realities. But the "not knowing" can be disorienting, even frightening. *It is what you do at this point that determines whether you experience a breakdown into a problem or a breakthrough into a creative new solution.*

Figure 3.4. How identity destabilization leads to breakdown or breakthrough

1. Ego identity dominates until ...

2. Identity destabilizes (trauma, major stressors, life changes, intentional destabilizers)

3. Ego state collapses, primitive consciousness amplifies

4a. If primitive consciousness is engaged with neuromuscular lock (fight, flight, freeze, fold), symptoms ("negative trances") develop until ...

4b. Creative flow is established between primitive consciousness and ego

5. New identity is created

6. New identity stabilizes until ...

If the response is the neuromuscular lock state of "fight, flight, freeze, or fold," negative experience and behaviors will unfold. While this stress-based response is understandable and in some cases – such as trauma – unavoidable, staying stuck in it spells trouble. Trying ever harder to negate the experience – via dissociation, numbing, projecting – deepens a vicious cycle of self-violence in which *the more negatively you respond to your experience, the worse it gets.*

To transform the suffering, a positive relationship of creative flow with the primitive energies of the creative unconscious is essential. This requires moving to a generative state of consciousness. The remainder of the book focuses on how this can be done – how you can become centered, relaxed, and aware; how you can be attuned to a space beyond the problem, thereby not getting locked inside of it; and how you can engage in a mindful, creative, and transforming way. These are some of the generative forms of the somatic, field, and cognitive minds, respectively, and they can allow you to live life as that great journey of consciousness.

Summary

The "three minds, three levels" model gives a practical way to develop generative trance. We need to move the reality-creating filters of the body, the intellect, and the relational fields to generative levels. At the generative level, self-awareness is united with systemic wholeness to enable transformational consciousness. The generative state is distinguished by centering, an open state of mindfulness, subtle awareness and energy, musicality, positive intention, and creative engagement. In such a state, problems can be transformed into resources and a great journey of life can be lived.

Chapter 4
The Four Steps in Generative Trance

One step at a time is good walking.

Chinese proverb

All great masters are chiefly distinguished by the power of adding a second, a third, and perhaps a fourth step in a continuous line. Many a man had taken the first step. With every additional step you enhance immensely the value of your first.

Ralph Waldo Emerson

I was once talking with a well-known fiction writer about how he wrote his books. One of his main strategies for "receiving" the story was to find a quiet place, get settled, and close his eyes to sense a gentle, dark field all around him. He would wait with curiosity until, slowly but surely, from different directions various characters would begin to emerge from the darkness and interact in a space in front of him. He would "transcribe" the events as the basis for the book, adding other strategies (such as editing) along the way.

To work in such a creative way, the conscious mind must be in harmonious partnership with the creative unconscious. The conscious mind is responsible for setting intentions, creating and sustaining the proper conditions, receiving the communications from the creative unconscious, and then translating them into classical language and action in the world. Your creativity is only as good as your underlying state, and the conscious mind is responsible for creating and maintaining that state.

This chapter describes how this state of "disciplined flow" can be developed and maintained for generative trance work. Four basic steps are distinguished in Figure 4.1. They describe how to first develop (and then maintain) a generative state; how to include and rhythmically connect all the important parts of the goal-defined work; how to bring the parts into an integrative whole that creates new identity maps; and how to transfer the "trance-formations" to the everyday world. We will explore each in turn.

Figure 4.1. The four basic steps of generative trance

1.	Preparation (of a generative state)
2.	Welcoming and weaving the identity parts into generative trance
3.	Integration and transformation
4.	Transfer learnings into real life

Step 1: Preparing a generative state

I always like to finish the job before I begin.

Milton Erickson

Figure 4.2. The preparation step: three positive connections

1.	Positive intention (generative cognitive)
2.	Centering (generative somatic)
3.	Resources (generative field)

To "trust the unconscious," you must first develop the requisite context. The simple form of this preparation step involves establishing the three positive connections listed in Figure 4.2: *positive intention, centering,* and *resources.* In the triune mind model, these connections are simple versions of generative levels of the cognitive, somatic, and field minds, respectively. The order and manner in which they are developed is variable. I will overview some straightforward ways, and then introduce *self-scaling* as an invaluable technique for working with these connections.

Connect to positive intention

To operate at a generative level, you need a strong connection to a *positive intention*. Otherwise, it's easy for the unconscious to drift in free association or get caught in a negative undertow.

In generative trance work, a well-formed intention meets three conditions. First, it is *positive*, specifying something a person wants to do or experience. People often begin with negative goals: "I don't want to feel this way," "I want to get rid of that experience," "I want to stop doing this behavior". While understandable, giving primary attention to a negative image often unwittingly reinforces it. Thus, it is generally better to identify what someone actually wants instead:

> What do you want to be feeling?
> What do you want to be doing?
> What do you want to develop?

It is usually good for the goals to be clear and specific:

> I want to write this book.
> I want to exercise every day.
> I want to feel calm when I talk with my parents.

However, sometimes the goal can be a general intention. For example, Dave was a man who went through a harrowing mid-life crisis that included a divorce, job change, and family deaths. Emerging from the crisis, he was surprised to discover how unhappy and unhealthy he had become. He decided to do self-hypnotic work each day with the "mantra":

> I want to be healthy and happy.

Within a week he found himself changing his diet significantly; after several more weeks, he gave up drinking alcohol. He then found himself curious each day about what really brought him happiness – which turned out to be reading, meditation, and daily exercise – and committed to those activities. What was especially interesting for him was how these changes arose "spontaneously" from his creative unconscious, stimulated by his daily self-hypnosis suggestions.

A second well-formedness condition is that an intention be *succinct*. I generally use a *five words or less* rule for stating an intention. With more words, the quality and the clarity of the intention usually deteriorate, muddied by explanatory stories of the type, "I want X because Y but I'm afraid that Z might happen so ... ". These stories often function as low-grade trance inductions that divert attention away from the base intention. So while the stories may be important at some level, it is generally important to differentiate them from the primary intention: "I want X".

When working with clients, I usually enforce this rule in a playful but strict way. I ask them to state the positive intention in the form of:

> What I want most in my life is X.

They then have five words or less to express X, while I hold my hand up and count with my fingers the number of words used. As soon as the five word limit is exceeded, I playfully sound a "beep" to let them know they are over the limit. Many people are quite surprised at the difficulty in being succinct about their goals, but find that doing so really clarifies the intention.

The third condition for a well-formed goal is *resonance*. That is, the speaking of the goal should touch something inside both the speaker and listener(s). Without this felt sense, there is no mind–body connection, and words have no power to change lives. So when working with people with generative trance, I am closely tracking what is happening in my somatic sensing as well as my clients' – not only during goal-setting, but throughout the session. If a person says something of apparent importance but I feel no resonance, I will let them know, saying something like,

> I sense you're speaking about something important, but I'm not feeling any deeper connection to it. I'd like to invite you to slow down, take a breath, sense what you're speaking about, and tell me again.

I will continue this until I can feel the resonance, which is the signal that the creative unconscious is active. This connection to somatic resonance leads us to our next positive connection.

Of course, it is equally important for the client to experience felt sense. Gendlin (1978) found that it best predicted the helpfulness of a session. That is, when a person experienced a somatic resonance when talking about a problem or goal, then the talking was helpful; if not, talking about it wasn't helpful. Somatic resonance indicates the mind–body connection that makes words magic.

Connect to center

While positive intention is a characteristic of the *generative cognitive* mind, *centering* is a core element of the *generative somatic* mind. In the next chapter we will explore centering in detail – its various functions and how it is developed and used. For now, we can generally define it as *a mind–body connection to a core sense of well-being that is deeper than any momentary experience*. One way to activate the center is through revivification of positive memories, since such experiences usually involve feeling centered. A general way to do this is to first invite general relaxation and then say:

> And as you can continue to breathe in and out … relaxing and opening … in and out … what a nice thing to know that you can begin to allow a positive memory to come into your mind … a time in your life when you felt deeply connected … deeply whole … deeply confident … no need to try to remember, just let it happen … breathing … wondering and letting your unconscious begin to remember an experience when you felt really deeply connected … perhaps an experience in nature … or when you were with someone you really love … or when you succeeded at a challenging task. Just let such a positive memory come into your awareness … (pause). And when you have one, you can let me know by nodding your head … (continue until head nods).

> And as you remember such an experience, let yourself tune into the sensory details – where you were, who was there, different details, and so forth … and as you do so, you can let yourself feel that experience fully again in your body … each breath bringing the experience more strongly into the present moment … so that you can begin to sense those feelings now … and as you do, you can begin to notice where the core, where the center of that deep experience is … so that if you were going to speak from that core feeling, walk

from that core experience ... think from that core feeling ... where is the center? (pause) And as you sense it, let yourself take a hand, or perhaps both hands, and gently touch your center ... And as you touch, let yourself feel a connection between your center and you ... a very positive connection ...

The next chapter will detail other ways to center, as well as ways to check and strengthen the connection when needed. For now, the important point is that centering gives a stabilizing, content-free connection "underneath" thoughts, feelings, and perceptions. It calms and clarifies awareness, allowing an integrated way of being with something. Along with the other positive connections, we thus consider it a necessary condition for generative work. Any significant work should only be initiated once centering has been established, and tracking occurs throughout a session to ensure it is maintained. At any time it is lost, other work is suspended until it is regained, since working in trance in an un-centered way is not wise.

Connect to resources

The third positive connection is to *experiential resources*. A "re-source" is anything that gets you back to your source (or center). Jung used to say that everyone should know who is in their "community of saints". By this he meant sensing who in your life really loves, supports, and cares for you. You can carry these positive presences with awareness, thereby offsetting and "opening beyond" any negative presences. They can be used as reminders, protectors, guides, supporters, advisors, models, and so on.

To identify resources, here are some basic questions or suggestions that might be used.

- Who in your life really loves and supports you? (They could be living people, no longer living beings, ancestors, spiritual beings, pets, friends, family members, teachers, etc. Let yourself take a few moments to notice what or who comes to mind.)

- When you really need to reconnect with yourself, what do you do? (e.g., cooking, listening to music, reading, going for a walk.)

- When you need to feel safe, what do you do?

- In terms of the goal(s) you have, take a few moments to let your unconscious come up with any people, experiences, or symbols that can support and guide you in this process.

In this way, a set of experiential resources can be identified and helpfully used to keep a person open to a positive field that can support and guide the journey.

It is important to appreciate that everybody has some resources. If a person can't access any, the likely reason is a state dependency caused by neuromuscular lock, which can be remedied by relaxation or absorption. With some people, you have to dig a little. I worked with one woman who had suffered horrible childhood abuse and didn't believe she had anything positive inside of her. I asked where she went as a child when things got really bad, and she mentioned hiding in the forest near her home. As we explored this further, she had a special tree that she would climb, which at some point housed a precious nest of chicks with which she very closely bonded. The forest and the tree and its nest of birds became exceptional resources in her healing work, helping her to learn how to connect with her resources before opening to anything else (such as her goals or challenges).

Once resources are identified, they can be sensed spatially in a surrounding trance field – for example, sitting next to you, standing behind you, or resting in your heart. This sort of spatial imagination opens awareness to a larger field filled with positive connections, into which the problems and challenges can be invited. This allows a person to stay connected to a creative space, and not fall into neuromuscular lock.

The use of self-scaling to assess and track connections

The success of generative trance work rests in no small part on the presence of these positive connections of intention, centering, and resources. Careful attention should be given to how to best develop these connections in each situation. This is not a race won by the swift, so take the time needed to properly set up and maintain the state. The three connections give the proper grounding and positive constraint needed to "let things happen" in a deep way.

Figure 4.3. The Positive Connections Scale

The connections are not all-or-nothing phenomena, and they can fluctuate significantly. To assess and track their levels throughout a session, a simple self-scaling technique can be very helpful. One version is a 1–10 scale that can be used to rate the present (or desired) level of an experiential process. For example, Figure 4.3 shows a "scale of positive connections" that can be used to track the levels of centering, positive intention, and resources. It is very helpful to use this scale throughout a session. Focusing on a connection – for example, centering – the suggestion can be given:

> On a scale of 1–10, where 1 is the low end and 10 is the high end, let a number come to your mind that best represents how much you experience X right now.

Notice the invitation is to "let a number come" rather than "what number do you think ...?". This encourages the rating to come from the creative unconscious.

Whatever number comes, be appreciative that it is possible to know exactly where you are on a given dimension at any point in time. The scale can then be used to *suggest a shifting of the intensity level*:

> Do you think it would be interesting to discover how you could increase (or decrease) that number just a little bit – perhaps one or two points – just enough to let your unconscious begin to make a meaningful shift?

It is generally best to suggest small changes: they are easier to accomplish, and also don't polarize a situation into "all or nothing". Assuming a person is interested, the process can then *invite the unconscious to increase the intensity level*:

> So when you're ready, let your eyes close ... and take a nice deep breath ... and as you close your eyes ... let your creative unconscious bring to you whatever experiences ... positive memories, people, symbols, colors, songs, other awarenesses ... that allow you to develop a deeper connection with X ... just a little bit more ... just enough to begin to allow your unconscious to shift into a deeper level of creative activity.

This simple scaling method can be very helpful. Observing the maxim that *the capacity for creative change is a function of the quality of the state*, it gives a straightforward way to assess and track important dimensions of the state.

Of course, the technique can track other relevant paramenters in addition to the three positive connections – for example, how much you believe you deserve something, level of trance, feeling of safety, completion of goal, level of anger or fear, and so on. Such information is central to successfully guiding a creative process.

In using the scales, we generally seek *optimal* rather than *maximal* values. Thus, a relaxation level of 7 might be better than a 10 for certain activities. For practical purposes, we can see that very low ratings on an important dimension – for example, a 1 or 2 on "connection to center" – indicate an unreadiness for significant work. Similarly, the scales will fluctuate during any challenging work – for example, it is easy to become un-centered when touching into difficult experiences. By observing signs of neuromuscular lock – for example, muscle tension and breathing inhibition – scaling questions can be used to ascertain the level of centering (or other parameters) and then, if needed, to increase the state level.

Self-scaling can be used throughout a session, and also informally throughout the day. The tool allows you to monitor and shift state levels to optimal values. For many people, it is a revelatory awareness that they have direct access to their ongoing states. Such feedback is invaluable in creating and maintaining generative states.

Step 2: Welcoming and weaving identity parts into generative trance

Once the generative state has been prepared by the three positive connections, the trance work proper can be initiated. This second step has two main parts:

1.   Invite relevant parts into a generative trance field

2.   Weave the parts into a generative trance

Inviting parts into a generative trance field

Generative trance is not created through artificial, standardized suggestions, but rather through the emotionally relevant pieces of a person's identity. This ensures that the language of trance will be the very language that a person uses to create and maintain their identity, thereby making change easier and more lasting. (When a "foreign" language is used, what might be called the "psychological immune system" will reject it as not belonging to the system.)

Some relevant parts include:

1.   Goals

2. Problems

3. Resources

4. Negative parts (criticism, fear, objections)

5. Identity associations (job, family, hobbies, etc.)

A core premise is that *each part is integral and important to the system as a whole.* Creativity and growth are properties of the whole, not of the parts. This can be seen in systems such as musical groups, sports teams, families, marriages, and business teams. It is only when the different parts are in harmony that creativity emerges. In a problem state, key parts are in conflict and disconnection with each other, thereby creating a degraded identity state that produces problems. Remembering our guiding principle of transforming neuromuscular lock into creative flow, we become interested in how each part can be welcomed, positively engaged, and brought into connection with the other parts. The resulting identity state will be a generative field that gives rise to solutions and creative responses. This is the essence of generative trance work.

At first glance, it may seem inadvisable or impossible to invite all the relevant parts to become members of the solution team. The negative parts may seem so destructive and without merit that it appears the only hope is to remove them by any means necessary. By the time a person approaches generative work trance, this intra-system violence has been attempted in various ways with negative outcomes, so the real hope lies in transforming different parts and bringing them into a deeper systemic wholeness. Remembering the two-stage theory of experience, which states that an experiential pattern at a core level is without any fixed meaning and carries the potential for any form, we see trance as a way to de-frame negative parts to find their positive value, then open a generative field where all the disparate parts can become a cooperative team.

One of the great values of trance is as an experiential field where multiple, contradictory values can be held and integrated. We noted how the first step in this is to create a generative state based on centering, positive intention, and a resource field. The second is to invite the relevant parts into an interacting trance field. For example, Hank had been through a painful divorce but now, after several years, was dating a woman. Things were going well, until Hank started experiencing fears that he would be hurt again. For the generative trance work, the parts were:

1. Goal: "I want to experience an intimate relationship"

2. Problem: "But I feel distrust and fear"

3. Resources: professional success as an entrepreneur; daughter, Katie; connection to the ocean

4. Negative parts: memory of painful divorce; critical voice, "Don't ever trust anyone"; dread of financial ruin

We moved through the preparation step, and Hank was able to develop good connections with centering, positive intention, and resources. After briefly reviewing the above parts, I suggested a trance process where he would explore the relationship between the parts via moving his arms (with palms facing upwards) through four different positions. When the right arm was slowly lifted to shoulder level, he could attune to his goal; when it moved down a foot or so, he could attune to his resources. For the left arm, moving to shoulder level could activate different experiential aspects of the problem; and when it moved down a bit, the negative parts would be accessed. Note that this is a simple way to create a field with places for the four relevant parts. (It's not necessary to include all parts in every trance process, just those that seem most relevant.)

Creatively weave the parts into a generative trance

Once the relevant parts are given places, a generative trance can be developed by weaving them together. For example, with Hank I suggested, once he'd established the three positive connections, that he slowly lift his right arm to the shoulder position, to attune to the goal:

> And as you let your arm move to the shoulder position, let it almost float by itself ... you can begin to attune to all the different experiential aspects of your goal of intimacy ... breathing ... relaxing ... letting different images, feelings, thoughts come and go ... all having to with that goal of intimacy ... images of a future intimacy ... feelings and desires ...

This was elaborated for a bit longer, then attention was directed to the "problem part":

And as you let the right arm move back down ... you can let your left arm slowly lift up to shoulder height ... that's right ... slowly lift up to shoulder height ... so that as your left arm lifts, you can begin to attune to ... to welcome ... to allow different parts of the prob- lem to be sensed ... fears ... *I don't want to* ... concerns ... and yet even as those parts of the problem occur, you can feel your center ... remember your positive intention ... all the while making room for all the different parts of the problem ...

Notice that as the problem parts are invited, the underlying positive space of trance continues to be developed, so that *in generative trance there is always a positive holding space for any negative content.* To reiterate, success depends on the presence of this positive context, so primary attention is given to developing and maintaining it, especially when negatively toned material is being touched upon.

In this general way each of the parts can be invited into trance. Once each has its place, the next step is creatively weaving connections between them. This is where things get interesting, as the creative unconscious is invited to explore how to begin to make new connections between the parts. With Hank, I suggested that his unconscious begin to move his arms, such that it could guide the flow of which parts needed attention at which point, Thus, he stayed with the goal (right arm up) for about 30 seconds, then shifted to negative parts (left arm lower) for about 20 seconds, then over to resources (right arm down), and so forth. In this way, his creative unconscious led the process, with me following along and feeding back each position touched, while encouraging his unconscious to allow new understandings and more integrated ways of being in intimacy.

Generative trance elements of parts weaving

The weaving of the parts into a generative trance is an aesthetic practice. Many examples of aesthetic weaving exist: the blending of ingredients to make a good meal; the unfolding of a story, with its different characters and themes; a symphony orchestra; decorating a house; creating a dynamic business organization or sports team; a beautiful garden. In each instance, the weaving of disparate parts into an integrated whole is a central chal- lenge. When it happens, something special occurs: a beautiful aesthetic field opens that lifts consciousness to a higher level. This is what we're looking to do in generative trance: create a space where all the different identity parts can integrate into a deeper wholeness.

The following principles are especially helpful in this process:

1. *Limbic attunement.* Generative trance always involves two levels of consciousness. The first is an underlying contextual mindful awareness; the second is the different content elements of the work. Limbic attunement and resonance provide the first so that the second can creatively flow.

2. *Positive welcoming.* Each part is positively welcomed and absorbed into the process; while there may be unacceptable behaviors, there are no "bad parts". Doing the work while in a generative state (center, positive intention, resources) gives both the curiosity and safety needed to do this congruently and effectively.

3. *Aesthetic spacing.* Welcoming each part into the field is not simply a process of throwing them all together in a heap. To realize the goal of integrating the different parts, they must be aesthetically balanced in different ways – for example, how differentiated they are, the rate of shifting between parts, and the relative intensity levels. Often, one part may be more dominant than the others, thereby making creative flow impossible; or two parts may be too entangled together.

    Thus, the generative trance practitioner must have the skills of a dinner hostess or a team manager, sensing proper placing for the different parts so they can find a differentiated wholeness within the generative trance. Of course, this involves connections with each part and communicating in ways that get them to be part of the overall team.

4. *Musicality.* In Chapter 3, we touched upon musicality as the first language of human being, and an integral part of a generative state. Weaving words into trance fields is a musical patterning of sounds, silences, intonations, rhythms, breath, repetitions, resonances, and other nonverbal patterns. Special attention is given to how the words move through the body, and how to awaken the sensual intelligence of the somatic mind.

A training method I often use (to be explored in Chapter 6) involves students doing trance inductions with each other based entirely on made-up nonsense syllables. In groups with international students, I encourage people who speak a language that the client doesn't know to periodically move into that language while doing trance work. These experiments are surprisingly powerful experiences for speaker and receiver alike, as they demonstrate how trance can be deeply developed through nonverbal patterns.

Even when comprehensible words are used, people in trance are often not consciously listening to them. It is very common for a person to reorient from a trance I've been guiding and tell me something like, "That was great ... I didn't hear a word you said, but I felt this energy presence that allowed me to go into these amazing places". This is not to say that words are unimportant; it's that in trance we're letting our verbal meaning-making become secondary to the deeper energies and patterns of the creative unconscious.

5. *Symbol elaboration.* Finally, experiential elaboration of symbols can be used to foster trance. One of the basic differences between the conscious and creative unconscious minds is that the former treats a pattern as a sign, having one fixed meaning; whereas the creative unconscious treats that same pattern as a symbol, having multiple (even contradictory) meanings. To open the creative unconscious into a generative trance flow, we therefore playfully riff off certain words to make meaning shifts, jokes, and other word plays. For example:

And you can be *a part of* that experience and *apart from* it at the same time. And you can *know no* and *know yes* now, you know ...

And you can *be it* ... feel the *beat* ... *be* it ... feel the *being* ... the *beat* ... the *be*-ing *be*-fore ... *be*-cause bee in the bonnet as you move through trance.

The attitude here is pleasurably witnessing each word, image, symbol, feeling, and movement passing through mind–body awareness, curious about the multiple pathways that can be taken at any given point, even in mid-word or mid-sentence. As long as there is adequate rapport and trust, treating each word or image as a symbol that can open in infinite ways fosters play and curiosity while relaxing the neuromuscular lock of literal, linear, body-dissociated processing.

Step 3: Integration and transformation

The purpose of creatively weaving the parts into a generative trance is to allow new parts of the self to be born. This occurs through a transformational integration that occurs at the peak of any aesthetic progression – for example, when a team clicks into "the zone," the music rises to a crescendo, or the different parts of a suspense come to the exciting climax. Such a transcendent shift opens a space of consciousness beyond words and history, and a new identity can emerge.

This step is the culmination of the careful work of the preparation step and the creative work of the "trance weaving". With all the relevant identity parts in creative play, the experience is gradually intensified, as in a piece of music. This can include accelerated tempo and accelerated rate of shifting between parts, as well as heightened intensity. All this must be done in deep rapport, the conscious mind and creative unconscious engaged in mutual influence. Here's an excerpt of the trance work with Hank:

> And you can experience the goal … *I want intimacy* … the changing faces and feelings of the shyness … *not too fast* … all the resources … your work … *the ocean* … a curious shifting understanding of the critical voices … shifting … moving … increasing … on the one hand … on the other hand … and in a moment, when next I say the word "now" you can let yourself drop into a deeper level of trance … where all these experiential patterns can integrate together into a new positive identity … a new way to know … to trust … to experience intimacy … and let yourself drop deeper and experience that integration *noww*!

The last word ("now") is drawn out to sound like "the winds of change" blowing through a person's world. Interestingly, many people report this to be one of the most powerful parts of their trance experience. Coming at the point of integration, it provides a sort of a "trance slide" through space, opening many deep experiences.

Usually it's good to give about five minutes for the integration process.[5] During this time, few words are used, so as not to take away from a person's deep inner process. To ensure a holding field, some general trance suggestions (e.g., *that's it, that's good ... just letting it happen ... new future*) may be gently interspersed as background support. After about five minutes or so, attention can turn to the final step of returning to the ordinary world.

Step 4: Transfer learnings to real life

The goal in this final step is to ensure that the changes made in trance make it into a person's everyday life. Don't assume that this transfer will happen automatically. Figure 4.4 shows the basic elements of this step of orienting the trance changes into the real world.

Figure 4.4. Connecting trance changes to real life

1. Marking out key learnings

2. Imagining the positive future

3. Commitment/vows

4. Gratitude

5. Reorientation

6. Feedback

7. Incorporate feedback

---

5   Occasionally, the integration process will not happen. A person might open their eyes suddenly or display signs of tension or conscious thinking. This typically indicates that proper preparation has not been done (e.g., a person does not feel sufficiently relaxed or safe, or an important identity part has not been included). Simple inquiry and observation can usually reveal the source of any problem and open ways to resolve it.

To illustrate, here's how it was done with Hank:

Marking out key learnings

And so as you enjoy feeling all that you have experienced here today
... let yourself take a few moments to review the different experiences ... your goal of intimacy ... the fears ... all the resources you
have ... and just notice what changes you have begun here today
... and as you notice those changes, let yourself mark out the most
important learnings ... If there are one or two things you most want
to remember from these experiences here today, what are they?
Just let yourself silently note them ... breathe them in ... give them
a place inside of you (allow a minute or so).

Imagining a positive future

As you sense those new learnings, let yourself take a few moments to
sense yourself opening to the future ... to tomorrow, to next week ...
to next month ... and opening to that future ... you can enjoy seeing
yourself in that future ... seeing yourself ... feeling yourself ... enjoying yourself in experiences of intimacy ... integrated ... fulfilling ...
experiences of intimacy ... (this can be elaborated a bit further).

Commitments and vows

And in sensing that positive future ... seeing yourself already in
that future ... let yourself sense what vows you most deeply want
to make to yourself ... regarding your life ... regarding your future
... what simple vows ... what simple commitments ... and you can
sense those in simple ways ... *My deepest commitment is to* ... What
commitments to yourself ... to your world ... do you want to make?
... And as you sense them ... let yourself feel them deeply vibrating
in your center ... You may want to touch your center ... (pause) feel
your center ... and silently speak those vows ... practicing each day

... remembering each day ... the deepest life you want to live in this world.

Gratitude

And then finally, before wrapping things up, take a few moments to sense any gratitude you wish to express ... to yourself ... to any people or presences in your life that have given you the support ... the love ... the opportunity ... to live this amazing life ... let yourself sense anybody ... including yourself ... you would like to sincerely express gratitude for supporting these positive change you are making ... You can imagine that person and simply say, touching your center ... *Thank you* ... *Thank you* ... *Thank you* ...

Reorientation

And then when you are ready ... let yourself begin to gently prepare to bring closure to the experience ... perhaps you'd like to wrap a "second skin of light" around your body ... giving it protection ... giving it blessing ... to carry all these intimate learnings as you walk in the world in the coming days and weeks and months ahead ...

(Voice and resonance begin to shift to waking state "musicality") And then when you're ready ... let your creative unconscious return you back in the room here ... a breathing shift ... a gentle reorientation ... and opening of the eyes ... and coming all the way back now.

Reorienting should be done clearly but gently. Often a few minutes are needed to fully return, especially from a really deep experience.

Feedback

Post-trance feedback can then be elicited, unless a person feels a need to stay silent for a bit. (In self-trance contexts, journaling, or otherwise writing down the experiences can be very helpful.)

It may be helpful to note what seemed to help the trance process, and what interfered with it. Hank shared, for example, that the resonance of my voice felt like it was inside of him, giving a profound experience that he was not alone. He also described how the rhythmic movements between the problem (fear) and resources (his daughter) were really helpful. Every time he would feel scared, the sweet and silly presence of his daughter would "pop him out" of some "bubble trance of fear" that seemed really young, and the "trance waves" gave him a way to relax even in the face of the fear. He was surprised at how deep and young the "fear bubble" was, and was grateful for becoming aware of it.

Inquiry about *interferences* may reveal experiences such as a critical internal dialogue or inability to relax. Every trance is a good teacher about what a person's full needs and styles are, so all feedback should be received gratefully. For example, the critical voice would be regarded as a significant identity part to be included in subsequent work.

Feedback will also reveal that often the most meaningful experiences were never suggested by the practitioner; or that it was a seemingly small and inconsequential detail that turned out to be the most important part of the trance. This should not be surprising, as *the main task for the conscious mind in generative trance is to develop and maintain the proper conditions for the creative unconscious to lead the way*. This requires close attention to feedback at every step of the process, and a willingness to be guided by it.

Incorporate feedback for next cycle of work

Such feedback also guides subsequent work. For example, Hank's attunement to the "fear bubble" of his younger self led to significant further work around re-connecting and transforming the younger self. All in all, in generative trance work the conscious mind becomes a humble but attentive student to the creative unconscious.

Summary

We have explored here the four basic steps of generative trance work: (1) the preparation step of establishing positive intention, centering, and resources; (2) welcoming and creatively weaving identity parts into a trance field; (3) transformation and integration; and (4) incorporating the trance learnings into real life. There are infinite variations on how to perform these steps, with a person's ongoing experience guiding and shaping how the work unfolds. But within this creative weave, the four steps indicate an underlying deep structure for the work.

They thus provide a map for how to proceed, and an assessment tool for when things aren't working well. For example, if a person can't relax or doesn't feel safe, it suggests insufficient presence of the core positive connections of the preparation step. Or if an impasse is reached, it suggests that some relevant part is not being included. So if you're having difficulties, the four steps allow you to sense where and why you're having difficulties, thereby suggesting remedies.

Part II

The Methods of Generative Trance

Chapter 5
"Drop into Center": Somatic Attunement in Generative Trance

There is more wisdom in your body than in your deepest philosophies.

Friedrich Nietzsche

The physical world, including our bodies, is a response of the observer. We create our bodies as we create the experience of our world.

Deepak Chopra

Generative trance is a higher state of consciousness distinguished by a subtle field of mindful awareness that pervades the contents of classical consciousness – the thoughts, actions, embodied presences, and social and physical environments that make up our everyday experience. An experience of creative flow results, such as when an athlete is "in the zone" or a person is absorbed in deep concentration. Time disappears, worries dissolve, absorption deepens, and spontaneous yet skillful intelligence is activated.

One of the main ways to reach this higher state is through the body, which might be said to be the first "unconscious mind". The body carries and attunes to the history of consciousness, not only at a personal but a species level. It knows how to heal, how to intuitively think with what Gendlin (1978) calls "felt sense," and how to relationally attune and engage with extraordinary sensitivity.

Unfortunately, somatic intelligence is typically inhibited by the neuromuscular lock of ego consciousness, reducing the body to an "it" to be exploited, a machine to be programmed, or a dumb animal to be coerced into action. On work days, it is startled awake by the early morning alarm, fired up with caffeine and pushed out the door to worry and hurry through the day. At night, it descends into a torpor of food, television, and per- haps alcohol, then dragged to bed to sleep. Mind–body dissociation reigns supreme, with little trust or sense of the potential wisdom of the body, and no direct experiential connection with the world. Is it any wonder that we too often walk around feeling numb, scared, angry, or depressed?

The good news is that each person has the capacity to move to a generative level, where the body is experienced as subtle energy capable of healing and wisdom. Most people can remember such somatic "flow" experiences – for example, when engaged in aesthetic activities like reading a good book, listening to a beautiful piece of music, walking in nature, or gently holding a loved one. At such times, the body is not experienced as a half- witted ass, but rather as a sensitive intelligence that is the base for all meaningful thinking, acting, and feeling.

This is especially relevant to trance work, where traditionally (in Western hypnosis) the body is slumped or cataleptically stiff. Such somatic pattern- ing may release a person from his or her own ego control, but replaces it with the ego control of the external hypnotist. In effect, the physical body is still isolated from its creative base. In generative trance, we dissolve neuromuscular lock to open a subtle body that "transcends yet includes" the physical body and its experiences. Figure 5.1a illustrates how at the ego somatic level, neuromuscular lock isolates the body in classical con- sciousness, depriving it of a connection to the creative unconscious. The result is being stuck in anger, fear, dissociation, or tiredness. Figure 5.1b shows how, in contrast, at the generative level a subtle body opens up that is connected both to the quantum field of the creative unconscious and the physical body and its somatic consciousness, thereby making it a sort of "body of bodies" able to contextually hold many possible states of the physical body.[6] The fact that it is subtle and energetic, not physical, means that it is unwounded and unwoundable. How can you wound light? As such, this subtle field is an exceptional generative context for transforma- tional consciousness.

---

6   For an excellent overview of the history and present applications of subtle energy/ information to healing in Eastern, Western, and integrative medicine, see Dale (2009).

Figure 5.1a Ego-contracted somatic self. Person neuromuscularly locked in physical body without access to the creative flow of the quantum field

Figure 5.1b Generative somatic "body of bodies". Person centers and opens connection to the quantum field of the creative unconscious, creating a subtle body that can fluidly attune to both worlds

Lest you think this too esoteric, I would reiterate that any time we feel at our best, this embodied sense of wholeness and light is present. In optimal performance, it feels like this "greater presence" opens around us and moves through us; we must remain present and intentional, but also receptive to its intelligence.

This chapter explores how to develop and make use of this subtle body in generative trance. We first examine the general principle of mind–body centering, seeing how it allows attentional stability, connection to a mindful presence more basic than thought or action, an intuitive channel, and an integral base for unifying the disparate elements of experience into a powerful expression. We then move to exploring the different somatic dimensions of generative trance, emphasizing how a creative state arises from optimizing levels of relaxation, absorption, musicality, openness, and groundedness. In all of this, we are guided by the principle that reality is created from a state, so you want to be in the highest possible state to create the most rewarding experiences.

The generative principle of centering

We dance around in a ring and suppose,

But the Secret sits in the middle and knows.

Robert Frost, "The Secret Sits"

Centering is an experience of mind–body unity wherein all the dimensions of experience and expression are integrated into a calm, powerful, and mindful state. The distinction is especially found in performance arts such as dancing, acting, martial arts, and sports; it is also crucial for creative leadership, optimal performance in a challenging situation, and navigation through emotional difficulties. High-level performers know how to "drop into center," find the non-cognitive base of awareness "beneath and before" thinking, and use it to steady, relax, inform, and guide creative action. Centering is a core dimension of generative trance.

The first base of centering is somatic. You feel the physical center point of your body, attuning to it so all your movements can coalesce and be unified around it. In primarily movement domains like martial arts or dancing, the center is located right below the navel, as this is the actual physical center (if you were measuring with a ruler). For other activities, the center may be most felt in the heart or the gut, or even the "third eye". All of these chakra centers lay along the mid-line, so that the right and left sides may be in balance.

Just as the center is physical, it is also mental. It is not based on muscular tension but rather on subtle awareness attuned with a physical center. Free of neuromuscular lock, it allows consciousness to flow with relaxed concentration.

The values of centering

Figure 5.2 lists the important values of mind–body centering. Let's consider each in turn.

Figure 5.2. The values of centering

1. Attentional stability
2. Calm alertness
3. Non-judgmental experiencing
4. Connection to life force (*chi*)
5. Gateway to creative unconscious
6. "Sanctuary" or container for disturbed experiences
7. Allows cognitive/experiential differentiation/integration

Attentional stability

We need stability in one way or another in order to function well. The most typical ways involve neuromuscular lock around a fixed content. We cling to a rigid belief or ideology (fundamentalism); we need a person to always be there in a certain way; or we assume that a past experience represents what will always happen. While it may seem puzzling as to why someone would operate so rigidly, it makes sense when we appreciate that it satisfies the need for stability.

Centering is a superior stabilizer since it is content-free; it doesn't require a neuromuscular lock on some content. Consequently, you are open to the creative unconscious and free to have a stable and intentional attention that can creatively flow through many possibilities.

This is especially needed in trance work. Trance unbinds the identity filters defining the conscious mind, thereby opening to the vast networks of the creative unconscious, where you can "go anywhere from anywhere". By centering, you can keep a stable awareness and self-connection even while in deep or difficult waters.

Calm alertness

Centering both calms you and heightens your awareness. When your primary attention is resting in your somatic center, you are not stressfully reacting to the "soap operas" of everyday life. The "one point" of attention allows you to stay connected with each changing moment, with the relaxed attunement needed to creatively engage with whatever comes up.

Non-judgmental experiencing

In the non-dual awareness of centering, you are not caught up in "good vs. bad" evaluations as primary; you are able to sense things more directly. Of course, you can still discriminate and operate intentionally, as evidenced by centered high-level performers. It is just that you are not lost in your head and its judgments, and are more directly attuned to the wholeness of each moment.

Connection to life force

The mind–body unity of centering moves self-awareness out of ego contraction, back to the primitive fields of nature and mind. This results in a more creative flow of *chi*, the subtle life force that is immanent in all living consciousness. This enhances happiness, health, healing, and whatever work you want to do in the world.

Gateway to creative unconscious

A fifth value is that centering opens the subtle door to the creative unconscious and all its (ancestral) archetypal resources. When not centered, we are neuromuscularly locked in the limited history of our personal self. From there, all that is possible is versions of our past experience. Centering opens a sort of transduction channel into the quantum field of the creative unconscious, thereby allowing many new resources to be utilized.

In thinking of the center as a translucent gateway to the creative unconscious, two levels should be distinguished. The first is the empty (content-free) channel; the second is the particular content that is flowing through that channel at a given moment in time. When we are not centered, the primary channel is shut down. But when we center, our attention can rest in the primary channel, with a mindful and creative relationship to the secondary level of the content of awareness. This type of relationship is encouraged in the core trance and meditation idea of "just let it happen," inviting a process of witnessing each moment with curiosity, thereby allowing a more integrated and intelligent response.

"Sanctuary" or container

The primary (content-free) space of the center can also provide a sort of "safe place" or "sanctuary" for vulnerable or unintegrated experiences. The idea is that to transform any experience, it must first be given a home. As we will see, a core question in dealing with problematic experiences is:

> Where do you feel it most in your body?

Some basic settling down – breathing, slowing down, relaxing tense areas – might first be needed to allow access to somatic awareness. The felt sense is usually located in one of the main somatic centers – heart, solar plexus, or stomach.[7] As we will see, this felt sense can then be developed so that the negative emotional content – for example, fear – is held within a safe somatic center. When this happens, the negative experience of the emotion usually begins to spontaneously shift, as it encounters positive, kind human presence.

Centering can also be used as a sanctuary for archetypal (or other positive) resources – e.g., a healer self or higher power. One of the values of opening a generative trance is that it gives access to a field of positive resources. When a difficult experience arises, a resource self can be accessed and placed in the center as a consciousness that can hold, receive, and transform the difficult experiences. For example, Marianne was a woman who was trying to integrate childhood experiences from various ages – very young through adolesence – characterized by the feeling of never being seen and needing to take care of others. She felt unwilling and unable to be the caretaker for this wounded self – that was the function she wanted to release – so I suggested she allow a "higher consciousness" resource to appear to her. She was visited by the deep experiential presence of a "Divine Mother" with loving, open arms. I suggested that she invite this healing presence into her heart center, and allow her wounded selves to be held and healed by that presence. This was an extremely powerful process of discovering that she could surrender and trust in deeper parts of creative consciousness.

---

7   There is an important difference between the felt sense of a center and the emotional content of muscular reactivity. The former is the primary experiential response, and the latter is the secondary reaction to it. So fear and vulnerability may arise as a feeling in my stomach, and I might respond to it by tensing my shoulders and gritting my teeth. If caught up in this reactive posture, I will usually answer questions about felt sense with these secondary feelings (e.g., tension in the shoulders). To connect with the core feeling, we first need to relax the muscular locking.

Cognitive/experiential differentiation/integration

Centering allows a content-free mindful awareness to be differentiated from the contents of awareness. In other words, you can "be with something without becoming it". Thus, you can mindfully notice negative thoughts, images, and feelings without reactively identifying with them. This differentiation allows skillful, transformative relationships with such content. For example, if a feeling of panic shows up, you can mindfully open a space to welcome it, and then become curious about how to "be with it" in transformative ways.

All of this suggests that mind–body centering is a crucial dimension of generative consciousness. In harmonizing and unifying somatic and cognitive consciousness, it lifts both up to a generative level, where all the above positive qualities begin to emerge. When you are centered, you feel the subtle body, with its superior capacity to limbically attune, receive from the creative unconscious, stay connected, track subtle patterns, and be in optimal flow. In trance work, this allows you to stay intentional, relaxed, grounded, and accessible to resources, thereby allowing your goals to be realized.

Methods of centering

Figure 5.3 shows the three methods used in generative trance for centering: somatic attunement, positive memories, and negative experiences. Each will be considered in turn.

Figure 5.3. Three methods for centering

1. Somatic attunement
2. Positive memories
3. Negative experiences

Centering through somatic attunement

One of the easiest ways to center is by moving through a simple mind–body progression. To initiate this, the following straightforward process can be used:

1. *Settle in, settle down.* Take a few moments to find a comfortable posture where you can be both relaxed and aware at the same time ... as you do, let yourself settle in and settle down ...

2. *Shift from thinking to breathing.* And as you begin to settle in and settle down, let your awareness move from your thinking to your breathing ... just notice how the waves of your breath move in ... and move out ... move in ... and move out ... just like the waves of the sea.

3. *Release muscle tension.* And as you allow your breath to move in and move out, you can enjoy discovering how your muscles can begin to relax ... begin to release tension ... so that your breath can flow in ... and flow out.

4. *Breathe through vertical axis.* As you relax your muscles and follow your breath, see how you can allow your breath to move up and down through your spine ... as you breathe in, let the breath move up, inside the spine, all the way to the crown of your head, and continuing all the way to the heavens above ... and as you breathe out, you can sense the breath moving down through your spine, down through your body, down your hips and knees ... down through the soles of you feet ... dropping all the way down to the center of the earth.

5. *Relax and drop hips.*[8] And as you sense the subtle flow of the breath moving up and down your spine, you can relax your muscles a little deeper ... especially curious about how your hips can really relax and drop lower and lower ... your hips relaxing and opening and dropping down ... so you enjoy a beautiful sense of grounding and feeling more and more calm and present.

---

8   It can be said that a boy becomes a man, and a girl becomes a woman, when their consciousness drops down through their hips. Until then, they are up in their head, feeling like they need to please and impress others, not really knowing their own power. When their center of gravity drops, a calm groundedness opens up. A person can be present without having to perform, and can discover a new type of intelligence and power.

Each of these steps can be elaborated and modified according to individual needs. For centering through somatic attunement, the following communications could be added:

> And from that place, let yourself sense where in your body you most feel your core, your center. If you were going to move from that place of inner connection ... if you were going to speak from that place of inner knowing ... where would your center be? ... In your heart? ... In your belly? ... In your solar plexus? ... Just sense where the core of that place is, a center that would give you a deep sense of presence ... and when you feel that place, go ahead and place one of your hands there ... very gently ... very mindfully ... letting yourself sense how placing your hand and awareness there can help you become even more *centered ... even more attuned ...*

The strength of the center can be assessed and monitored by the self-rating scales described in the last chapter, where 1 represents the low end ("none or very little") and 10 is the high end. The simple request is:

> On a scale of 1 to 10, let a number come that represents how much you feel the presence of your center now.

This can be assessed before and during a challenging task. A low rating means more centering is needed before continuing. The basic idea is that when you remain centered, good things will happen; when you lose your center, all bets are off.

Centering through positive memories

Centering can also be developed by revivifying positive memories – for example, a time when you felt a really deep connection with yourself and the world. To do this as a trance process, you could start with the five-step process used above, then add:

> And let yourself begin to allow a positive memory come into mind ... a time in your life when you felt deeply connected ... deeply whole ... deeply confident ... perhaps an experience in nature ... or when you were with someone you really love ... or when you succeeded at a challenging task. Just let such a positive memory come into your

awareness. And when a memory comes, let me know by nodding your head (elaborate until head nods) ... Great, and I'd like to thank your unconscious mind for bringing forward that memory into the present experience. And as you sense that memory, let yourself notice and enjoy all the sensory details, breathing them in, letting them attune you to that state once again ... You can notice the place ... who was there ... the most interesting feelings and details ... And with each sensory awareness, let yourself feel that experience fully again in your body ... each breath bringing the experience more deeply into the present moment ... so that you can begin to sense those feelings now ...

After such an invitation, you can ask about what a person accessed, where it somatically resonates most in their body, and the present intensity level. Finding out about the content provides positive trance techniques to be used throughout the work. For example, if a person remembers walking in the forest, this content can be added into the trance "song" at various times in a session (such as when positive resources are needed or trance needs to be deepened). The centering can be deepened by having a person touch their hand gently to the center and breathe into it to develop an aligned harmony. Self-rating could similarly be used to identify and modify the degree of centering experienced.

Centering through negative experiences

A third way to center is through negative experiences. Since such experiences are not uncommon when a person is exploring meaningful work, it is important to be willing and able to skillfully utilize them for different positive purposes, including centering. Such experiences are often neuromuscularly locked in the center, thereby shutting down creative flow and forcing a person to live away from their core. This makes sense within our two-level theory of experiential construction: whenever a new resource is needed (that is not available within the ego state of a person), the creative unconscious activates and sends some core archetypal patterns through the transduction channel of the center. As they emerge into the world, they are met by human presence, either a person's own or other people. If met negatively, the core experience freezes in the somatic center with a negative form and meaning. (Remember, a core energy or pattern has infinite possible meanings in the creative unconscious; it collapses into one particular form by virtue of the human connection with it.) The person now feels alienated from their core, fearful that if they relax or open to it, some horrible (often primordial) fate will befall them. This is a main reason why so many people live away from their center. Unfortunately, the locked content means that each time the person engages in that area of their life, the unintegrated negative experience will automatically fire off. What is important to appreciate is that such experiences are trapped in the center, shutting down its open channels and frightening a person away from their core consciousness.

By being willing and able to skillfully engage with the disturbed energies in the center, a tremendous shift can occur. When doing such work, it is very important to realize that the *primary connection is to the unwounded (and unwoundable) core of the center*. The outer face of the experience – the content of fear, pain, or anger – reveals a conditioned history of negative human relationships, but the inner energy reveals that the unconditioned light of the spirit is still active at the core. (Were this not the case, there would be no suffering, merely a passive resignation to the outer injustice.) So we train ourselves not to get "hypnotized" by the surface content, instead resonating with the positive life force inside of it.

Figure 5.4. "Relational mantras" for engaging negative experiences

1. That's interesting
2. I'm sure that makes sense
3. Something is trying to heal or wake up
4. Welcome

This requires applying positive and respectful curiosity to each experience connected to the somatic center, whether positive or negative. Figure 5.4 shows four core "relational mantras" helpful in this regard. (By this I mean a word or phrase that, when repeated silently, can help in a transformational conversation.[9]) Here's a brief example of how it was done to help a woman use her "panic" as a means of centering.

---

9   The etymological roots of *mantra* are the Sanskrit words *man* ("to think" or "of the mind") and *tra* ("instrument" or "tool"), thus giving the literal translation of "instrument of thought", or something that improves the quality of mind.

Alexandra: It's really hard for me to relax. I feel this sense of *panic* start to happen.

Gilligan: (takes a deep breath, slows down) That's interesting ... I'm sure that makes sense. (gentle twinkle in eyes) So when you go to relax, this presence of what you're calling *panic* shows up ... Is that right?

Alexandra: Yes.

G: That's interesting... I'm curious ... Where in your body do you most feel the presence of this experience you're calling *panic*?

Alexandra: (touches heart and chest) Here.

G: (pauses, breathes, looks to feel resonance with the somatic presence in Alexandra's heart) Thanks for letting me know that that's where she is right now[10] ... And on a 1 to 10 scale, where 1 is the low end and 10 is the high end, how much do you feel the presence of *panic* right now?

Alexandra: About an 8.

G: 8 ... That's interesting ... I would like to say to that presence inside of your heart, *welcome* (voice softens) ... *Welcome*. I'm glad you've joined us. (pause) And what do you notice when I say that?

Alexandra: It seems ambivalent. One part seems to calm down, the other gets more worried.

G: One part more calm, the other more worried. *I'm sure both sides make sense, I'm sure they each have deep integrity* ... And what happens when I say that?

---

10 The use of the personal pronoun ("she" or "he") is often helpful in shifting the meaning of an unintegrated negative experience from the dehumanizing "it" language of traditional psychotherapy to the humanizing "thou" language. The idea is that each negative energy represents a cursed soul presence or human part of a person, which can be transformed into its positive form by humanly valuing it. Shifting to personal pronouns can help in this regard. But if using them seems a bit too strange for a person (and there is indeed a skill in introducing such a language), there are other possibilities, such as: "There is a part of you that feels X" or "There is a presence inside of you that is filled with X" (e.g., anger). Using the third person also differentiates the experiential part from the observing ego, thereby making it easier to have a clear, curious relationship.

Alexandra: Well, it gets a little calmer.

G: That's great, it gets a little calmer. (Takes a breath, slows down, quiet attunement with client.) And whatever that presence is in your heart and chest, I really would like to invite her into our conversation ... because I'm sure she has tremendous integrity and tremendous importance for you. So again, *welcome* ... What's happening now?

Alexandra: It feels calm in my heart ...

G: That's great ... thanks so much for sharing that ... And perhaps you'd like to place your hand on your heart ... just taking a few moments to *enjoy that calmness, to breathe into that deep center of your heart* ... where I can sense you carry so much wisdom ... so much delicacy ... so much love ... that needs understanding ... protection ... and listening. Isn't it nice to know that your heart center carries so much beautiful wisdom?

Alexandra: Yes.

This illustrates how by adopting a centered, positive curiosity about the core of a negative somatic experience, you can transform it to its positive form. To do this skillfully requires tremendous sensitivity and flexibility. For example, sometimes you can only spend a few moments touching a negative experience before shifting attention to some positive focus (e.g., a pleasant memory), so that overloading doesn't occur. But by attuning to the positive inner core, you can gently and carefully open its lotus blossom back into the world of being.

As in all generative trance work, the relational attunement and musical resonance of the communication is of primary importance. Whether doing this with self or others, the intent is to resonantly join with the core presence. The resulting limbic resonance becomes the primary guide in each moment. When resonance increases, move in that direction; when it decreases, release the direction and sense where the better (more resonant) path may be.

Somatic elements of generative trance

It is only by grounding our awareness in the living sensation of our bodies that the "I Am," our real presence, can awaken.

George Gurdjieff

We might think of the subtle body of the generative somatic mind as a quantum field with many diverse energetic qualities dancing within it. Figure 5.5 shows five basic somatic elements that we seek to optimize for a generative trance.

Figure 5.5. Somatic elements of generative trance

1. Relaxation

2. Absorption (concentration)

3. Musicality (rhythm and resonance)

4. Openness

5. Groundedness

The importance of the first element is perhaps self-evident: if you don't have a decent level of *relaxation*, creative consciousness is not possible. It's interesting to listen to interviews with top athletes; when asked what they were thinking before or during a big competition, many say they weren't thinking, they were just trying to relax and get into a rhythm. Such relaxation, of course, is different from what you find in a person drinking in a bar or someone slumped in front of the television. Generative relaxation is more like what you see in any creative performer. It is a centered relaxation with lots of awareness to go with it.

Thus, a second element is *experiential absorption*: to be creative you need good concentration. Unfortunately, trance is too often thought of primarily in terms of relaxation, so people sometimes think that if they just sort of collapse into a heap and drool, good things will happen. They won't. A generative trance embodies a good balance of relaxation and concentration. A *cardinal feature of creative consciousness is the capacity to think without neuromuscular lock*, and relaxed concentration opens this experience of creative flow.[11]

A generative trance also has *musicality*, with its various dimensions of rhythm, resonance, fluidity, and play. You need to be able to creatively flow through many experiential possibilities in generative trance. Locking into a single view is the kiss of death for good trance work; you need to stay flexible, always delighting in the twists and turns of creative trance experience.

A sense of play is especially important. Life is much too serious to survive without a good sense of humor. Without play, it's hard to be creative. Interestingly, Milton Erickson was probably the most playful person I've ever met, especially in his therapeutic sessions. He delighted in jokes, plays on words, surprises, and other shifts that would move consciousness into a high level of creative play. As he would say, clients come into therapy because they are rigid, and your job is to help them get un-rigid. Fluidity and play are therefore essential ingredients in this process.

A fourth element of a generative somatic state is *openness*. This means that somatic attention is radiating outwards, attention stopping nowhere. This is in contrast to the neuromuscular lock of most concious thinking, where the mind–body constricts onto the object of its focal attention. By making the peripheral field dominant, you don't lock into any content of consciousness, and can stay connected to the creative unconscious.

A final element is *groundedness*. To creatively engage with difficult emotional experiences, it's important to feel settled and connected to the earth. It's also important as you open to the flow of many experiential images that move across many different frames of reference. Being grounded allows you to witness what is happening without neuromuscular lock.

---

11   It is interesting to note that Milton Erickson's polio rendered him completely paralyzed during the formative years of late adolescence, thereby forcing him to learn to think without muscular tension. In this way, what for most people is the "unconscious mind" became, I believe, his primary or conscious mind.

The somatic mixer model

Our bodies are our gardens – our wills are our gardeners.

William Shakespeare

Health is the result of relinquishing all attempts to use the body lovelessly.

A Course in Miracles

Along with centering, these five elements are the somatic base of a generative trance state. A creative state has an optimal blend of relaxed, focused, resonant, open, and grounded attention. To achieve this, the self-scaling method introduced in Chapter 4 can be used in a process I call the *somatic mixer model*. An image of the somatic mixer is shown in Figure 5.6, with each dimension represented as a parameter that can be adjusted from "1" to "10". The process can be done via the self-scaling method introduced in Chapter 4. A given element – for example, *relaxation* – can be experientially optimized by identifying its present and desired levels, then asking the creative unconscious to make make the shift from the former to the latter.

Figure 5.6. The Somatic Mixer Model

To reiterate, small changes (1-2 point increases) are generally more help-ful than big changes, and optimal values are preferred to maximal values. Thus, a 6 or 7 on the relaxation scale might be better than a 10 for cer-tain tasks where you wouldn't want complete relaxation. Similarly, a 10 on playfulness might be a bit much for a challenge needing seriousness as well. Thus, each person can find which intensity levels are optimal for a given task.

For generative trance work, the somatic mixer model can be used in differ-ent ways. Figure 5.7 outlines how the four steps of generative trance could be used in this regard.

Figure 5.7. Self-scaling of somatic state

Step 1: Preparation

    a.   Center

    b.   Set intention

    c.   Invite resources

Step 2: Develop generative trance via client resources

    a.   Select one dimension (e.g., relaxation) and identify present intensity level (1–10 scale)

    b.   Suggest small increase in intensity level

    c.   Invite person to close eyes and discover how that can happen (via images, memories, etc.)

    d.   When rating increases, suggest brief trance exploration of goal

    e.   Repeat with second dimension

Step 3: Transformation

    a.   Creative weaving of experiential associations around goal development

    b.   Integration

Step 4: Return into external world

    a.   Future orientation (imagine self with realized goal)

    b.   Vows/commitments

    c.   Gratitude and appreciation

    d.   Reorientation

    e.   Feedback

Step 1: Preparation

We start with the preparation step of developing the three positive connections: centering, positive intention, and experiential resources. The order in which these connections are developed is variable. For example, some people might best start with a goal, others with centering, still others with resources. It is also possible to be shifting among the three levels – for example, starting with intention ("What do you want?"), then shifting to centering ("Where do you feel it most in your body?"), then back to intention, and so forth. The important thing is not to follow a fixed protocol but rather the unique unfolding process of each person.

When a coach is working with a client, both need to move into a generative state. So whatever the coach says to a client, he or she moves through his or her own somatic consciousness. As we will explore further in the next chapter, this locates the trance in the interpersonal field, and allows the coach to be equally an observer and participant in the process. Here's a straightforward example of the step with a man wanting a better marriage. After a few moments of social pleasantries, the preparation step is introduced.

> Gilligan: So shall we get to the work at hand?
>
> Allan: Sounds good.
>
> G: Great. Let's each take a few moments to go inside and settle in and settle down ... Let's get a comfortable position, relaxed yet aware ... straight spine, relaxed shoulders ... Take a few deep breaths ... settle

in and settle down ... switching from our social performance mask to our inner core ... that's it ... that's good.

And from that place of deeper inner connection, let yourself tune to the most meaningful goal you'd like to set for the work. I'd like to suggest you use the following form: "What I most want in my life is _____" and then use five words or less for the goal.

Allan: (pause) I want to be a happy person.

G: That's great. You want to be a happy person ... (pause, breath, somatically attune) And as you sense that longing, that goal, notice where in your life this would be most meaningful. There may be many different areas, but just notice which area seems most important for developing happiness.

Allan: (brief pause) In my marriage ...

G: Great, that's good ... (pause, resonance attunement) When I listen to you say that, it touches something deep and resonant in me, and it looks like it does for you, too ... Is that right?

Allan: Yes.

G: That's great. Thanks for sharing this important part of your life with me.

Allan: You're welcome.

(Having touched a place of resonance, about 30 seconds of silent attunement occurs. When relationally connected, this simple process and deepens a shared trance field.)

G: Now for our second step, I'm going to invite you to close your eyes, and take a few moments to find your deepest core center from which you can create this happiness in your marriage. You can let go of thinking about the marriage for the moment, instead letting yourself close your eyes ... *that's good* ... and just breathe ... *that's good* ... and let go ... *that's good* ... and let yourself remember an experience in which you felt a deep connection with wisdom, with positive motivation, with a good feeling ... Let whatever experience of confidence and wisdom come to you ... And when you have one, you can take a nice deep breath, open your eyes again, and let me know what you discovered ...

(After 30 seconds of silence, Allan takes a breath and opens his eyes.)

Allan: It's interesting, I was remembering a conversation with my mother, who just died in this last year. She was very ill, but we had some great connections and conversations.

G: Wow, that sounds powerful ... Let's breathe with that a bit ... (brief silence with relationally attuned breathing) That's great, thanks ... And in the memory you recalled, what was happening?

Allan: She was telling me that I could do whatever I wanted, that I could be whatever made me most happy ... (tears well up)

G: That's great, thanks for sharing that ... and notice as you take a few moments to breathe with that memory ... feeling its presence deep in your body ... notice where in your body you most feel its core center ... just breathe ... just notice ... where is that positive feeling of confidence most felt in your body?

Allan: (touches his heart) Here ...

G: Yes, I can see that very deep experience is centered in your heart. Just take a few moments to continue to touch your hand there, finding a way to deepen your connection with it ... deepening your connection to your center ... That's great ... that's good ...

(As Allan absorbs in the centered experience, I slow down to open a space for it, and adjust my resonance to join more deeply with it.)

And on a scale of 1 to 10, how much do you feel the presence of that center now?

Allan: 10.

G: 10 ... That's great ... And by the way, how much do you feel your connection and commitment to the goal of finding a deeper happiness in your marriage ...

Allan: About a 5 ... (pause) Wow, that's a bit surprising. I thought it would be higher.

G: About a 5 ... that's good to know! That *right now* it's a 5. Who knows what it will be in a short while? But it's great to know that you can sense exactly where you are in relationship to an experience inside of you ... anytime, anywhere ... Isn't that good to know?

Allan: Yes, it really is ...

G: Now do you think it would be interesting to discover how you might increase that connection to your goal just a little bit more – perhaps one or two points – just enough to feel it move to a deeper place inside? Do you think that would be interesting?

Allan: Yes ...

G: Good ... When you're ready, close your eyes and take a deep breath ... that's it ... a nice deep breath ... letting go ... and as you let go, you can let your inner creative self begin to send into your awareness any images, memories, people, places, symbols, colors ... that will help you deepen your connection to your goal ... perhaps to a 6 ... or a 7 ... just notice how your inner self can help you to do that.

(Allan smiles.)

And what do you become aware of there?

Allan: It's strange, I became aware of playing as a child. I was about 9 or 10, and my older brother was telling me I had to be more serious, and I remembering thinking, no, I need to play ... (smiles) *I need to play* ... and so I went and played out in the fields with my dogs.

G: And as you attune to those memories, notice your present intensity level regarding the intention.

Allan: 8.

G: 8 ... that's great ... So you discovered that when you need to increase your connection to a goal, you can ask your creative unconscious to help you ... and this time it helped you by bringing a long forgotten, pleasurable memory of needing to play ...

So right now your intention is at an 8 ... and how about your connection to your center ... your mom saying, "You can do whatever makes you happy" ... how much connection to your center?

Allan: 10.

G: 10 ... that's great ... Now in addition to developing a good connection to your center, and to your positive intention or goal, I want to make sure you are also connected to some of the many resources that are in this world to help you on your journey ... Of course, resources can be of many different types ... so just close your eyes ... take a deep breath ... center ... sense your goal ... and ask your creative unconscious to send into your awareness whatever resources might best help you on this wonderful journey of finding deeper happiness in your marriage. The resource might be a family member ... or a friend ... perhaps a teacher ... a special place in nature ... an animal ... a spiritual being ... ancestors ... just notice what comes up ... And what do you become aware of?

Allan: It's very interesting. I first saw waves from Hawaii ... (smiles) ... I felt this awesome freedom and happiness of watching those waves ... I'm not sure why ... it was just there ...

G: Great ... waves in Hawaii ... Do you surf?

Allan: (smiles) Yes. It's one of the happiest things that I do.

G: Great. So somehow your creative unconscious is trying to get the happy Hawaiian waves into your marriage ... Isn't that interesting? (smiles)

Allan: (smiles) Yes, indeed. It feels somehow very important.

G: Great, the Hawaiian waves are very important. Is there anything else?

Allan: Yes, I became aware of these memories of my wife and me in the first year of our relationship. We had these long, beautiful talks about our lives ... what we wanted to do with them ... how we wanted to be together and live and support each other on our journeys.

G: Great, so the presences of you and your wife, from the early days of the relationship, came to visit you. That's wonderful. I would like to say to them: *Welcome ... welcome, Allan and Eliza ... thanks for joining the journey here.* (pauses) And what happens when I say that?

Allan: I feel their presence increase ...

G: Where do you sense them in your present field? Are they inside of your body? Hovering over your head? Behind you? Just notice where in the present space you sense these important resources.

Allan: It's very interesting. I can feel them over my right shoulder.

G: Yes, that's very interesting. (looks over Allan's right shoulder and gently waves) Welcome to both of you. Thank you for coming forth to guide Allan on his great journey of deepening happiness in his marriage. Now Allan, how much do you feel the presence of those resources?

Allan: About 8 or 9.

G: 8 or 9 ... that's great ... Now before concluding our preparation step, I'd like to invite you to close your eyes again, take a deep breath ... settle in ... settle down to your deepest state of awareness and presence ...

And then attune first to the goal ... *I want a happy marriage ... I want a happy marriage ... I want a happy marriage ...* and just notice how much you can feel that connection ... *that's good ... that's good ...*

And as you feel the positive connection to your core goal, let yourself feel also your connection to your center ... (Allan touches heart) ... *that's good ...* and just breathe in and through your heart center ... noticing where you are on the 1 to 10 scale ... and enjoying how you can always shift the level as needed ... just feel that connection to your center ... that's good ...

And as you feel the deep positive connections to your goal and to your center, let yourself also sense the different resources you have to give support ... encouragement ... protection ... positive examples ... to allow you to realize this deep intention of a happy marriage ... Notice who shows up ... perhaps the waves in Hawaii ... your mother

... yourself at a younger age ... always curious as to the many creative resources that can offer support ... that's good ... that's great ...

Finally, just let yourself take a few moments to shift among the three positive connections ... *intention* ... *center* ... *resources* ... ... until you can begin to feel them weave together ... as a great base for your journey.

And from that place of integrated wholeness, take a few moments to notice the few most important learnings you have made here today ... the few most basic learnings to take forward into your journey ...

And from that place of awareness, perhaps you'd like to make a simple vow ... a sacred commitment ... regarding your participation in your marriage ... As children we usually make negative vows ... of who we don't want to be like ... of what we don't want to happen ... And what a nice thing to know that as we become grownups, we are called to make the positive vows, the positive commitments ... of how we will live our lives ... how we will be in our relationships with ourselves ... and with others ... So just take a few moments to sense what vows you feel called to make ... then a few moments to express gratitude to yourself and any others in your life that have given support for this important part of your journey ... and then when you're ready, take a nice deep breath, and come on back into the outer world.

(Allan opens eyes and smiles.)

G: Hi! Welcome back ...

Allan: Thanks!

Allan shares how he made some deep connections in the experience. He expresses surprise about some of the images (e.g., the Hawaii surf) and is moved by the memories of the early intimacy in his marriage.

The preparation step is elaborated here to emphasize its importance as a precursor for generative change. Developing and sustaining the three positive connections generally ensures good outcomes, though it is easy to lose the connections. Thus, ongoing monitoring and maintenance of the connections is of primary importance. Again, we are always tracking two levels: the content of the process (i.e., how to create the desired changes) and the underlying state in which the process is occurring. A disturbance in the state results in a diminished outcome. This is the main purpose of generative trance: to open a creative state in which difficult challenges can be positively addressed. That is why we give even more attention to the quality of the state than its content.

Step 2: Develop generative trance via client resources

Once the preparation step is achieved, the generative trance can be further developed by optimizing the different elements in the somatic mixer. I recommend starting with relaxation, as it forms a base for the others. In an hour session, you usually have time for perhaps one additional element. This can be selected by sensing which additional element might be most beneficial for a person's state and situation. For example, a highly serious person might be most helped by increased playfulness, whereas a reactive person's state might be best improved with greater absorption. Of course, you can also simply ask the person to identify which additional element would be the most helpful addition to their state.

The process for optimizing a somatic element is similar to that used for the preparation step.

> G: So Allan, let's move our attention to this wonderful question of how you can find more happiness in your marriage.
>
> Allan: OK.
>
> G: Take a few moments just to settle in and settle down once again ... and let yourself sense those positive connections again ... to your center ... that's it ... to your positive intention of a happy marriage ... that's it ... and to the many resources ... waves ... beaches ... good memories ... Hawaii ... and much more ... and when you've reconnected well with each of those, you can let me know by nodding your head ...
>
> (Allan nods head after about 20 seconds.)

G: Great. Thank you. And now before you fully discover how to begin to find more happiness, I want to make sure you're in your best possible state, connected to the very best of who you are and who you can become ... And one component of that best possible state is being deeply relaxed, relaxed enough so you can allow a deep learning experience. Does that make sense?

Allan: Yes, it does ...

G: Great. And to find your best state of relaxation, let's start with your current level. Using that same 1 to 10 scale we used earlier, where 1 is the low end and 10 is the high end, I'd like you to just tune into your inner state, notice your level of relaxation, and let a number pop into your mind that represents your present level of relaxation. Just let the number pop in – you don't have to effortfully think about it so much ...

Allan: The number 6 just came to me ...

G: Great. 6. Isn't that good to know that anytime, anywhere, you can sense just how relaxed you are?

Allan: (smiles) Yes, indeed ...

G: And do you think it would be interesting to discover how you might increase that level of relaxation just a little more – perhaps one or two points on the scale – *just enough to allow a deeper state of relaxation to develop in which your creative unconscious can begin to develop positive new changes?*

(Allan nods head.)

G: Not *too* much. (smiles) You can save the 10 for another time. *Just enough to go into a creative trance where the positive changes can begin to develop.*

Allan: That would be interesting ...

G: Great, so when you're ready you can *close your eyes again and take a nice deep breath ... and as you take that nice deep breath*, and let your creative unconscious begin to bring forth whatever images ... memories ... songs ... associations ... feelings ... symbols ... that allow you to *relax just a little more now ... just enough to begin a creative trance-formation ...*

(30 seconds of silence, to allow accessing to develop. As during the whole process, the coach is an observer-participant who is fully sensing his or her experience in the mutual field.)

And what number comes to mind now, representing your present level of relaxation?

Allan: 8.

G: 8 ... That's wonderful ... What a nice thing to know you can deepen your level of relaxation anytime, anywhere ... And what did you notice in terms of experiential associations?

Allan: I felt a warmth in my body and I saw an image of a lion lying in the middle of a field ... (smiles) I was surprised, but it felt really deep and interesting ...

G: Great. So when you asked your creative unconscious to help you relax, it brought you a feeling of warmth and a symbol of a lion.

Allan: Yes.

G: That's interesting.

This somatic mixer process was repeated with the element of playfulness, chosen because Allan was a bit over-serious. He started at 3, then moved to 7, via the creative unconscious images of diving in a pool and the American childhood song of "Do the Hokey Pokey". (Notice again that all the experiential trance shifts are generated by a person's own creative processes.)

Step 3: Transformation

The first two steps of (1) developing positive connections and (2) optimizing the somatic state, create a generative trance field wherein new brain maps can be born. In Chapter 3 we touched upon some of the (COSMIC) dimensions of this state: Centered, Open (and mindful), Subtle awareness, Musicality, Intention (positive), and Creative engagement. In this creative field, many different elements of identity can be mixed and re-mixed into new mandalas of identity.[12] Some of the most important are (1) the positive future goal, (2) resources, and (3) relevant memories and beliefs. It is not important that all the elements be positive, as the presence of a generative state opens a non-dual field beyond "good vs. bad". However, it is important that there be a balance of energies on different levels, just as in a piece of music, a good book, or a dance.

Here is a sample of how Allan was invited to experience this transformational step:

> And as you allow yourself to release ever more into a creative state ... feeling the center ... remembering the intention ... so many resources flowing ... you can feel each different part of your marriage ... your understanding of it ... your history in it ... all the related aspects of it ... to begin to whirl and swirl in that beautiful sense of trance-formational music ... music to the ears ... music in the eyes ... music for the future ... all the different notes and chords ... accords and past discords ... music of new harmonies forming ... different memories, each a different note in the symphony ... different feelings, each a different tone ... moving in time, in breath, in center, in deeper trance-formation ... times of love ... times of fear ... beautiful jewels ... old wounds ... all swimming in time, glimmering in rhyme ... unfolding ... enfolding ... refolding into a new image of intimacy now and in the future ...

> And as you continue to feel all the relevant images ... memories ... beliefs ... needs ... intentions ... regarding your marriage ... each reflecting a different light ... each sounding a different note ... in a moment you can allow yourself to go a little deeper, deep enough to allow a full trance-formational integration of all these different experiential dimensions ... letting them coalesce into a new pattern, a new mandala, a new brain image of a positive marriage ... as you take a deep breath, you can let that integration begin *nowwwwwwww!*

In this several minute period of integration, any communications offered are just to support the space in which the integration is occurring. Gentle

---

12 I believe this is what Erickson meant when he described therapeutic trance as an experiential learning state where a person could reorganize and re-synthesize learnings to better reflect the needs and capabilities of the present self.

support suggestions can be offered – for example, "that's it," "a deep integration," "a new pattern from within," and so on. After several minutes of integration, the final step can be done.

Step 4: Return into external world

The third step is about using generative trance to create a new identity map as the base for forging a more positive future. The fourth step is about extending this new map into the world. Here is an abbreviated version of how this was done with Allan:

Future orientation

> And as you enjoy all the new changes you've created here today ... sensing a new, more positive relationship to your marriage ... you can take a few moments to let yourself orient into the days and weeks and months ahead ... looking forward in time to the coming future ... seeing a beautiful light guiding the way ... and you can allow one of your subtle bodies, one of your imaginary selves ... to move forward, through time, into that positive future ... perhaps several months from now ... and as you sense that imaginary Allan in the future, you can see him ... you can feel him ... you can enjoy him enjoying his marriage ... a sense of happiness ... and you can see him looking back through time, and signalling you ... connecting with you ... calling you ... guiding you ... towards that future with a sweet happiness.

Vows and commitments

> And as you see that positive future ... as you feel the deep important experiential changes you've experienced here today ... as you sense how deeply important a happy marriage is to you in your life ... you can take a few moments and just notice whatever simple, deep vows you'd like to make to yourself ... whatever simple commitments you want to make to your marriage ... deep in your heart ... deep in your

soul ... living from simple, deep, positive vows of how you want to live your life ... how you want to be in your marriage ... how you want to grow in this world.

Gratitude

And in sensing what you've learned here today ... what you've realized here for today and tomorrow and the rest of your life ... in sensing the possibilities and committing to creating the actualities of a happy marriage ... just let yourself sense whomever you'd like to thank ... for whomever you have gratitude ... for helping you in living a happy marriage ... perhaps yourself ... your wife ... teachers ... friends ... just notice who you'd like to thank.

Reorientation

And then when you're ready, you can find yourself taking a nice deep breath ... and open your eyes ... and come back into the outer world.

This is one example of the somatic mixer method. Endless variations are possible. Each trance is unique, and each moment may bring a surprising or unexpected development – this is the nature of the creative process. The important point is that centering and somatic attunement are integral parts of generative trance, and the somatic mixer method is a very helpful means to optimize their values. When we find the aesthetic "sweet spot" in which different experiential dimensions are properly balanced and integrated, special things happen. This is our goal in generative trance work.

In using the somatic mixer and self-scaling, action is no longer determined by a fixed protocol. With a positive goal in mind and resources at hand, somatic resonance may become a primary navigator, as it indicates a mind–body (cognitive/somatic) unity. An increase in resonance is a green light, while decreases mean slow down or stop. Resonance can tell when an important experience has been activated, when words fit, and if a new direction has promise. This close attunement to the somatic mind allows one to "trust the unconscious" with a disciplined intuition.

When we are no longer imposing rigid control, each experience has its own unique unfolding. This applies not only to what happens in trance, but afterwards as well. Changes made in trance are the beginning not the end of the transformational process. Thus, special attention is paid to what happens in the days following a trance session. Sometimes positive changes occur immediately, but require further attention to be sustained and elaborated. Sometimes nothing significant happens, which suggests that proper motivation has not been developed, or that hidden parts or beliefs have not been identified and transformed. And sometimes something a bit unexpected might happen, suggesting issues that need to be addressed in order for the desired changes to occur.

For example, Allan enjoyed a few days of sweet connection with his wife, but then found himself in uncharacteristic arguments with her regarding household responsibilities. Attending to this need opened a new level of marital intimacy.

Thus, one should not expect trance work to be an instant cure that provides immediate and permanent enlightenment. Rather, it allows new reference structures and motivation to develop, enabling a person to get back into the creative flow of a challenging life. By meeting each new development with the relational mantras (e.g., "I'm sure this makes sense" and "Welcome"), and by using further trance work where appropriate, an integrated consciousness grows more strongly into the world.

Summary

A generative somatic state is the base for creative trance work. It can be developed by mind–body centering and the optimizing of the somatic dimensions of relaxation, concentration, fluidity, openness, and groundedness. The resulting trance is a creative field of "disciplined flow" where old identities can be released and new identities forged.

As we noted in Chapter 3, the generative state is a higher level of consciousness wherein emergent properties appear. It "includes yet transcends" the ego level where the body is primarily physical, opening a subtle "body of bodies" that can move fluidly through many possible somatic states in a creative manner. This is what is meant by being in a "creative flow" state or being "in the zone". It is also a main component of generative trance. In these heightened states of awareness, many new things are possible.

Chapter 6
"Open Beyond": Subtle Fields in Generative Trance

Doctor, you say that there are no haloes

around the streetlights in Paris

and what I see is an aberration

caused by old age, an affliction.

I tell you it has taken me all my life

to arrive at the vision of gas lamps as angels,

to soften and blur and finally banish

the edges you regret I don't see,

...

I will not return to a universe

of objects that don't know each other.

Lisel Mueller – "Monet Refuses the Operation"

We may therefore regard matter as being constituted by the regions of space in which the field is extremely intense ... There is no place in this new kind of physics for the field and matter, for the field is the only reality.

Albert Einstein

The last chapter described how creative trance may be developed by moving somatic consciousness to a generative level. This chapter explores how field consciousness can also be elevated to a generative level. We start with a general overview, noting the two different levels of field awareness. We will then concentrate on different methods for opening the higher level of field awareness, a quantum space that contains virtually infinite possibilities.

Opening to a generative field

In Chapter 3 we saw how generative consciousness involves self-awareness of a whole field of relationships, whereas ego consciousness can at best identify with, and have awareness of, only parts of the field. This difference is especially relevant in challenging situations. In a problem state, a person generally locks attention onto a specific object – a thought, person, feeling, and so on. Thus, you might get caught up in a belief of inadequacy, a negative memory, or a threatening person in front of you. When this neuromuscular lock occurs, a difficulty degrades into an irresolvable problem, persisting until the neuromuscular lock is released.

One way to release the neuromuscular lock is to widen attention beyond the problem. This is the most practical meaning of "opening the field". In the martial art of aikido, a major training principle is,

> Never give your eyes to the attack(er).

If you do, you also give your center and mind away to the problem, and lose connection to everything else. Thus, to transform a problem into a solution, open attention to a wider field and the many resources beyond the problem.

An interesting example of this was shared with me by a student of Tohei Sensei, one of the great aikido teachers. It involves the advanced aikido practice of *randori*, where a student is attacked by multiple assailants from all directions. Before the practice, Tohei Sensei sends the student out of the *dojo* (training hall). He then posts on the *dojo* walls four pieces of paper, each with different information written on it. The student is then invited back into the room, whereupon the *randori* immediately commences. To pass the test, the student must succeed on two counts: (1) effectively respond to the attack and (2) report what was on each piece of paper. Obviously, this requires that the student develop a wide peripheral field awareness, unattached but creatively responsive to the different focal points of the field. This is the same interest we have in generative trance.

A similar approach can be found in the therapeutic approach of eye movement desensitization and reprocessing (EMDR) (Shapiro, 2001). This approach was originally developed for trauma resolution, but subsequently expanded to other areas as well (Shapiro, 2002). In the original version, the client attunes to three aspects of a traumatic memory – a visual image, a somatic feeling, and a negative internal self-talk (e.g., "I deserve this"). They then hold the three modalities while (visually) tracking the hand movements of the therapist as they move across the client's horizontal field. After a 45 second cycle, the client is invited to rest, share their awareness, and then usually encouraged to "go with that" while moving through another cycle of eye movements. A typical result is that somewhere in the process, an experiential "pop" occurs and the client feels free of the "negative spell" of the trauma field. It no longer feels like it's happening in the moment. It's a memory, a bad one, but nevertheless something that is now over.

The pattern in both the aikido and EMDR examples is similar. Faced with a daunting challenge, a person orients primary attention to the peripheral field beyond the challenge, while moving (eyes or whole body) in rhythmic, resonant patterns. This unfastens the neuromuscular lock that is inadvertently holding the negative event in place, while opening an accelerated learning process of the creative unconscious. This is precisely what we're looking to do in developing generative trance, and is generally what is meant by "opening to the field".

As with the somatic center, there are two levels of fields. The first level is the multiple dynamic contexts for our ongoing experiences. The physical environment is a field, as is culture, social context, personal history, family, vocational "field," and so on. In quantum terms, they are "non-local selves" in our identity space, having no fixed location or self-awareness, but powerful influences (cf. Goswami, 1993). At any given moment, any of these fields may be active, guiding and constraining behavior and experience. Figure 6.1a shows how when we are in the neuromusuclar lock of an ego contracted state, we are generally at the mercy of the fields.

Figure 6.1a. Neuromuscular lock in a field. Person contracts and isolates within classical field, cut off from creative consciousness

When we move to a generative level, we include yet transcend the patterns of these fields. They are still there but we are not causally determined by them. Consciousness extends to the creative unconscious while also pervading the classical field, thereby allowing a capacity to move in "creative flow". A core triumph in the hero's journey is transcending – and in doing so, often transforming – major field constraints. This might be Edmund Hillary climbing Everest, Nelson Mandela challenging apartheid, or Milton Erickson learning to walk after polio paralysis. But it can also be an ordinary person transforming a key life area – a family "trance," a professional challenge, a personal difficulty. Breakthrough experiences are available to everyone.

In making these transformational shifts, a second field level opens up, which I call a generative *field of fields*. As Figure 6.1b shows, it is a subtle field that "includes yet transcends" the dynamic fields of the conventional world, opening a new level of consciousness. In other words, we can hold in a mindful field of subtle awareness a sense of ourselves and the contexts in which we are situated, as well as multiple ways to move within them and possibly transform them.

Figure 6.1b. Generative consciousness in a field. Person centers and opens to creative field, thereby 'including yet transcending' the classical field

This is the core generative principle at the heart of this chapter: generative trance is a subtle field of non-dual unity in which all the elements of a challenge can be integrated into a deep level of creative wholeness, thereby allowing new identities and skills to emerge. Figure 6.2 lists the five methods covered in this chapter.

Figure 6. 2. Methods for creating a generative field

1.   The energy ball
2.   The energy ball and archetypal resources
3.   Generative trance as a quantum field
4.   "Second skin" as a generative field
5.   Celtic cross

First method: The energy ball

This first technique basically involves sensing subtle energy flowing between the hands. In traditional hypnosis this is the "magnetic hands" technique. Subjects are asked to extend both hands forward, palms facing towards each other. It is then suggested that a magnetic force be felt between the hands, so strong that the hands begin to move involuntarily. While such a technique hints at the subtle energy found in generative states, the traditional way in which it is usually done suggests that (1) the energetic current is created by the hypnotic suggestion and (2) a subject who feels the magnetic current is "under the control" of another person (i.e., the hypnotist). Obviously, neither of these premises supports the generative view of a person mastering mind–body processes at a creative level of consciousness.

A more helpful version can be found in Eastern mind–body approaches. In both *qigong* and *tai chi*, a practitioner attunes to a subtle "energy ball" held in the hands. This is not seen as an artificial "hallucination" produced and controlled by external hypnosis, but attunement to the *chi* or subtle life force pervading the living world.

Similarly, in aikido there is a training technique called *Tai no Henko*. Here the practitioner centers and then extends his arms out, as if holding an energy ball. When a person attacks by, say, grabbing the wrist, the practice is to "keep the ball alive" while moving in a way to draw the attacker's energy inside of the ball. In practical terms, this is a process of developing a mind–body center in which calmness, strength, and groundedness are maintained. The energy ball provides feedback about whether you are staying centered and bringing all relational connections into that center. It is easy to observe in practice: if the connection to the attacker collapses your energy ball, you have lost your center – that is, your mind–body unity – and hence your creative potential. On the other hand, each time you maintain your energy ball while absorbing whatever comes at you, you are made stronger and more present by the connection.

This is the challenge we face in generative trance work: how to stay centered, open, and connected to resources while engaged with a problem or challenge. The energy ball technique is a nice way to learn this. It is an excellent metaphor for appreciating what it means to develop and sustain a generative field. Figure 6.3 shows how the energy ball can be developed and utilized in generative trance work.

Figure 6.3. The energy ball technique

Step 1: Preparation

    1.   Center

    2.   Positive intention: goal to achieve *or* problem to transform

    3.   Resources

Step 2: Shift into generative state

    1.   Extends hands out to sense "energy ball"

    2.   Focus on space between hands, "frequency tuning" the subtle energies

    3.   Open attention beyond ball

    4.   Make first commitment to "keep the ball alive"

Step 3: Transformation

    1.   Bring image of goal/problem into the energy ball

    2.   Invite "creative unconscious" to transform image to generate desired state

    3.   Slowly reach inside ball, move transformed image to somatic center for integration

Step 4: Return to outer world

    1.   Vows and commitments

    2.   Gratitude

    3.   Review important learnings

    4.   Reorientation

The following is a transcript from a group process.

Introduction

So let's take a little time to explore one of the basic, very interesting experiential processes of creative trance. This is called the "energy ball" experience. What it involves is centering and then finding a good balance between relaxation and extending your awareness into the world. You'll be exploring how you can sense yourself holding the energy ball, then placing something inside of it that you'd like to work with – either a positive future you want to experience or a problematic situation you'd like to heal or transform or understand differently. We'll see how developing the ball provides a sort of a sanctuary, a sacred holding space, which allows you to creatively engage with that part of your life. We'll then see later how to extend this further and do transformational work with the content of the energy ball.

Please do not think of this as me hypnotizing you. I am merely offering some coaching suggestions for you to find that creative process within yourself. This is not some supernatural process or some experience where you're being controlled from outside. On the contrary, it's a process for you to find that balance point, that "sweet spot" in your mind–body tuning where you can open up a space to be with whatever is going on in your life, and then find some creative new ways to engage with it.

Let yourself think like an artist or an athlete, someone who is tuning their nervous system to let something flow through, tuning the frequencies of your consciousness to allow some creative process to move through you. If you're too relaxed, you won't be able to be that channel, but if you're too tense, you'll block the creative process. So you're going to be sensing where the balance point is in your attentional awareness, that place where *yin* and *yang* combine to open a natural path to new possibilities.

Step 1: Preparation

To begin, just let yourself find a good place to settle in and settle down. A place where you can both relax and stay aware and open to the field beyond you. You want to be either standing up or sitting down with a straight spine – whatever feels best for you. And as you tune into your body, let yourself make the first shift of moving from thinking to breathing, thinking to breathing. Let the breathing move up and down your spine, from heaven to earth, and upwards again, then dropping down again, until you feel your center.

As you feel your center, you might begin to explore a few, very slow and graceful movements. Let your hands come to your center, then lift your hands from your center, opening and extending into the world beyond. Do this very, very slowly, like a *tai chi* movement, at least four or five times slower than a normal movement, letting your hands find a way to move on their own. Dropping down into center, opening out in the field ... Let yourself do this at least four or five times, seeing if you can sense the subtle energy that can go with that.

And as you continue to drop into center and open into the field beyond, you can begin to sense whatever goal you have to work with today. It could be something you want to become in the world – succeeding in your business, being healthy and happy in the world, or enjoying an intimate relationship. Whatever that desired future might be, just let yourself sense an image of that desired future self.

Or perhaps there is something you want to heal or change or shift your relationship with in the present ... something you've been struggling with ... a part of yourself that you want to change ... or something in another person that you're struggling with ... Whatever it is, just allow yourself to sense an image of that problem you want to transform ...

And then let yourself return to centering ... breathing ... opening to the field beyond ... feeling the rhythm of the creative unconscious ... breathing ... dropping into center, opening into the creative world beyond ...

And as you do that, you can invite and notice any resources that can help you on your journey today ... any resources ... people ... places ... ancestors ... symbols ... that can guide and protect and encourage your journey here today ...

Step 2: Shift into generative trance

In the second step, the energy ball is opened:

Connecting with those resources, drop back down in your center ... very slowly opening your arms from your center ... into the field ... very slowly ... at least four or five times slower than a normal moment ... like releasing a bird from a cage ... and just let yourself become curious about the movement ... Let it be a voluntary movement in one moment ... and then allow it to be movement, all on its own, flowing from within ... Your conscious mind directing, then your creative unconscious opening ... dropping ... opening ... releasing ...

Then at some point when you drop down to the center with your hands, this time when you open to the field ... let your hands extend out in front of you, palms facing towards each other ... just as if you are holding an energy ball. Relax your elbows, relax your face, relax your shoulders, extend your arms, drop your hips ... and let yourself begin to explore how to tune into that pleasurable feeling of an energy ball ... breathing ... one part of you looking into the ball ... another part of you extended beyond the ball, watching and feeling the energy ball in your peripheral awareness ...

Let yourself discover ... with a gentle, subtle, almost imperceptible movement and attunement ... the feeling of the energy ball between the hands ... a ball of light ... a ball of life ... a sphere of infinite possibilities ... discovering all the subtle vibrations in the ball ... the many textures ... colors ... dimensions ... open space ... an energy ball ... a safe place ... a sanctuary ... You might move your hands ever so slowly around the ball ... gently holding it from the sides ... holding it top and bottom ... looking inside of the ball ... another part of you looking beyond the ball ... a feeling of pulsation in the ball ... when you breathe in, the ball gets a little bigger ... when you breathe out, the ball contracts a little ... the ball harmonized with your breath, the deepest part of your creative unconscious ... relaxing ...

The communications can, of course, be elaborated and modified as needed. Body and breathing should be monitored closely, since any muscle tension will tend to block the flow and the subtle awareness needed to experience the energy ball. Simple suggestions for relaxing any tense areas can be gently used; also, the quality of musical tones, playfulness, and rhythm can be modified to deepen experiential absorption.

Step 3: Transformation

In the third step, the future self (or problem self) is placed inside of the ball to begin a transformational process:

As you continue to put your primary emphasis on sensing the ball, keeping the ball alive ... tuning into the ball ... opening your awareness beyond the ball ... you can also sense that the ball is a safe place ... a sanctuary ... a ball of light and life ... into which many different important presences can be brought ... For example, that special goal that you have selected for today's journey ... that future self (or problem) that you want to have creative, positive connections with ... But even as you begin to sense that goal, keep your first attention on keeping the ball alive ... maintain your first attention to the ball, not to whatever is inside the ball ... let what is inside the ball be in your secondary awareness, your peripheral awareness ...

And with that in mind, let that image of the self you want to create (or the self you want to transform) move inside the ball ... Let it enter into the energy ball, gently, into the very "center of centers" in the ball ... while you give your first attention to keeping the ball alive ... breathing ... relaxing ... extending ... absorbing ... opening beyond ... as you sense that in the very center of the ball is the self you most want to create – or transform.

And be curious about how you can continue to feel the ball ... making the light brighter ... more radiant ... a feeling of flow ... an experience of glow ... And as you continue to keep the ball alive, you can give permission for whatever is inside of it to begin to transform ... a beautiful home ... a fertile place where something new is born ... a birthing of a new self ... while you keep the ball alive ... looking far in the future, infinitely beyond ... sensing the presence inside of the ball become more integrated ... more whole ... more happy ... more free ... more a part of your future ...

And then when you are ready, you can very slowly, very gently let your hands reach inside of the ball and take hold of that precious presence ... carefully ... full of care ... gently take hold of that future self ... and when you're ready ... moving gracefully, ever so slowly, let your hands bring that self into whichever center of your being that can best give it a place ... Perhaps your hands will move to your heart ... or to your belly ... perhaps to your third eye ... just letting the hands bring the self into that center ... and as it enters inside of your being, you can find yourself taking a deep breath that can allow an ever deeper process of integration ...

Step 4: Return to outer world

In the final step, the experiential changes are directed into the everyday life of the person:

And, letting your hands gently touch that center, you can sense and bless the beautiful presence that it holds ... you can breathe with it ... you can allow it a deep place within ... And in breathing with it, you can sense what you've learned from this journey today ... sense the learnings you've begun to develop about yourself ... your life ... and as you sense those learnings ... you can sense also whatever vows you'd like to make ... whatever promises you want to make ... to yourself ... to the world ... to life ... about how you will live this life you have been given ... what positive promises you will live by ...

(Silent pause to allow vows to be made.)

And with those vows guiding your thoughts, your actions ... your feelings ... in the days ahead ... you can also sense how you can open the doors into the future ... you can sense yourself ... and opening beyond the moment ... opening a path into the future ... you can allow that self to move forward in time ... allowing one of your subtle bodies to move forward into that future ... until you can see him (or her) in that happy place ... in that happy time ... in that place of wholeness ... waving back to you, guiding you forward ... a beautiful north star to navigate by ...

And as you sense yourself having crossed the threshold, committing to this positive journey ... take a few more moments to express any gratitude at all to those who support you on your path of awakening. To yourself ... to others ... who have provided support, love ... good examples ... protection ... encouragement ... let yourself say, *thank you ... thank you ... thank you.*

(Silence for gratitude.)

And then, when you're ready, you can take a nice deep breath and gently return back into this world, bringing with you all the positive learnings you have made.

The energy ball can allow a person to move from the ego level of identifying with a particular position in a field – for example, feeling depressed or angry – to the generative level of the field. Placing primary attention on "keeping the ball alive" is especially helpful in ensuring that a person doesn't collapse back into the problem state. By attuning to the subtle field of the energy ball, freedom is given to self and the experiential process to creatively flow into transformational change.

Second method: The energy ball and archetypal resources

The energy ball technique can be elaborated by adding the *archetypal resources* of tenderness, positive fierceness, and playfulness (Gilligan, 1997). In previous work, I proposed these energies as core resources for creative consciousness. That is, optimal performance requires the *yin* (receptive) skills of tenderness, soothing, kindness, and gentleness; the *yang* (active) skills of positive fierceness, focus and commitment, a good "bullshit detector," and taking life seriously; and the shape-shifting wizard skills of playfulness, nimbleness, and generativity. In a stuck state, at least one of these energies is missing or in its dark (neuromuscularly locked) form; so by adding them into a trance field, these resources can be transformative.

Figure 6.4. Energy balls and archetypal resources

1. Identify problem pattern or desired goal
2. Preparation step
3. Develop energy ball
4. Place goal/problem into ball
5. First revolution (around ball): add resources of tenderness
6. Second revolution: add resources of positive fierceness
7. Third revolution: add resources of playfulness
8. Fourth revolution: blend all resources
9. Reach into ball and bring integrated self into center
10. Future orientation
11. Reorientation

Figure 6.4 shows an outline for doing this with the energy ball technique. The process is done standing up. The first part is as in the previous technique: you do the preparation steps, develop the energy ball, and then place the goal inside the energy ball. The new part involves slowly walking around the ball four times. In the first revolution, resources of tenderness and kindness are extended to the "self-presence" in the ball. In the second, resources of positive fierceness – protection, support, commitment – are extended. Next, resources of playfulness are offered. In the final revolution, all resources are blended simultaneously. As with the previous exercise, the presence in the ball is then brought into the client's center, and a future orientation completes the process.

Also, as before, all movement is done very slowly and gracefully, at least four or five times slower than an ordinary movement. The "trance dance" itself is especially helpful, unbinding the neuromuscular lock – in posture, breathing, thinking, point of view, and so on – that freezes consciousness into a problem state. By circling a challenge with a slow dance, the creative flow of generative consciousness is activated, and new learnings arise as a result.

When a coach is helping a person with this process, the coach is responsible for creating and maintaining the proper conditions for the work. This includes "protecting" the space within which a person is turning. I usually move with the person, adding shifting rhythms and musical tones to open a trance space. If at any point the person might bump into something, a gentle hand is used to guide them into safe space.

This process was explored with Peter, a man beset by procrastination. He was starting a new company, his third in ten years, and felt overwhelmed by the myriad details and challenges. He would find himself locked into anxious, self-critical processes. His goal was to shift his negative state to a positive one of confidence and creativity.

The first four steps were done in a manner similar to the previous example of the energy ball. The transcript begins after the preparation step is completed. Peter is invited to open the energy ball and bring the presence of his "worried self" into it.

Develop energy ball

> You can close your eyes again, Peter ... and just take a few moments to again settle in ... settle down ... and center ... *that's it* ... releasing ... *that's it* ... connecting to your intention ... *that's it* ... and really sense that this is your journey ... this is your time ... a time to leave normal time ... and enter a special time ... a time with many times ... a time of many places ... a time with infinite possibilities ... this time ... there are many times ... and many places ... many experiences ... that can help you ... and guide you ... on your own ... hero's journey ... into a new relationship with yourself ... regarding the new business ... So let go a little more now ... and move into the deeper time

... move into the deeper space ... My voice can go with you. You can utilize it ... as a friend of the soul ... in your own hero's journey ...

When you're ready ... you can let your arms extend out in front of you ... palms facing towards each other ... so you can begin to tune into the energy ball. You can begin to sense the energy ball ... a beautiful ... sense of feeling ... the sensations in the one hand ... all the sensations in the other hand ... the sensations *between the hands* ... a space between your hands ... a space beyond your hands ... perhaps you can notice different variations of color ... tuning ... turning ... tuning to an exquisite awareness of lights glimmering ... shimmering ... different colors within one color ... that's it ... that's it ... that's it ... and when you feel a deep sense of that energy ball, you can let me know by nodding your head ... (he nods his head) That's it ... that's great ... that's it ...

Bring self-image into energy ball

You can feel not only the energy ball ... and also the feeling of the energy ... moving ... through the tips of your fingers ... light shooting through the fingertips ... and an awareness beyond the ball ... so your awareness of the ball is in your peripheral vision, in front of you yet in your peripheral vision ... When you're ready, you can take that image that you have brought here today ... your difficulties at work ... and you can gently release it ... inside ... of the energy ball ... You can be curious how the energy ball is able to absorb the image in a spongy ... wonderful ... way ... so it has a safe place ... for you ...

As you look towards the ball and also ... beyond the ball ... an awareness ... that's opening ... beyond the ball ... so that whatever is inside ... is almost secondary ... to the feeling of an expanding ... awareness ... beyond ... the inside ... of the ball ... Part of you is seeing into the great openness ... beyond the ball ... Part of you can see ... in your peripheral vision ... what's inside ... the ball ... and be able to hear ... my voice ... and the nice feeling of seeing ... all the different ways that today you can transform and form trance ... in a way that ... your shoulders relax ... you can feel a sense of an expanding world ... so that your mind opens beyond the image ... even as you sense peripherally inside the ball. And when you have that sense of the image inside of the ball, you can let me know by nodding your head again ...

(His head nods after about 20 seconds.)

He is now invited to walk around the ball four times, each round bringing different resources to his "worried self" inside the ball:

When you're ready ... in just a few moments ... I'm going to ask you to begin a circular rotation ... around the ball.

(Peter turns very slowly; the coach stays beside him and turns with him.)

First revolution: resources of tenderness

And as you move circularly around the ball ... creating a *wider* ... *wider* space ... that's it ... relaxing ... *opening wider* ... that's good ... that's good ... As you begin that rotation ... you can bring to yourself resources of kindness ... sending to yourself, inside the ball, beautiful energies of kindness ... of support ... emanating from your heart ... Tenderness ... a tender, sweet support ... Notice yourself breathing with that sense of kindness, of support, of relaxation ... watching how it allows you to work effectively ... happily ... creatively ... in the days ahead ... so much to look forward to ... as connections of kindness and support develop between the deep self ... and the self inside of the ball ... heart energy filling him, protecting him, relaxing him ... so that whenever he finds himself ... in any challenging relationship ... it really can be a good time ... to be filling him ... at an unconscious level ... with a beautiful sense of kindness ...

(Peter completes one full circle.)

That's good ... and take a few moments to take a nice deep breath and feel that integration of resources of kindness into your work self ...

Second revolution: resources of positive fierceness

And then when you're ready, you can begin the second rotation around the ball ... very, very slowly ...

(Peter turns spontaneously in the other direction, accompanied by me.[13])

That's it ... seeing yourself inside the ball ... from many changing perspectives ... many different points of view ... many new understandings ... and this time as you turn, you can bring to yourself many beautiful resources of positive fierceness ... a sense of protection ... a sense of positive support ... *You can do this ... I will protect you ... you can do this* ... you can support yourself ... see yourself ... from so many different perspectives ... being in front ... standing to the side ... sensing the creative world beyond ... and bringing to yourself ... a positive fierce support ... sending him ... beautiful positive support ... *I am with you now ... I am with you now ... I will give the support ... to fly free ... and easy ... and confident* ... See and feel ... how much protection ... he's always needed ... how much protection ... you might send ... that's good ... So as you complete this second circle ... you can pause and take a deep integrating breath and feel yourself integrating all those resources ... those images ... that future filled ... with positive fierceness ... that's good ... that's great ... that's it ...

Third revolution: resources of playfulness

And then when you're ready ... you can let yourself so slowly ... so freely ... so happily ... begin a third rotation around the ball ... this time ... bringing so many resources of play ... (the coach's voice and movements become more playful) so much to play, to enjoy ... (Peter's movements shift, moving one way, then another, as if dancing happily) That's it ... exploring ... letting your body be free ... sending so much playfulness to yourself ... for work ... for happy creativity ... A sense of bringing play from your heart ... Let him be wildly free ... all the different funny things ... all the different

---

13   Such spontaneous shifts often occur (especially during the playfulness round). Many variations of the circle are possible.

pleasurable things ... all the different wonderful ... things ... of playing ... that he can discover ... and enjoy ... Moving around ... playing
... energy ball ... playing ... really enjoying ... being able to move ...
Float like a butterfly ... with a sense ... a beautiful feeling ... round
and round ... feeling of play ... all the support ... behind you now
(holding a hand behind Peter's back, letting it go down very slowly)
... Support is in front of you ... from all sides ... feeling ... of play ...
feeling ... sensing ... a new connection ... new understandings ... new
possibilities ... new experiences ... that's it ... that's good ... that's it
... So as you complete this third circle, you can let a nice deep breath
bring happy waves of integration ... rhythms in the body ... rhythms
of change ... different waves through the ball ... feeling ... integrating ... so that as you sense your self inside that ball ... you can see
yourself happy and connected to all the spirits of play ...

Fourth revolution: blend all resources

Then when you're ready ... you can begin the fourth circle. This time
... you can bring all those important energies ... tenderness ... positive fierceness ... and playfulness ... Tender ... fierce ... playful support ... of yourself ... Feeling balanced ... tender, fierce playfulness
... Bringing all ... swirling ... integrating ... Allowing that self ... to be
born again ... Watching him, seeing him ... in so many ways ... he's
with you now ... he's within you now ... he's within your field ... He
belongs with you ... so that as you see him ... as you sense him ... as
you provide a second skin ... for him ... he can grow and change and
feel confident and creative within that field of self-love ...

Bring integrated self into center

And then when you're ready ... you can let yourself very slowly ...
very gently ... reach inside of the ball ... and take gentle hold of him
... and then let your hands slowly bring him inside of your body ...
in whatever center your hands most want to move to ... your heart
... your belly ... just trust your creative unconscious to select out
which center to bring him ... (Peter's hands begin to move towards
his heart) That's it ... that's good ... breathing ... giving him a home

> ... breathing ... so when your hands touch your heart ... you can feel a deep breath of integration ... bringing him ... into you ... a new space around him ... (Peter's hands touch his heart and he takes a deep breath) That's it ... that's it ... just letting that integration take you deeper ... And as you do, a deep path towards a positive future ... begins to unwind in space ... a beautiful path of success and learning ...

The final five minutes of the process focused on noting key learnings, making commitments and vows, gratitude, and future orientation. Peter reported a really powerful experience. The circular movement released him from any fixed positions, and an extraordinary "soul journey" opened up. As is typical for most generative trances, the most important experiences for him were not directly suggested by the trance communications.[14] He described sensing himself as a young boy, alone in a field, crying for help. As the resources were added, he found his father appearing and holding the boy gently, speaking encouraging words. This father/son healing was elaborated further in the trance and was the most important experience for Peter, as he had felt unloved by his father.

While each archetypal energy is integral to creative conscious, most people find one to be especially helpful. For Peter, playfulness was the most significant resource, both during the sessions and afterwards. His re-connection to his father released a happy playfulness, an energy he reported having forgotten for some time. In reclaiming it, both his personal happiness and his work performance increased significantly.

---

14   Remember, generative trance is a poetic language where a person translates symbols into their own meanings. This was central to Erickson's work: he would often suggest at the outset of a trance that a person could translate his words into their own meanings, translate his voice into another voice (e.g., a childhood teacher), or translate his English into their own primary language (e.g., Spanish). I often say that the work only begins when the client's response is very different from the coach or therapist's suggestion, as this is the point where the person's creative unconscious is primary.

Third method: Generative trance as a quantum field

Out beyond ideas of wrongdoing and rightdoing,

there is a field. I will meet you there.

Rumi

Some of the most profound experiences of my life came during trance sessions with Milton Erickson. They are difficult to describe in words. I would sense myself in some amazing space of infinite possibilities, without boundaries or dualism. Each experience was perfect within itself, each moment a new learning or discovery. At some point I would find myself wondering who and where I was. I would then be startled to realize that the field that was holding me was Erickson! And his presence was clearly "inside" of me, inside the boundaries I had so carefully constructed to deny anyone access to my deepest self. My budding anxiety over this realization would be almost immediately met and assuaged with a kind reassurance (from Erickson's nonverbal presence) that I needn't worry, everything was safe, and this was a place of unconditional acceptance.

Given their unorthodox nature, I didn't share these experiences for many years, but I feel happy to do so now. They have stayed with me as beautiful reference structures for generative trance as primarily an experience beyond words; the human presence and musicality – the textures, rhythms and resonances – mattering the most. What we look to do in generative trance, then, is to establish, with deep human respect, a sort of musical field with limbic resonance that can absorb a pattern and allow it to transform to its highest human potential.

Exercise

I use the following exercise in workshops as an exploration of these values. It uses poetic language and nonverbal rhythms and resonance to unfold a generative trance field. In it, one person is the *explorer* and two other people are *guides*. The exercise is generally done in three rounds, with the roles changing in each round. Each guide has three communication tasks, as shown in Figure 6.5.

Figure 6.5. Developing a generative trance field

Guide 1:

1. Identify then feed back explorer's goal: *You really can do/ experience X*

2. Resonant connection: hand gently on explorer's shoulder

3. Grandfather drum: *boom boom*

Guide 2:

1. Nonsense syllable induction

2. Childhood songs/nursery rhymes

3. Interspersal of generative trance ideas

Thus, the first task for Guide 1 is to identify, before the trance is developed, the explorer's simple goal statement. The goal (as always) should be positive, resonant, and succinct. For example: "I want to feel positive about my future," "I want to write this book," "I want to be happy and healthy". This is then offered them back as trance "suggestions," in the form:

> You really can do/experience X.

The second task for Guide 1 is, with the explorer's permission, to place a hand gently on the explorer's shoulder. It is not to control or dominate, but to attune to a relational resonance.[15] When done properly, the guide will equally feel *sending* and *receiving* with the partner: *sending* communications such as resonant relaxation, trance rhythms, positive curiosity, and gentle sensing; and *receiving* (through a partner's breathing) much subtle information and energies to guide the process well. This limbic attunement provides an excellent medium for sensing how to be a deep observer/participant in the relational mind of the creative unconscious.

---

15   I should note that when I work alone with clients in my office, I rarely touch them, given the need for impeccable boundaries and trust within the intimacy and vulnerability of therapeutic trance work. However, in a workshop setting where many witnesses constitute a type of "chaperone," touch is more possible.

The third task for Guide 1 is gently speaking the resonant and repetitive phrase of *boom boom*. The guide's voice here is like a grandfather (or grandmother) drum that marks out the underlying beat of the trance music. It is best when timed with the explorer's breathing, and attuned to heart rate and pulse rate. This drumbeat helps to synchronize all communications to breath and beat, which are the heart of opening a trance field. As with all trance communications, the resonance of the drumbeat is looking to gently reverberate through the body, to create a limbic connection. Thus, the coach needs to be relaxed and in tune with his own heartbeat and breath, letting the words and their rhythms synchronize with them.

So during the trance process, Guide 1 offers these three communications:

1. A gentle hand on the shoulder

2. The breath-synchronized drumbeat of *boom boom*

3. After every three or four *boom booms*, the simple suggestion, *You really can X*

At the same time, Guide 2 has three different tasks. The first is the use of nonsense syllables to make a sensual, non-rational, trance-absorbing song. It is a bit difficult to convey the lyrical resonance of the musical sounds in words alone: *sha ba boom de la boom, dawa shooooon brawba* ... But listen to jazz singers scat singing or young babies babbling.

Part of this process is to help both coach and explorer let go of needing to make sense with words for a while, and instead become the musicality of creative consciousness. It may at first feel a little silly, especially in the contemporary consciousness that has so deeply separated from the rhythms of life, but it really helps all parties in trance-formation. When we are willing to temporarily release our tense addiction to verbal communications, a whole new world opens up.

The second task is to periodically shift into childhood songs or nursery rhymes. It generally doesn't matter if the songs and rhymes are from a different culture – they still work. The intent is to access what Erickson called the "early learning set" of enchanted consciousness. Examples would be the "Happy Birthday" song, the alphabet song, "Itsy Bitsy Spider", or "Do the Hokey Pokey".

The final task of Guide 2 is to intersperse simple ideas that are the "spices" of a good trance. For example, phrases such as:

- *Trance is a learning state*

- *Trust your unconscious*

- *That's it, that's good, that's right*

- *Relaxing, a little deeper*

- *Safety, resources, your own place*

At the outset, trance is framed as an experiential learning state belonging to a person's own creative process, with the roles of the guides being to support and encourage the person in the journey. Any special interests, requests, or needs of the explorer are solicited, and the simple goal statement to be used as the "trance suggestion" is identified. Next, all three team members take a few minutes to move through the preparation phase of attuning to center, positive intention, and resources. The explorer is then asked to nod when ready to begin.

The first guide, once permission has been given, gently places his or her hand on the explorer's shoulder. Usually, there are some silent moments to breathe and develop relational resonance, and then Guide 1 begins with the first *boom boom*. As in all trance communications, the drumbeat should be resonant, so it vibrates through the mind–bodies with a deep but gentle energy.

As this occurs, the second guide begins some gentle nonsense rhythms. The two guides are part of the same musical group, with each looking to synchronize, balance, and harmonize in ways that allow a deeper "music" to emerge. As in all generative trance process, the guides are both observers closely attuned to the explorer, but also participants playing in the same trance field. This dual relationship gives both an "inside" and "outside" perspective, which is very helpful for all.

A primary concern is to ensure that the explorer is enjoying a safe and positive experience. If any hints of neuromuscular lock develop (e.g., inhibited breathing, tension in the forehead or shoulders), the guides slow down, become more gentle, and emphasize simple suggestions such as *safety, resources, and security.* Any suggestions for deeper experiences are always dependent on a person feeling in a safe, resourceful place.

It is hard to convey in text alone the nature of the interaction, but here is a sample. The first guide's words are in regular font, while the second guide's are in italics. The explorer's goal was to experience healing in her body.

> (Guide 1 gently places hand on explorer's shoulder) *Boom boom ... that's it ... Boom boom ... jabaushimoo daba shiwas ... Boom boom ... shiBAAAshiti dabaji muwa ...* You really can experience deep healing in your body ... *That's it ... a little deeper ... Boom boom ... shaabiwaja jidurwas ... Boom boom ...* A, B, C, D (alphabet song) ... *Boom boom ...* E, F, G ... You really can experience deep healing in your body ... H, I, J, K, L-M-N-O-P ... *Boom boom ...* Q, R, S, T ... *shannnnaw bejubija ... Boom boom ...*

When performed well, the "trance music" carries many interesting qualities: it is gentle, playful, non-linear, sensual, rhythmic, non-rational, entrancing, and child-like. Participants share a subtle trance field that allows freedom, curiosity, and creative exploration. This trance field is not inside of any person; rather, *each person is inside it.* Generative trance does not come from a single location; it arises from the harmonious relationship between different parts of a field – as does any aesthetic experience.

Core to the integral creativity of generative trance is its underlying musicality. In the present exercise we are weaving a variety of simple techniques to foster this nonverbal harmony: a drumbeat, gentle touch, breathing harmony, songs and non-rational words, simple core suggestions, and general contextual suggestions (e.g., *safety, deeper*). *It is this rhythmic musical field that allows the creative unconscious to transform and integrate major identity patterns.* This is not to say that words are unimportant, but rather that good trance work involves a creative integration of mind and body, verbal and nonverbal, stillness and movement. As we will see in Chapter 8, it is when the opposites integrate that transformation occurs. Such magic is only possible within a unified field of musical consciousness.

Fourth method: Second skin as a generative field

Another example of a generative trance field is what might be called *the second skin*, a subtle field that opens around the physical body. At the ego level we primarily identify with the physical body. But in states of well-being and peak performance, we expand into a subtle body that provides boundaries while also allowing connection.

Thus, generative trance looks to activate a subtle body that provides not only a safe container, but also a superpositional quantum field of multiple possible states. This allows the specific state of the physical body – its movements, emotions, response patterns – to vary freely. In other words, when you're identified with a subtle consciousness of infinite possibilities, you can let the specific contents of classical consciousness shift freely and creatively. This certainly describes optimal performance states, where one can fluidly move among many possible states to find and express an optimal response. If you're tense and locked into your physical body, you can't do this; if you're relaxed and attuned to your subtle body, you can.

The need for a second skin around the physical body has been found in research on "body buffer zones" (Horowitz, Duff, and Stratton, 1964). This work confirms the intuitive awareness that we need to experience a private space around our body. If this space is physically or emotionally violated, it is usually met with intense neuromuscular lock (anger, fear, immobility, or collapse). With the presence of a second skin, such intrusions can be more creatively engaged.

We are not born with "second skin"; it developmentally unfolds over time. When we're children, our family and community are responsible for providing the second skin. Everyone has seen a child playing with carefree abandonment with trusted others, then suddenly freeze when a stranger walks into the room. Invariably, the child immediately looks to mama or papa (or caretaker) as the second skin. When reliably provided, children slowly grow their own individual second skin that allows them to walk confidently and freely in the world.

The second skin is a dimension of the "subtle body" (see Dale, 2009). This non-physical body has been noted in many traditions. In sports psychology, training with the "imaginal body" is considered crucial to optimal performance. In hypnotic work, it is experienced in ideomotor phenomena such as hand levitation and finger signals, where the hand (or finger) is felt to be detached from the ego identity. Also, a person in trance can separate, and from a safe distance watch, their physical or emotional body in helpful ways. I earlier noted research on phantom limbs that shows that an amputated arm or leg often feels like it is still there, sometimes even moving on its own. In Oriental medicine, it is considered the "body of *chi*", the source of good health and well-being. And when a person is happy, we can sense a sort of radiant "body of light" opening into the world.

Of course, second skin may not always be fully present. Neglect can weaken it and trauma can rip a hole in its sheathing. When this happens, a person feels "exposed" and unsafe. To find adequate boundaries, they might withdraw into solitude, numb with addiction, or develop the "body armor" of anger or dissociation. Having no healthy boundaries, they are more at risk of further abuse or misuse.

Boundaries based on neuromuscular lock typically lead to negative outcomes. Fear contracts boundaries, anger breaks them (in self and others), immobility dissociates, and apathy collapses them. Students of aikido are taught that a better way to protect the life – both one's own and others – is to "drop into center, open into field". This means that you connect with the *ki*[16] (subtle energy) of your primary core and then extend it into the world, even under inhospitable circumstances. At first, it seems deeply counterintuitive to open when danger is present, but *the practice is opening into the world, not giving yourself to another person.*[17] Thus, attention extends beyond the attacker, opening a space of presence and confidence that is helpful to self and hopefully to others as well. In extending our subtle energy into the world (as a second skin), our boundaries expand beyond the body into a field. These extended boundaries allow us to achieve what in aikido is called *ma-ai*, roughly translated as "harmony of space". This is what Martin Buber (1923) described as the "between space" that allows

---

16   The Japanese call this life force "*ki*," which is derived from the Chinese word "*chi*". Since aikido is a Japanese art, I am using the former term here.

17   This distinction of opening into the world rather than to a specific person is not possible in childhood, where to move into the world we must go to and through a caretaker. Unfortunately, if the caretaker meets us with a negative presence, it freezes us into a neuromuscular lock that can persist indefinitely. Within this contracted state is not only our own life force but also an image/belief that it is not safe to bring ourselves into the world. Part of growing up is realizing we don't need anybody's permission to be in the world, we can do it ourselves. This allows us to appreciate that while we want support from others, there will be stretches in the road where we don't get it. If we know that we can survive those stretches, it allows us freely to come into the world.

self and other to experience an "I/thou" relationship. In other words, you feel the connection with another person between you, not primarily inside of you. It allows a person to sense: "There's a spaciousness here, there's safety. There's an openness that allows me to face whatever challenges I'm facing, and to open my sensitivities into connection".

Figure 6.6 shows a simple procedure for doing this.

Figure 6.6. The generative field of second skin

---

1. Identify a *threshold challenge*

2. Step into experience for a moment and feel the patterns

3. Step out and develop second skin:

    a. Preparation step
    b. Energy ball
    c. Distribute energy around the body to create a second skin

4. Step back into the challenge and navigate with second skin

5. Future orientation

6. Reorientation

Here is an example of this process, done with Beth, an entrepreneur. Both coach and client are standing during this process.

Coach: Good afternoon, Beth. How are you?

Beth: Good, thank you.

Coach: And what is the challenge you want to work with here today?

Beth: Well, I'm having this difficulty with these guys I have to deal with in my work. They are very aggressive and I get shut down when I deal with them. My goal is to stay open and fully resourceful when I am with them.

Coach: That's good. That sounds like a great goal. Let's just take a few moments to breathe ... to let that important goal sink in and be received and held in all parts of your creative consciousness ...

(30 seconds of silence.)

Coach: Great. Thank you. So the process I'd like to guide you through here today involves first sensing what happens in that context now, then taking a step back and developing some resources in terms of an energy field or second skin that you can develop around you, so that you feel both safe and fully present. Once you have that second skin, I'll ask you to step back into the situation and notice any new changes.

Beth: Sounds good.

Coach: Great. So what I'd like to ask you to do, Beth, is when you're ready, step forward into that place, that relationship, for a moment, just to let yourself feel what happens in your body.

Beth: (takes one step forward, pauses) Hmmm, I feel very uncomfortable ...

Coach: That's good to notice. Anything else?

Beth: I feel immobile, like when my father used to lecture me.

Coach: Like when your father used to lecture you ... That's good to know. Just notice how you are in that space and then, when you're ready, take a step back and step out of that space and back into the present moment.

Beth: (takes a step back, breathes deeply, opens her eyes) Wow, that was interesting ...

Coach: Yes, very interesting. So this is one of those stuck places when old patterns don't quite work. These are precisely the places where we can use generative trance to develop new identity maps and new resources. Does that sound like a good idea?

Beth: Yes, very much.

Coach: Great. A trance can be a place to take a step back from performing, find our inner resources, then step back into the challenging area. So for this generative trance process, we're going to do two basic steps. The first is the preparation step we've done previously, where you'll connect with your center, your positive intention, and any resources. Remember that?

Beth: Yes.

Coach: Great. And then in the second step, I'll be inviting you to develop a second skin for yourself, a sort of protective energy field that allows you to feel safe and also allows you to extend your presence deeply into the world. You get two benefits with one technique!

Beth: (smiles) Sounds good!

(The coach guides Beth through the preparation step of developing the three positive connections of center, intention, and resources.)

Coach: When you feel those three connections, let me know by nodding your head. (Beth nods head)

Coach: Good, thank you. And now let's see how you can develop that second skin as a resource. We're going to start with tuning into the energy ball. When we did that process with the energy ball this morning, how did that go for you?

Beth: It was really good, I felt it.

Coach: Great, let's see how you can call that energy ball back into your awareness. Just let yourself breathe ... through your whole body ... You may find it helpful to imagine some light or some presence above ... moving down ... like a waterfall ... entering through the crown of your head ... and purifying you, cleansing you, opening you to a deep sense of being filled with subtle awareness ... with self-love ... with confidence ... Just breathing that sense of the golden light through your whole body ... through your arms ... through your legs ... through your fingertips ... And when you feel that, just let your hands begin to extend out in front of you ... slowly ... gently ... with deep absorption ... relaxing your hips ... relaxing your shoulders ... extending your awareness through your arms ... until you can begin to sense yourself holding the energy ball ... and let yourself just really feel ... just the right distance, how big the ball is ... its texture ... its color ... how it breathes with your breath ... its pulsation ... just totally tune yourself to that subtle force of light ... In fact it's a beautiful presence of your life force.

And when you ... have that feeling ... you can go ahead and nod your head ... (Beth nods) Good ... that's really good ... And when you're ready, Beth, I'd like you to gently reach in and gather all the energy inside of that ball ... and in a slow, loving way ... move it all over your body ... your skin ... let your hands move over each part of your body, layering it with this amazing second skin of subtle energy.

(Beth begins to slowly move her hands over her body, at a distance of about three inches from her physical skin.)

That's it, you really can begin to create a second skin all around you, a beautiful energy field that protects you and allows you to safely extend into the world ... And as you move across every area of your body ... you may notice that some places in particular need special attention ... need special protection ... need special blessing ... extending the second skin all around you ... a beautiful sense ... of a field that provides ... a whole new level ... of safety ... a whole new level ... of spiritual intelligence ... a whole new level ... of creating a place for you ... All of your thoughts ... all of your patterns ... all of your feelings ... protected ... held ... within this second skin ... so that they belong to you ... not to anybody else ... so that they are all of *your* thoughts ... all of *your* patterns ... all of *your* feelings ... *safely* held ... in the second skin ... that is developing all around you ... So that as you move in the world, you can move within the second skin ... *a beautiful sheathing* that allows you to come into the world ... and allows the world to come into you ... through the spiritual filter ... through the generative sheathing of the second skin ... a translucent field ... a boundary that can breathe ... really let yourself breathe it in, let it become second nature ... second skin ... second nature ... Take as long as you need.

(Beth's hands have now moved around her whole body, and she is standing with arms at her side, palms open into the world.)

And then when you're ready ... I'm going to ask you to again take a step forward ... step into that old situation ... with new connections ... with your connection to the second skin ... far more basic than your connection to what's going on outside of you. (Beth steps forward) That's good ... Taking a step forward into a new connection with yourself ... into a new, positive connection with others ... noticing what's happening outside of you ... those aggressive men ... but feeling that sense of a second skin ... keeping you safe ... curious ... centered ... aware ...

And as you observe with that wonderful feeling of a second skin ... you can notice all the different ways that you can confidently move in this situation ... all the different awarenesses that keep you *centered ... confident ... relaxed ... resourceful ...* And as you feel that sense of wholeness ... within the second skin ... all of the different possibilities for new ways of being ... some perhaps with tenderness ... (brief pause to allow exploration) Some perhaps with fierceness ... positive ... loving ... warrior fierceness for yourself and others ... (pause) Some perhaps with playfulness ... a beautiful sense of how to play within the safety of your second skin ... (pause) Always staying connected to the wholeness of being ... within you a whole new sense of boundaries ... of growing ... of healing that second skin ...

(Another pause, then brief communications are given for noticing new learnings, making vows, extending self into positive future, and gratitude.)

And then when you're ready ... you can gently take a step back once again ... into the starting place ... the center of your self ... (Beth steps back) Great, you did so well. You did such a good job for yourself. Really great ... And just take a few moments to enjoy that new sense of connection ... an appreciation for a job well done ... and then when you're ready, take a nice deep breath and open your eyes and return back into the room.

(Beth takes a deep breath and opens her eyes.)

Coach: (smiles) Welcome back!

Beth: Thank you ... That was really an amazing experience!

Beth shared how powerful it was for her to give herself a second skin in which she could feel present and unperturbed as she imagined the aggressive men. She sent me an e-mail several weeks later, happily noting how she was continuing to practice extending her second skin and that it was really helping her to feel free and confident in her work place.

This is one of many possible ways to cultivate the subtle field of second skin. In exploring others, remember that this subtle field opens naturally whenever you feel centered and integrated. It is a natural product of feeling whole and present. We lose it each time we contract our consciousness with neuromuscular lock. Each of the methods in this book is about realizing the creative wholeness that will allow our second skin to return.

Fifth method: Celtic cross

The Celtic cross technique is another example of creating generative trance fields of mindfulness. A Celtic cross is a traditional cross with a circle at the intersection point. Carl Jung and Joseph Campbell both suggested it as a mythological symbol wherein the four directions of the cross represent the world as a whole (field), while the circle in the middle represents the emergence of (generative) self into the world. We are using it here in this mythological sense, not as a religious symbol. (If the cross symbol is not resonant for you, alternative symbols include the tree of life, the four directions as used by Native Americans and Tibetans, or Leonardo da Vinci's *Vitruvian Man*.)

Figure 6.7. The Celtic cross

Step 1: Preparation

   1.   Center

   2.   Positive intention

   3.   Access resources

Step 2: Shift into generative state

(Repetitive hand movements done very slowly and gracefully)

   1.   Open vertical axis

   2.   Open horizontal axis

3. Open depth axis from center into world

4. Move between three axes with very slow, graceful movements, opening up the generative subtle field of the Celtic cross

Step 3: Transformation

1. Bring intention into center

2. Slowly, repetitively lift desired self into world

3. When ready, release fully into field, letting deep integration "beyond form" occur

4. Bring transformed self back into center, integrate further

Step 4: Return to outer world

1. Notice important learnings

2. See desired self in future

3. Vows and commitments

4. Gratitude

5. Reorientation

The Celtic cross consists of three intersecting axes: (1) the *vertical axis*, representing the polarities of heaven/earth, above/below, conscious/ unconscious, spirit/soul, north/south, etc.; (2) the *horizontal axis*, representing east/west, yin/yang, feminine/masculine, etc.; and (3) the *depth axis*, which represents the inner/outer polarity of the self coming into the world (and the world coming into the self).

The Celtic cross can be used as a means to open subtle awareness along the vertical and horizontal axes. Moving attention into this subtle field releases the neuromuscular lock of contracted attention and thinking, opening a space for a creative process to arise from the center. Figure 6.7 shows a step by step process by which this might be done. The illustrative transcript below is from a group process.

Introduction

OK, let's get settled and ready for the process. I want to encourage you to approach this experience, as with all trance processes, as a delightful experiment in how you can attune your mind–body frequencies to the most subtle, sublime level. In this way, you are like any other creative performer. For example, if you were a piano player wanting to play a beautiful piece of music, you would sense and attune to subtleties of all sorts: how you sit, how you breathe, how your hands touch the keys, how your fingers lift off of the keys, how your body and ears sense the textures and emotional nuances of each note, and so forth. This is the same sort of "experiment in consciousness," an exploration of just what is possible for you to experience and create in your life. So please don't think of this in terms of someone hypnotizing you, or in terms of some mystical disembodied experience, but rather as a natural exploration of how to attune to subtle awareness, and then use that subtle awareness for creative purposes.

Today we'll be working specifically with the Celtic cross technique, which involves opening the four directions of life: north, south, east, and west. When you do this, move slowly, about four or five times slower than an ordinary movement. See if you can attune the movement to your breath, and keep opening a "space beyond," being curious about what pleasurable developments may occur by doing that. Once you set up your four directions, I'll invite you to connect with your center, wherever you most feel it – your heart, your belly, your solar plexus, maybe your third eye. Then I'll ask you to sense your goal – that aspect of yourself that you most want to live in the world – and bring it into your center. Then, and only in a way that keeps the four directions of the Celtic cross open, I'll ask you to open what Jung and Joseph Campbell call the "fifth direction," the emergence of your soul presence from the center into the world. You'll be making slow, repetitive movements with your hands and arms, bringing a new presence within you out into the world ... lifting it into the world, guiding it, encouraging it, sponsoring it. After we do that for a while, we'll do an integration experience before reorienting. Any questions?

After addressing any questions, the usual preparation step follows, which develops positive connections to center, intention, and resources. Next we shift into generative state, experientially developing the three axes of the Celtic cross in the following way:

> So having connected to your center ... your intention ... and your resources ... let's make positive use of those connections to do some great soul work for yourself ... the work of bringing the deepest part of you fully into the world ...
>
> So get yourself comfortable, stable, centered, aligned, and open. Sit up straight ... relax ... open ... and develop good experiential absorption. Sense your relaxation process just as if you were an athlete or an artist preparing for a creative performance. It's not like watching TV or sitting in a bar relaxation. Let yourself begin to sense a finely tuned relaxation. This process is not for others; it's not about looking good for others, or about pleasing others ... It's about honoring the deep soul gifts within you, by connecting with them and bringing them into the world. So let go of the need to perform for others, and make this a soul performance to life itself. The sacred life of which you are a part ...
>
> And in stepping outside of performing for others, you can step inside of an inner space where you can feel yourself and your creative possibilities at the most intimate level ... Make sure you have a straight spine and a relaxed body ... breathing ... relaxing ... attuning to your spine ... and beginning to breathe inside the spine ... so that as you attune to your inner awareness, all the outer parts of your body ... all your muscles ... can begin to relax ... as you shift from thinking to breathing ... from acting to sensing ... all your muscles can release as you find a more basic connection to your breath ... nothing to do in the body except relaxation ... nothing to cling to in the mind ... release, let go.

Open vertical axis

> And as you release, you can begin to attune to how the breath moves up and down the spine ... with each inhalation, you can feel the awareness moving up the vertical axis ... your awareness lifting up ... and with each exhalation ... you can feel the breath moving down the spine, down the vertical axis ... and just follow that for

a while, attuning to the sensual awareness of your vertical axis ... moving up ... north ... to heaven ... to the sky ... and down ... dropping down ... deep into the earth ... deeply down ... and really sense the balance between those two energies ... the ascendant ... and the descendant ... perhaps like two snakes wrapped around each other ... like a double helix of awareness ... inhaling up ... exhaling down ...

And as you find the balance, that pleasurable balance of heaven and earth ... you can feel where your own center is ... where the balance point is in your body ... the place where the two worlds meet ... the center you feel most connected to ... It could be your heart ... or your belly ... or your solar plexus ... whichever you feel most drawn to ... Let your hands gently move to touch with that center ... to sense it ... to unify with your center ... to breathe with it ... in a way that allows you to let go and go a little deeper ...

And when you're ready, you can begin to open the vertical axis of the Celtic cross by very gently ... very, very slowly ... about four or five times slower than a normal movement ... letting one hand *lift up* ... up on the vertical axis ... while the other hand begins to very slowly *move down* from your center ... opening the vertical axis all the way down to center of the earth ... that's it ... one hand *slowly lifting up* along the vertical axis ... opening ... gently sensing ... tracing ... feeling the subtle thread opening up ... up through the crown chakra ... all the way to the heavens ... and the other hand slowly opening the thread downwards ... deep into the life of the earth ... deep into the soul and all of its dimensions ...

You can find the quality ... the texture ... the lightness of the movements ... a slow ... curious ... sensual ... dimension of your creative unconscious can begin to awaken ... so that at some point ... the hands may seem to be actually moving on their own ... At one moment you can move them consciously ... and the next moment let them move without conscious effort ... continuing this movement all the way up and down at least three or four times ... feeling openness through the fingertips ... openness through your wrists ... relaxed flow through your shoulder joints ... the weight of the movement allows you to do it in a slow, sensual, curious way as you begin to discover how you can do it, so your hands actually begin to move on their own at some point.

Once you move all the way up and down, the hands can move back slowly. And sometimes you are moving them so slowly and consciously it may not even feel like they are moving, even though they are, until they touch each other again ... and then you can repeat it ... and feel open fingertips, openness through your wrists, openness through your elbows ... a beautiful sort of *tai chi* movement ... all the different frequency fields ... all the different waves ... opening along the vertical axis ... flowing up and down ...

Open horizontal axis

And then at some point, when your hands come back to the center point, you can begin to shift and open outwards, to the right and left, on the horizontal axis. Let the hands open slowly on the horizontal axis ... very slowly ... at least four or five times as slow as a normal movement ... opening the horizontal axis ... opening your awareness infinitely to the east ... infinitely to the west ... until you are completely open ... a feeling of light flowing through your fingertips ... a radiant openness of yourself to the universe ... breathing in and breathing out ... and let yourself continue that movement at least three or four times ... stretching the horizontal axis open to the infinite periphery ... and then bringing the world back into your center ... feeling the fabric of the universe opening to you ... opening through you ... you aligning with it ... opening out ... bringing back home ... opening outwards ... bringing back home ...

(This can be elaborated further.)

Alternate between vertical and horizontal axes

And then at some point, you can allow the hands to alternate ... moving up and down through the vertical axis ... returning to center ... and then opening the horizontal axis ... a beautiful subtle thread of opening into the creative unconscious ... returning to center ... and moving back and forth between the two axes ... opening up the four directions ... opening the infinite radiance of the Celtic cross ...

the four directions and the subtle fabric of the universe opening the four directions ...

(This can be elaborated further.)

Open depth axis

As you feel the four directions, north and south ... heaven and earth ... east and west ... you can feel in the core of your center ... a beautiful sphere of light ... a beautiful ball of awakening energy ... the fifth direction of the Celtic cross ... the opening of self-awareness into the world ... and to create a path for self-awakening ... a path for self-realization ... you can let your hands touch your center ... and then gently open them forward ... ever so slowly ... into the world ... into your future ... into living consciousness ... like freeing a bird ... like offering a beautiful gift into the world ... Relax through your wrists, your shoulders, your elbows ... Let your fingertips be open, with a feeling of golden energy flowing from them ... and let yourself begin to feel how to bring that energy into the world ... how to support it ... bless it ... align with it ... breathe with it ... be within it and all around it ...

(This can be elaborated further.)

Integrate self into world

And then you can begin to move through each axis ... the vertical ... the horizontal ... the depth ... like a Balinese trance dance ... opening the three dimensions ... opening the four directions ... opening the Celtic cross ... opening the generative field ...

And as you *feel that opening* ... the vertical ... the horizontal ... a generative field allowing *something deep* to come through ... *something deep to be born* ... let yourself sense what it is you most want to bring into the world ... what it is you most want to be in the world ... opening to the horizontal ... as above, so below ... radiant openness ... and the sense of the deepest part of you that you want to bring into the world ... and when you're ready, let yourself reach into your center of centers ... your deepest inner place ... and connect with that self you most want to live into the world ... and then let that slow movement of your hands into the world ... guide ... bring ... give birth ... free ... that part of your self ... bringing from inside of you ... your deepest self ... to live happily ... freely into the world ...

And at any time you feel any interference ... any blockage ... just move back to opening the horizontal ... and then the vertical ... keeping the space open ... keeping the field open ... then bringing that desired self into the world through the opening ...

Return to center

And then when you see that your deepest self, your truest self, your most authentic self ... has a place in the world ... you can also let him/her know that there is also a home within you to return to ... to rest ... to heal ... to be at home ... so when you're ready, you can gently reach out and take hold of the self that you have released into the world ... and gently connect with that self ... and slowly, gently ... let your hands bring him back into your center ... an integration ... a coming home ... a welcoming ... a giving of place to that free spirit of your being ... breathing that presence in ... giving a safe place ... his own way, her own life ... and as you sense that place deep within your center, you may want to just notice the most important message you want to give to yourself ... Let yourself communicate that message through your breath, through your heart, through the innermost part of your silent voice and feel that connection within you to that presence ...

The final step of future orientation completes the trance process:

And then take a few moments to just sense what you have experienced in this process ... what you have learned ... what you most want to remember ... the most important positive learnings ... and open a path to the future ... many roads to many futures ... and in each future ... see yourself doing more of this positive action ... learning more of this positive self ... freeing more of your self into the world of self-realization ...

And noticing those learnings ... and seeing those futures ... you can sense any simple, deep vows you want to make to yourself ... to life ... any promises about how you live ... about how you will be with yourself ... about how you will be with others ... just sense whatever simple ... positive ... core vows you want to make ... Our life is lived from our vows ... you can sense which vows you want to make ... and make them ...

And then before you come back, you may want to take just a few moments to express any gratitude ... to yourself ... to all those who have supported you ... in so many ways ... on this amazing journey ... who have helped you on your path ... people who have gone before you ... ancestors ... teachers ... spiritual beings ... presences in nature ... a mountain ... a tree ... a forest ... people who are with you ... family ... friends ... pets ... It's nice to know how much support you are given ... and to be able to say, *thank you ... thank you ... thank you* for this beautiful journey I am living.

And then when you are ready, you can slowly head on back to the outside world knowing that you now have the rest of the day to share and enjoy the fruits of your labors, so you can enjoy looking back at the end of today with that sweet smile of satisfaction ... finding yourself saying: "Now, that was some day!"

(As the trance ends, it is usually good to have at least five to ten minutes for processing.)

While the above is a more extended version of the process, you can also use briefer forms of this mind-body attunement process during the day. This is especially helpful when you're preparing for a performance, or you're scattered and lost in ego contractions. Just take a few moments to settle, center, breathe, then move your hands through the vertical and horizontal axes until you can feel a shift back to a creative flow state. Then sense what you're wanting to bring into the world, feel its center, and "trance dance" slowly through the repetitive movements of bringing it into the world. Remember, you're opening into the unitary wholeness of the world, not to a particular person; and your movements are very slow, like a tai *chi* dance or a hand levitation. It's a simple way to release and return to yourself and the world.

I was once lucky enough to participate in an extraordinary tea ceremony in an ancient monk's home in Kyoto. Each of the six participants knelt in a circle as the hostess and her son prepared and served each cup of tea in that very formal but achingly beautiful Japanese way of ritual. Receiving the tea, you meditate a bit, then lift the cup to contemplate the nature scene painted upon it. The cup is then raised to the field, a bow is made, a sip is taken, the cup is placed down again, and a short meditation completes the cycle. A fresh cup of tea is made for the next person, until each person has been served. During the whole time, the unified field is silently and resonantly honored.

Afterwards, we adjourned to another room where a brief history of the tea ceremony was offered and questions were accepted. When I asked to whom or what one was bowing when raising the teacup, the hostess, dressed in traditional kimono and still in a formal role, could not quite contain the astonishment that flickered through her eyes. "Why, you are bowing to *everything*," she kindly stated, which somehow I already intuitively knew.

When you are opening to the field, you are opening and bowing to everything. This non-local self is what allows you to creatively accept and engage with whatever is within the field. I hope the methods touched upon in the chapter support that realization.

Summary

In a generative state, consciousness moves from identifying with the contents of awareness to being the field of awareness itself. We examined different methods for "opening fields" in generative trance work: the energy ball, adding resources to a self-image in the energy ball, generative trance as a quantum field, "second skin," and the Celtic cross. Attuning to a generative field allows one to think and act without neuromuscular lock, thereby deepening the aesthetic intelligence and subtle awareness needed for creative performance. With this freedom, you can (1) be with problems without being attached or overwhelmed; (2) be open to the flow of the creative unconscious; and (3) remain calm, curious, and attuned while engaged in a challenging process. In short, a generative field allows significant improvements in happiness, health, work performance, and healing capacity.

Chapter 7
The Principle of Creative Acceptance

The inner being of a human being is a jungle.

Sometimes wolves dominate,

sometimes wild hogs.

Be wary when you breathe!

At every moment a new species arises in the chest –

Now a demon, now an angel, now a wild animal.

There are also those in this amazing jungle

who can absorb you into their own surrender.

If you have to stalk and steal something,

steal from them.

Rumi

We have thus far explored the somatic and field bases for opening the flow of generative trance. In the next three chapters, we turn to the cognitive relationships that foster creative experience and action. In generative trance, we identify five major principles of the generative cognitive mind:

1. Mindfulness (open curiosity)

2. Positive intention

3. Creative acceptance

4. Complementarity ("both/and")

5. Infinite possibility

The first two principles – opening a mindful space and holding a positive intention – have already been covered, especially in terms of setting up a generative state. This chapter focuses on the principle of creative acceptance, while the following two chapters address the principles of complementarity and infinite possibility, respectively. The principle of creative acceptance is the radical cornerstone of Milton Erickson's legacy. We will start with an overview of this principle, and then move to an exploration of four specific applications.

The generative principle of creative acceptance

As my sufferings mounted I soon realized that there were two ways in which I could respond to my situation – either to react with bitterness or seek to transform the suffering into a creative force. I decided to follow the latter course.

Hatred paralyzes life; love releases it. Hatred confuses life; love harmonizes it. Hatred darkens life; love illuminates it.

Martin Luther King, Jr.

A central premise in generative trance work is that creative consciousness requires (1) self-awareness and (2) connection to a non-local generative field. The corollary is that this creative flow is blocked by the contracted ego consciousness of neuromuscular lock, where we rigidly identify with one part of a field against the other(s).

Ironically, this contracted, divided consciousness is what we typically use when trying to change an undesirable state. We shut down in anger or fear, and with tense muscles attempt to force a change. It is in this sense that Watzlawick, Weakland, and Fisch (1974) observed:

The attempted solution becomes the problem.

That is, what we are doing in trying to change a situation becomes precisely what keeps it stuck.

In such situations, the seemingly paradoxical alternative is to accept whatever is there in order to activate the process of change. In other words,

To change something, first completely accept it as it is.

In generative trance we call this principle *creative acceptance*. The acceptance is not a passive submission or resignation to what's there; on the contrary, it's a deep and curious connection with something in a way that opens beyond it to further possibilities.

Milton Erickson was the great master of creative acceptance. A beautiful example can be found in the case of a young woman who came to see him. She was an office secretary who was so convinced that she was ugly and unlovable, and that no man would every marry her, that she was suicidal. A gap between her front teeth was cited as "obvious" evidence of this ugliness. Erickson asked her to commit to do a few things before she took any drastic action. Her first task was to go home each night and practice squirting water through the gap in her teeth, until she was able to hit a target at a goodly distance. She found this assignment frivolous, but complied. Erickson then learned that she was attracted to a single young man at the office, and he possibly to her, as evidenced by the fact that they just happened to meet at the office water cooler each day. (Of course, she was convinced that there was no way he could find her attractive.) To her horror, Erickson instructed her to notice when he was approaching the water fountain, run up and fill her mouth with water, squirt him (through her teeth) when he bent to get a drink, and then "run like hell". She did, he chased her and asked her for a date, and they ended up married with kids!

In this abbreviated but lucid example, you can see how a "problem" (the gap in the teeth) was used as the basis for a creative solution. It was accepted and then held in some curious way that allowed new positive meanings and pathways to open from it. This is the focus of this chapter: how to turn conflict into cooperation, and problems into solutions, via creative acceptance.

To begin to do this, we might consider how Erickson was able to sense the "gap in the teeth" as a gateway to intimate connection. Our two-level theory of reality construction again comes in play. At the first level, a pattern has infinite possible forms and meanings, all vibrating and shimmering in the quantum field. An observing consciousness then "collapses the quantum wave" into the second classical level of one particular state. At the quantum level of the creative unconscious, a pattern is a symbol, with multiple, contradictory possible meanings, many of which cannot be made explicit. (This is the essence of art.) At the classical level, the same pattern is a sign with one fixed meaning.

In Erickson's case, we can say that the woman was holding the "gap in the teeth" with the neuromuscular lock of the conscious mind. It thus had the fixed meaning that she was so ugly and unlovable that she would have to kill herself. (People interacting with her might be susceptible to the same trance process, coming to believe that it had the singular, negative meaning.) Erickson somehow opened his creative unconscious and absorbed the pattern into it so its many other possible forms and values could start to resonate. Holding the positive intention of utilizing the pattern to help the patient's development, his creative unconscious was able to discover (or create) a meaning that would realize that intention – namely, squirting water through the teeth.

This is an example of the generative level of the cognitive mind, where consciousness operates as a sort of "mind of minds," a content-free field of awareness that can absorb and be curious about whatever content patterns are present. This meta-mind can consider the pattern in many different contexts, and then choose a new context that best supports that content. It is like the "energy ball" described in Chapter 6, where a subtle field absorbs and creatively engages with a challenge.

This pattern is described in the four-step model shown in Figure 7.1.

Figure 7.1. Four-step model for transforming patterns

Step 1: Open quantum field of mindfulness

Step 2: *Creatively accept* negative pattern and absorb into quantum field

Step 3: Allow quantum field to unfold new possible ways to experience or express pattern

Step 4: Holding positive intention, choose new possible way

This process of *creative acceptance* can be practiced in many ways. Figure 7.2 shows the five methods we will cover in the remainder of this chapter.

Figure 7.2. Methods of creative acceptance

1. The suggestion loop of creative acceptance
2. Self-trance process of creative utilization
3. Unfolding trance from experiential resources
4. Relational mantras
5. Somatic modeling of problem patterns

First method: The suggestion loop of creative acceptance

The principle of creative acceptance begins with joining something as it is, not trying to change it. This is not merely an intellectual trick; complete acceptance means opening a generative field to receive it, absorbing it into your somatic center, and finding the cognitive associations (names, beliefs, associational networks) distinguishing it. This will bring the pattern into a generative space, where the creative unconscious can open new possibilities. To do it well, relational rapport and limbic resonance are more basic than the verbal words. In this way, the change feels like it is coming from within the pattern, not some external force acting upon it.

A simple way to practice this principle of creative acceptance is the suggestion loop of joining and leading, represented in Figure 7.3.

Figure 7.3. Joining and leading at the micro level

---

1. Pacing statement (*This is so*)

2. Pacing statement (*This is so*)

3. Pacing statement (*This is so*)

4. Leading statement (*And this can be so*)

5. Receiving back (*And what are you aware of now?*)

6. Feeding back feedback (*And you're aware of X*)

7. Return to Step 1

This is a micro-process, in that attention is paid to joining each small detail unfolding. Generally speaking, it is helpful to do some version of the preparation step for generative trance – centering, setting intention, and opening to resources. This allows mind–body rapport and positive curiosity to be present. Then attention is joined with whatever small details may be present in the moment. Such details might be simple external facts such as:

> … You're sitting in a chair

> … and you're looking at me

> … of course your hands are resting on your lap

> … your breathing is moving in and out …

Such statements are expressed with rhythmic attunement and deep connection with the person, as if nothing else exists in the world. A simple leading suggestion can then be given, such as:

> And you can relax just a little bit more …

The question can be asked:

And what are you aware of now?

Whatever the person reports can then be used for a further round. For example, let's say the person says that she is feeling a tingling in the hands. This response is used as the first statement in the next iteration. For example:

... That's good ... And as you feel the tingling in the hands

... and hear the sound of my voice

... and notice the feeling of breathing in your body

... and any other changing feeling in the hands ...

Then adding a leading statement:

... and you can relax a little bit more ...

A deep breath ensues, and a few moments of meaningful silence allow experiential processing of the suggestion. Then:

... And what are you aware of now?

This can be continued for however many more loops it takes to shift a person into a relaxed, absorbed state. That would signal that the person is ready for a next step, such as moving from statements about external facts to internal possibilities. Still, the process of staying carefully attuned to where a person is, and suggesting changes that could easily follow, is a general pattern to be used throughout trance work.

In doing this sort of joining, other types of experiential truths might be similarly used. For example:

(*Joining goal statements*) ... and you're really wanting to make a certain change ...

(*Joining doubts and resistances*) ... and you have some doubts about your capacity to achieve this goal. Voices wondering, "Can I do it? Can I do it?" Feelings of doubt coming and going ... Hesitations ... That's good to know ...

> (*Joining possible resources*) ... and you've got many resources to draw on ... your connections with your friends ... Paul and Sue ... your experiences in climbing mountains ... your spiritual values ...

In short, many different types of experiential values and truths could and should be included in a trance process. As was noted in Chapter 4, all relevant experiences and identity parts related to a goal should be invited into the trance field, especially during the second general step (of identifying and welcoming identity parts). This de-potentiates so-called resistances by including them and develops trance by entraining attention to each ongoing pattern.

In beginning trance work, it is often good to start with simple experiential details, making them part of a rhythmic circuit of linking to whatever is happening as the basis for desired experiences (such as trance) to unfold from that.

Here is a demonstration example, done with Walter, a workshop volunteer:

Coach: Good morning, Walter.

Walter: (smiles) Good morning.

Coach: Thank you for volunteering. What I'd like to suggest is that we explore a simple generative trance process. It involves seeing how we can work together to allow your creative unconscious to help you, and how you can explore a relationship with your experience that can take you deeper into a positive trance. Sound interesting?

Walter: Yes.

Coach: OK, great. We'll take a few moments to settle in and settle down. Then you'll signal me when you're ready to receive my statements. I'll offer three or four simple feedback statements, then add a suggestion to it, and give you an opportunity to see what happens with that. Then I'll ask you to note what's happening, and we'll do another "suggestion loop," this time starting with what you just noted. OK?

Walter: Yeah.

Coach: So let's just take a few moments to settle in and settle down ... (deep breath and a few silent moments) so that more than anything we can just see what is possible from listening to the creative unconscious ... and connecting with our own experience and beginning to sense our own inner intelligence ... and as you relax a bit, perhaps you'd like to set an intention, in terms of some experiential outcome you'd like to achieve here in trance today ... (pause to allow process) and then when you're ready, take a breath and open your eyes and come back out here.

(Walter opens eyes and smiles.)

(This brief opening emphasizes the experience as a learning experiment, with both persons curious as to which positive learnings may unfold.)

Coach: And what did you notice in those few opening moments?

Walter: When I closed my eyes, I became aware of the breathing in my chest and this area right here (moves hands around the area surrounding the chest) and that seemed to allow me to start to touch a trance.

Coach: Great. When you close your eyes ... (statement feedback) and begin to pay attention to your breathing (another statement feedback) and feel the growing awareness of the space around your chest (another statement feedback) it seems to help you to begin to drop into trance.

Walter: Yes.

Coach: Shall we go a little further?

Walter: Yes, definitely.

Coach: Great, let yourself close your eyes again when you're ready ... and take a few moments to center and settle in ... and when you're ready to go a bit deeper, you can nod your head ...

(Walter nods head.)

Great ... And as you attune back to your breathing ... And hear the sound of my voice ... And feel the sensation in and around your chest ... And all of the other experiential awarenesses that allow you to ... go a little bit more into an amazing trance ... (pause) And what are you aware of now?

Walter: (brief pause) I am noticing my breathing and the movement of my head.

Coach: Is it comfortable?

(Walter smiles and nods slowly.)

And what a pleasurable thing to notice all the different dimensions of your breathing ... the gentle, subtle changes in your head ... the shifting awareness in your hands ... your feet ... your body ... as you can go a little bit deeper into a wonderful learning trance ... (pause) that's it ... that's it ... And what are you aware of now, Walter?

Walter: I'm aware of some very interesting types of images flowing through my mind ...

Coach: That's right ... some very interesting images that flow through your mind ... some very interesting breaths than can flow through your body ... some very interesting sensations that can flow through your body ... and some very interesting trances that can begin to develop from deep inside of your creative unconscious ... and what are you aware of now?

Walter: (pause) Now I am aware of different kind of way of seeing ... it's an interesting sort of holographic blur ... swirling colors ... different patterns ...

Coach: Is it pleasurable?

Walter: Yes.

Coach: That's good to hear. So many creative changes unfolding from inside ... your breathing can change in positive ways ... the feelings in your body can change in positive ways ... your depth of trance can change in positive ways ... you can enjoy the deep experiential language of holographic swirls ... twirls ... whirls ... who knows what colors? ... (pause) Just enjoy all those positive changes unfolding from within and get to know the language of your creativity unconsciously at a whole new level ... And what are you aware of now?

Walter: I am aware of a tingling sensation in my lips ... and the small movements of my head ... and these interesting images ... kind of like surfboard shapes ... many surfboards ...

Coach: That's good ... that's very good. And just enjoy all those changes ... the lips ... the head ... the images ... an ocean of experiences to surf and glide through ... and you can enjoy moving to that best level of trance now that will allow you to attune to the intention that you set ... and then let your creative unconscious develop the first part of the realization of that intention ... moving through time, space, water, oceans, memories ... letting a solution develop ... a goal to be reached ... a new reality to develop ...

(Continues for several minutes, always with musicality and relational connection guiding the flow.)

And then when you're ready, you can sense what you've experienced ... what you've learned ... what you want to remember for your continuing learning ... and then when you're ready, gently and slowly let yourself open your eyes and reorient back into the external world.

(Walter opens eyes and smiles.)

Coach: (smiles) Hi!

Walter: Hi.

Coach: How was that?

Walter: Wow, really interesting ... The surfboards turned into a sort of moving, sparkling mandala pattern, kind of like a kaleidoscope ... but inside there were these figures ... sort of symbolic figures ... doing these interesting relational dances together ... (smiles) It's hard to put into words!

Coach: Yes, I know what you mean.

(Conversation continues a bit longer.)

This example indicates how the creative acceptance of the micro-experiences of each moment may unfold a generative trance. Again, the quality of such a trance is fundamentally different than one developed by standardized suggestions, as it is primarily generated by the client's own experience. Even beyond trance, this principle of creative acceptance suggests that when we can utilize whatever is there, interesting and helpful experiences can develop.

Conversely, we see impasses and other forms of stuckness as indicating that something in the field of experience is not being accepted. Sometimes this is obvious; we just notice what is being called "bad" or "stupid" or "unacceptable" – such negative terms indicate a neuromuscular lock that is freezing experience. As we will see, at other times what is not being accepted is more hidden and requires a curious contemplative type of awareness. In any case, once we include an experiential pattern, the musicality of the creative unconscious can make good use of it.

Second method: Self-trance process of creative utilization

The principle of creative acceptance can be used similarly in doing self-trance work. A formal technique for doing this was introduced to Milton Erickson's students by his wife, Elizabeth. She would demonstrate a simple process wherein one paid very close attention to each sensory detail, verbally noting it in a rhythmic and absorbed fashion. When done with COSMIC consciousness (Centered, Open (and mindful), Subtle awareness, Musicality, Intention (positive), and Creative engagement) – a beautiful trance may be developed and creatively used.

Figure 7.4 shows an outline for this technique. As usual, we begin with the preparation step of finding center, setting intention, and inviting resources. This provides the structural basis for the "disciplined flow" of generative trance.

Once the preparation step is done, a person sits in a centered, open position and attunes to each moment of sensory experience. A repetitive three-statement form is verbalized, either silently or aloud. The three statements identify visual, auditory, and somatic experiential content. For example:

Now I am aware that I see_____

Now I am aware that I hear_____

Now I am aware that I feel_____

For each statement, just note whatever content is in your awareness at that moment. The visual content could be external (e.g., *the chair in front of me, my hands on my lap, the color blue*) or internal (e.g., *an image of my dog Lucky, darkness, swirling colors, my friend Joe*). Examples of auditory content are *the sound of my voice, the air conditioner, silence, a beautiful song, the car noises outside.* Somatic examples are *my breathing going in and out, the tingling in the hands, tension in the shoulders, a golden glow.*

Figure 7.4. Micro-utilization of ongoing awarenesses for trance development

---

Step 1: Preparation

1. Center

2. Set intention

3. Invite resources

Step 2: Shifting the state

1. Begin induction: repeat cycle of statements, filling in new content each time:

   - *Now I am aware that I see_____*
   - *Now I am aware that I hear_____*
   - *Now I am aware that I feel_____*

2. Next cycle of statements:

   - *Now I am aware that I see_____ and I let it take me deeper into trance ... (breathe and relax)*
   - *Now I am aware that I hear_____ and I let it take me deeper into trance ... (breathe and relax)*
   - *Now I am aware that I feel_____ and I let it take me deeper into trance ... (breathe and relax)*

Step 3: Transformation

1. Once entranced, accept and allow each experiential form to contribute to solution:

   Now I am aware that _____ is happening, and I let it to move me deeper towards my goal ...

2. When ready, allow integration and movement beyond problem

Step 4: Bringing the change back to ordinary life

1. Sensing change in the future

2. Commitments and vows

3. Gratitude

4. Review important learnings

5. Return

As with any trance process, the musicality of the experience is most important. Eyes can remain open or closed; experiment with what works best. For trance absorption, it is generally best to speak in a slow, rhythmic, and resonant fashion, to allow experiences beyond the words to develop.

Just as in music, the relationship with the experiential content should be fluid and relational, not static. Many find it helpful to imagine extending their awareness to the content, then gently drawing it through their innermost spinal channel, then releasing it "beyond the self" to allow an experience to open. The feeling is often likened to a slide where the absorption of each image, sound, or feeling moves one deeper into an experiential field. This is especially helpful in the second round of statements, which include the elaboration:

Now I am aware that I see _____ and I can let it take me deeper ... deeper into trance ...

Now I am aware that I hear _____ and I can let it take me deeper ... deeper into trance ...

Now I am aware that I feel _____ and I can let it take me deeper ... deeper into trance ...

Each named content can be breathed through the inner spinal channel, then with a *whoosh* feeling allowed to slide into an experiential space beyond, opening pleasantly surprising experiences. During this time, the centering, repetition, and musicality keep the disciplined presence needed to balance the creative flow of the unconscious.

One of the really helpful aspects of this process is that anything can be included, including what traditionally what might be called inhibitions or resistances (e.g., internal dialogue, tension, blankness). A curious extension towards any content, grounded in the disciplines of the three positive connections (center, positive intention, resources), can transform it into a helpful experience.

These two induction cycles can be repeated to open a trance space of creative flow. As this starts to happen, the statements can be modified to:

Now I am aware that _____ and I can let this awareness move me deeper towards my goal ...

This sets the filter to creatively accept whatever comes up as a possible contribution to the goal. Often times what appears is unexpected and not fully comprehensible to the conscious mind. For example, a man was practicing this self-trance process with the goal of improving his professional success. He became aware of images of himself as a young boy, sitting in sadness. As he continued, images of a wizened old man appeared. A connection between the sad boy and the loving old man then developed, and the client felt a deep inner shift. It took him several months to realize that this involved an integration of a young depressed part of himself that carried a belief that there was no positive future possible.

Regardless of content, the intent is to allow different experiential contents to spontaneously arise. They are all absorbed into the quantum field of generative trance, where they can fluidly connect with many other experiential resources. When it seems that enough content has been gathered, a deep breath is taken, and the statement shifts to:

And now I can allow all to integrate into a generative solution …

In the musicality of the process, the different elements moving in the trance field can create a new mandala or mosaic of self identity. For example, the man who connected with the sad boy saw himself happy and confident in the future. Another person experienced the integration like "a rainbow of feeling colors" resonating deeply through her being, while for another, a series of gentle shakings ran through his body, followed by a deep calm. What is important during any integration phase is to let the creative unconscious guide the process. The observing consciousness gently holds the space, maintaining the three positive connections of the generative state.

After several minutes, attention is given to the final step of integrating back into the classical world: (1) noting what has been experienced and learned, (2) sensing these changes in terms of positive future orientations, (3) making vows or commitments to practice and realize the changes, (4) expressing gratitude (to self and others), and then (5) reorienting back into the room. Experiences may be discussed, perhaps noted on paper.

Self-trance can be used for many purposes. One value is steady cultivation of a generative state. To lead a creative and happy life, one must train the capacity, under virtually any condition, to *center, keep a positive intention, open beyond the problem, creatively engage with whatever arises, and make creative use of whatever is there.* This self-trance process is a helpful method for strengthening this capacity.

Another general use is as a daily restorative or attuning process. I highly recommend to clients that they practice 20-minute trance or meditation sessions each day, as a way to let go of neuromuscular lock patterns and to cultivate the generative flow of the creative unconscious.

Self-trance can of course also be used for practical purposes, such as preparation for a major event (childbirth, an upcoming test, a public performance) or new responses to difficult challenges (an ongoing problem at work or home, a chronic pain).

Third method: Unfolding trance from experiential resources

Milton Erickson began his formal study of hypnosis while an undergraduate student at the University of Wisconsin. The great learning theorist Clark Hull had set up a hypnosis laboratory there, and Erickson found in hypnosis many of the "trance-like" experiences he had discovered and explored as a child. However, he was surprised that the hypnosis theories of Hull and others regarded trance as strictly resulting from the artificial suggestions of the hypnotist. This was in stark contrast to Erickson's observations that trance seemed more natural and to arise from a person's internal experiences and resources. Of course, Erickson spent the remainder of his life demonstrating that his view had superior therapeutic value.

One of his early techniques involved asking a hypnotic subject to experientially recall a trance-like memory of pleasurable absorption (e.g., riding a train, taking a nice walk, listening to a beautiful piece of music). Erickson would invite the person to slowly describe the sensory details of the memory (e.g., sitting on a train, watching the scenery go by, talking to a friend, hearing the sound of the train, being absorbed in a book, beginning to feel sleepy). He would feedback each experiential detail in a hypnotic way, thereby having a person develop a trance based on their own experiential resources.

Figure 7.5 outlines a process by which this can be done in generative trance work.

The preparation step involves developing the three positive connections of a generative trance: centering, positive intention, and resources. In the second step, the person is invited to access a memory or symbol that would be a resource for achieving the goal/intention. The following is an excerpt from a trance session I did with Sofia, a woman who had the goal of "feeling more safe and free" in her sexual relationship with her husband.

Figure 7.5. Unfolding trance-like memories

Step 1: Preparation

    1.   Center

    2.   Intention

    3.   Resources

Step 2: Unfolding a generative trance

    1.   Invite memory or symbol to come as a resource

    2.   Slowly unpack each detail of resource to develop generative trance

Step 3: Trance-forming identity states

    1.   Open beyond experience to generative field

    2.   Weave trance elements towards integration

    3.   Integration

Step 4: Integrating back into ordinary reality

    1.   See changes in future

    2.   Vows and commitments

    3.   Gratitude

    4.   Review important learnings

    5.   Reorientation

(After preparation step)

Gilligan: And Sofia, you have identified as your important goal *feeling more safe and more free in your sexual relationship with your husband*. Is that right?

(Sofia nods head, with eyes closed.)

G: Well, that's good to know. And it's also good to know that your creative unconscious can help you to achieve that goal in so many different ways. What I'd like to invite you to do right now is let yourself take a nice deep breath and relax ... relax just enough ... that's good ... just enough to let your creative unconscious bring into your awareness a long forgotten pleasurable memory ... or perhaps a metaphorical image or symbol ... that your unconscious selects out as *a very helpful resource* to allow you to *achieve that goal* ... Just relax and let yourself perhaps be surprised at what your unconscious brings forward to allow you the *safety* ... the *strength* ... the positive confidence ... the gentle intimacy ... needed to *feel safe and free in your sexual intimacy* with your husband ... (pause) And can you tell me what you become aware of?

Sofia: (smiles) Well, it's a little strange, but I have an image of this smiling sort of warrior woman ... she's carrying a spear ... but she's really beautiful ...

G: That's so very interesting ... and I want to thank your creative unconscious for bringing forward this core self-image and resource to help you here today ... And as you sense that image, I'd like to ask you to take a deep breath and go a little bit deeper, deep enough to feel very connected with that warrior woman ... and what are you aware of now?

Sofia: She looks radiant to me ...

G: That's good ... and just let yourself experience that radiance of the warrior woman ... and breathe it in ... and let it flow through you ... (pause) And what are you aware of now?

Sofia: The look in her eyes is sparkling ...

G: Yes, just notice the sparkle in those eyes ... and breathe it in ... and let it take you a little deeper into your own sparkle ... (pause) And what are you aware of now?

Sofia: She's starting to do a movement with her spear ...

G: Is that pleasant?

Sofia: Yes, very ...

G: That's good ... and just let yourself attune to those movements of the spear ... and all the symbolic meanings therein ... and let yourself see them ... and then breathe them in and through you ... and let yourself go a little deeper into your dance of the spear ... that's good ... that's really good ...

In this way, a generative trance was developed with the client-generated resource of the "warrior woman" image.

In the third step, the positive symbols are used to deepen the creative space where old identities can be healed and new identities can be born. For example:

G: And as you feel ... the dance of the warrior woman creating a space ... opening the sources ... teaching you a new way ... to deeply be yourself in all ways good ... you can feel ... follow ... find ... those movements, experiences ... memories ... symbols ... future images ... resources ... needed to go even deeper now ... go even deeper into the healing world ... go even deeper into the dance of finding safety ... the dance of freedom ... the dance of connection with honor ... with love ... with fierce integrity ...

Letting yourself feel the turns ... the trances ... the images ... the new self-images ... of a safe free sexuality ... images from the future ... powerful healing images from ancestors ... powerful strengthening feelings from many times ... many places ... all integrating into the trance dance of fierce safety and freedom ...

The beating of a drum ... the breathing of the breath ... the fierce truth of the heart ... the desire to protect and be protected ... the desire to share and remain free ... the trance dance of the warrior woman ... the lover ... the healer ... the mother ... the woman ...

and so just let all these resources ... all these powerful feelings ... all these many images ... drop you into a deeper trance of integration ... letting yourself move into several minutes of integration ... of creating a new sense of self ... beginning *nowww* ...

Here the coach finishes with the "winds of change" (the word *now*, drawn into a long sound) a good method to gently "blow the mind" into new places. Generally, during an integration process there should be no new content presented, but it can be helpful to nonverbally support the process. The content-free technique of the "winds of change" can be remarkably helpful in this way.

After the integration process, the final step of shifting back into the classical world is done in ways we have covered previously.

Sofia reported a very meaningful trance experience. It deeply surprised her that the "warrior woman" image emerged in response to her need for safety and freedom. Even more interesting was how it positively embodied a fierce celebration of life along with the need to protect it. Her process continued over the following months. She remembered a number of childhood memories, ranging from some painful physical and emotional abuse, to long-forgotten memories of a strong tomboy who loved to play in nature. It also led her to a series of powerful new connections in her marriage, both sexually and beyond.

It is important to note is that all the core parts of the trance work were determined by Sofia. She set the goal, found her center, and connected to resources. Her unconscious then provided the core symbolic image – the warrior woman – as a crucial resource for achieving the goal. The post-trance changes also came entirely from her. As in all generative trance work, my task was to help her develop and maintain the creative conditions needed to realize these goals.

This method basically involves asking the creative unconscious to bring forth the resources needed to achieve a goal. The accessibility of such resources is a function of a person's state. The creative unconscious activates when we achieve the "not too tight, not too loose" balance of generative trance. Thus, if a person is having difficulty generating a resource, attention should attune to their underlying state. Usually, places of tension (shoulder, forehead, neck, etc.) will be obvious, or else a lack of absorption. Whatever the case, attention moves from the content level (e.g., trying to access a resource) to the underlying state (what is the mind–body state and how can it move to a higher coherence). By improving these state qualities – through shifts in somatic, field, and cognitive patterning – attention can be returned to the content level, this time with more positive results.

Fourth method: Relational mantras

In Chapter 4 we briefly touched upon the four *relational mantras*, or silent meditations, to practice while engaging in creative acceptance:

1. *"That's interesting!"*

2. *"I'm sure that makes sense"*

3. *"Something is trying to wake up (or heal)"*

4. *"Welcome!"*

When used in a generative state, they allow a person to begin to sense the positive intention and possibilities inherent in each experience. Remember, each pattern can have positive or negative value and form, depending on the human connection with it. Thus, when a negative experience or behavior is encountered, we first create a positive context and then bring the pattern into it, so that new, more positive forms and values are available. This is the essence of generative trance, and the relational mantras are at the heart of the positive cognitions that support this transformation.

For example, Dave was a 40-year-old engineer who came to see me, very shy and withdrawn. He vaguely mumbled something about procrastination being his problem. He rebuffed my efforts to get him to be more specific, just emphasizing that he wanted to do "trance for procrastination". It was only in the third session that he became more specific, announcing with great anxiety that he was a sexual pervert. When asked what this meant, he reported watching internet pornography for five to six hours daily. Multiple attempts to stop failed miserably, and he asked whether I could help him.

In my initial listening, I was visited (in my imagination) by my old Irish Catholic alcoholic priest, Father McCarthy. He was urging me to give the assignment of five cold showers a day, plus 50 Our Fathers and 100 Hail Marys. It didn't matter to Father McCarthy when I pointed out my client was Jewish; he insisted that one size fitted all. I could feel the degenerative state that this was inducing in me, so I thanked the good father for dropping by, then centered and attuned to the relational mantras. *This is interesting, I'm sure this makes sense, something is trying to wake up,* and *I welcome it.* Sensing in this way, the negative pattern became impressive: despite every effort made to live from his head, the symptom was insisting that sexuality also be included. That the sexual expression was negative was more of a comment on how it had been humanly treated, not its intrinsic nature. Thus, if a positive connection could be made to the sexuality, positive changes could occur.

Thus, when he asked if I could help him, I found myself saying, "Well, one thing I think we can say for sure: no amount of therapy or hypnosis will take away the fact that *you have an amazing sexuality!*" Predictably surprised, he responded with, "Yes, but I feel so much shame!" I breathed this in, welcomed the experiential presence into my heart center, cleansed its toxic overlay, sensed its positive core, touched it with human blessing, and then mirrored it back with the gentle affirmation, "Yes, as a sexual being you have shame ... That's good to know. And who else are you as a sexual being?"

We were limbically resonating with a shared connection, and he sheepishly looked down and said, "I'm really horny". This was received in the same fashion: welcome and absorb into center, purify, sense the core goodness, bless, and mirror back: "Yes, I see that as a sexual being you also are very horny. That's good to know ... (pause) And who else are you as a sexual being?" We continued in this way. Each time he noted a different dimension of his sexual identity – *I'm scared, I like to look at naked pictures, I'm confused, I'm lonely* – and each time it was positively accepted and fed back. After six or seven loops, he looked to be in a generative trance, his beauty as a man deep, vulnerable, and present. I gently suggested that this might be a good time to close his eyes and go on a ten minute healing journey, where his creative unconscious could take all these different elements of his sexual identity and begin to weave a new pattern, one that reflected the best of who he was in his present life.

He reoriented with a good feeling after ten minutes, returning the next week with two interesting reports. The first was that he had no urges to watch pornography during the week. Even more surprising to him was that he'd had many heated arguments with his wife, a high powered lawyer who was also pretty lost in her head. Things had been so cool between them that they were living in separate bedrooms. His reports suggested that the heat was moving back into their marriage, so I invited his wife to join us in the therapy. She did, and the remainder of the work was done with them as a couple, especially in terms of the sexual core of their relationship.

This case is an example of how creative acceptance can transform a very negative pattern (i.e., sexual addiction) to its positive core (of intimate sexuality). The pattern was welcomed into the quantum field of generative trance, along with different dimensions of his sexual identity. This fluid field can blend the multiple, often contradictory, parts of a person's identity into a new integrated whole. All the key elements of the generative trance were the client's own patterns, and the subsequent changes came from his creative unconscious. The four utilization mantras were the underlying cognitive aids for the transformational experiences. In using them, one finds a creative magic available for transmuting negative energies into positive ones.

Fifth method: Somatic modeling of problem patterns

The body says what words cannot.

Martha Graham

Creative acceptance can also transform negative patterns through a process I call *somatic modeling*. In this method, a negative pattern (e.g., smoking cigarettes, drinking alcohol, anger, anxiety) is represented in terms of its physical posture and basic movement, then repetitively expressed in a slow, rhythmic, sort of trance dance. Performing the "trance dance" of the problem allows one to understand its positive intention and then change it into a positive form.

Figure 7.6 shows the basic steps of this process. In the preparation step, the positive connections of centering and resources are developed, and the goal is expressed in terms of a particular negative pattern that a person wants to transform. For example, Kelly was a highly successful artist. Her complaint was that she was drinking two or three glasses of wine every night. She felt it was interfering with her life development, and was thus dismayed that her attempts to stop had not been successful. She wanted to either reduce or completely eliminate alcohol from her life.

Figure 7.6. Somatic modeling of problems

Step 1: Preparation

  1. Center

  2. Goal: *I would like to transform problem pattern X*

  3. Resources

Step 2: Unfolding a generative trance

  1. Develop somatic model of problem

  2. First pass: slowly and repetitively move through somatic pattern with utilization mantras

  3. Reorient and process

  4. Second pass: move back into expressing somatic patterns, this time developing generative trance by adding qualities of:

  • Centering
  • Slow, rhythmic dance
  • Sensuality
  • Grace

Step 3: Trance-forming pattern

  1. Allow the trance dance to begin to develop new ways to express basic need/intention of problem pattern

  2. Integration

Step 4: Integrating back into ordinary reality

1. Future orientation, seeing changes in action in future

2. Vows and commitments

3. Gratitude

4. Identify important learnings

5. Reorientation

In the second step, the person is asked to let go of all words, and instead represent and explore the negative pattern in terms of nonverbal physical posture and repetitive movement. For Kelly, the somatic model was simply one of sitting alone, and lifting an imaginary glass of wine up to her lips. To make this the basis of generative development, she was helped to center, slow down, and then very slowly repeat this movement, about five or six times slower than a normal movement. As she did so, I gently coached her absorption into a trance rhythm of repeating the behavior. Then, I interspersed the utilization mantras, saying something like:

> That's it ... just letting that movement repeat so slowly, so deeply ... with the curiosity: what is my unconscious trying to do here? Something is trying to be created, something important is trying to be fulfilled here ... what is it? And just move deeper into the feeling ... into the movement of the feeling ... into the language of your creative unconscious speaking through the movement ... beginning to sense the positive intentions of the behavior ... that's it ... relaxing and absorbing ... becoming more curious as you continue with that movement ...

After exploring this process for about five minutes, the person reorients and identifies any first learnings from the process – awareness gained about the positive intention, micro-elements of the pattern, and so on. Kelly was surprised to notice that when the (imaginary) alcohol touched the back of her throat, a deep field of warmth opened within her, connected to a powerful longing for "surrender". She had not been aware how deeply her use of alcohol was connected with this deep inner need. This is what we call *the positive intention of the symptom*. That is, while the surface structure of a symptom is negative, it carries a deeper positive intention. In trance we release the surface structure and move to the deep (archetypal) structure to find the positive intention, then generate new behaviors aligned with the positive intention.

The second cycle of exploration goes deeper and longer. Different dimensions of generative trance are added – centering, slow rhythmic movement, subtle and graceful flow, musicality, opening to resources, allowing new patterns to emerge, and so on. The movements are repeated very slowly – again, five or six times slower than a normal movement – thereby making it a sort of trance dance through the creative unconscious. The utilization mantras are interspersed throughout: *That's it, your unconscious is trying to bring you something, open to that and allow new patterns to develop*, and so on. This releases the neuromuscular lock binding the surface pattern, thereby making it possible for new patterns to be created.

This trance reaches its apex in the third step, where all the different weaves and sounds and images are musically moved to a climax of integration, and the creative unconscious is invited to develop new ways of satisfying the positive needs and intentions of the negative pattern. For Kelly, this meant asking her creative unconscious to develop new ways to bring that sense of warm surrender into her life.

The integration period usually lasts five or six minutes, followed by the final step of orienting to how the new patterns can be realized in a person's ordinary world. This involves noting and appreciating the important learnings made in the trance: sensing future images of performing the new behaviors, making deep vows and commitments to honor and make real the new learnings, expressing gratitude to those (including one's self) who have supported the transformational journey, and reorienting.

The somatic modeling process was very helpful for Kelly. Her attunement to what she called a deep spiritual need for surrender was both surprising and gratifying. She realized that using alcohol had become her major way to realize this need, and that she could and would develop better ways to do it. She gave up all drinking and began a daily practice of inner connection to a presence beyond her individual self – a process that continued to evolve over the next several years. It was especially helpful for her to notice any desire for alcohol as a signal that her spiritual longing was active, and that she best satisfy it mindfully, or else her drinking could well start up again.

The key to this transformational process is in the quantum and archetypal nature of the creative unconscious. The premise here is that when a challenge cannot be met with a person's historical resources, the creative unconscious activates and sends an archetypal pattern into a person's consciousness. An archetypal pattern can be positive or negative, depending on a person's relationship to it; and can be expressed in a virtually infinite number of possible forms. When we encounter a negative pattern – in Kelly's case, her alcohol habit – we see the seeds of positive intention and resources inside of that pattern. Generative trance opens a quantum field in which the old form can be released and a new form can be developed. Creative acceptance is a central cognitive relationship by which this transformation occurs. Bringing this sympathetic and curious attitude to each experience, whether it be positive or negative on the surface, allows much creative learning and development.

Summary

In this chapter we have touched on some of the ways creative acceptance can be practiced in generative trance work: accepting and utilizing each experiential detail as the basis for trance and transformation, unfolding and amplifying a simple memory or symbol into an elaborate field of resources, practicing the relational mantras (*That's interesting*, *I'm sure that makes sense*, *Something is trying to wake up*, and *Welcome*), and somatically modeling and transforming a negative pattern.

As with all generative trance processes, the success of these methods depends on the underlying mind–body state. Creative acceptance is not simply positive thinking, nor is it a passive process. It is a centered, field-connected, limbically attuned state that brings an experiential symbol or presence into a deeper field of consciousness. In this generative state of "disciplined flow," creative acceptance is a performance art where observer and observed engage in a relational dance of transformation. To support transformation in the "other," practitioners must receive and be transformed themselves. This makes the process ever interesting and intrinsically rewarding.

Several other points are worth mentioning. First, any time an impasse is reached, it suggests that something relevant to the process is not being accepted. The impasse indicates that there are two things pushing against each other: the ego interest on the one side, and an ego-antagonistic interest on the other side. The "negative other" can be identified by listening for pejorative language – what is being branded as "bad," "unacceptable," and so on. By replacing the pejorative framings with the utilization mantras, a creative acceptance of the "negative other" is possible and the impasse released.

Sometimes, however, it is not clear what is not being accepted. It may seem on the surface that all is good, but the lack of change suggests otherwise. This suggests a "hidden part" in the system that needs to be recognized and included in the process. Identifying a hidden part is a bit like the "tip of the tongue" phenomenon, where you can sense something is there, but attempts to identify it make it ever more elusive. At such times, it is best to let go of consciously trying to find it, and instead get centered and curious, silently asking whatever is hidden to come forward in its own best way. This more receptive attitude usually brings hidden parts forward, and the creative acceptance practices can then be used.

Second, the unwillingness or inability to creatively accept an experience suggests an underlying state of neuromuscular lock. We shut down many times throughout the day, and feeling stuck in an experience is a straightforward signal that this is happening. As long as we are in contracted consciousness, no new experiences are possible. By shifting attention to regaining a generative state, creative engagement becomes available.

Third, the point of creative acceptance is not merely to open to what's there, but also to absorb it into the quantum field of the creative unconscious. For example, say a person is stuck in an experience of failure. Creative acceptance means lifting that experience into a generative field that includes other experiences – for example, playfulness, success, being held. As in any systemic work (with families, groups, or teams), this involves consideration of aesthetic balance, spacing, musicality, and shifting attention. The existentialists have a saying: *psychopathology is precisely the study of loneliness.* In other words, when one part of a system becomes functionally isolated, bad things happen. By creatively accepting an experience, we bring it back into a larger systemic field where new meanings and possibilities are intrinsically present.

Fourth, it should be reiterated that the type of trance developed via creative acceptance is fundamentally different from those developed by artificial suggestion. Any experience, including trance, based primarily upon a person's values and associations will be more integratable to the psychological immune system of a person, and hence more therapeutically helpful.

Finally, creative acceptance is one of those deep principles that is never fully mastered. One can devote a whole lifetime to studying and practicing this principle, assured that at the end, the surface will have barely been scratched. By dedicated practice, one can enjoy the slow but steady unfolding of a deeper intelligence that guides us all.

Chapter 8
The Principle of Complementarity

[The soul] doesn't see joy and sorrow

as two different feelings.

It is with us

only in their union.

We can count on it

when we're not sure of anything

and curious about everything.

> Wisława Szymborska, translated by Joanna Trzeciak
> "A Little Bit about the Soul"

The separateness apparent in the world is secondary. Beyond that world of opposites is an unseen, but experienced, unity and identity in us all.

Joseph Campbell

The great quantum physicist, Neils Bohr, used to say that there are two types of truth: shallow and deep. In the shallow type, the opposite of a true statement is false; in the deeper type, the opposite of a true statement is equally true. In this chapter we will see how the deeper truth of *both/and* logic underlies the experience of generative trance, and how it can be creatively used in a variety of ways. We begin with a set of basic premises:

1. *Duality is the basic psychological unit.*

At its core, the cognitive mind is organized around dualities. Everything contains its opposite, and reality is constructed through a dynamic relationship between these opposites: breathing in and breathing out, self and other, stillness and movement, and so on. Figure 8.1 shows a simple figure of the interconnected circles of dynamic opposites. One of the basic differences between the conscious mind and the creative unconscious lies in this relationship between opposites: the conscious mind organizes around either/or relationships and gives preferential focus to one side of the complementarity over the other, while the creative unconscious holds a both/and relationship in which both sides are simultaneously engaged.

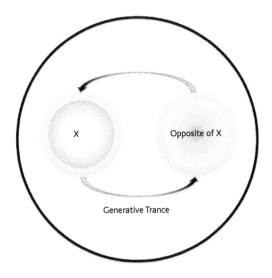

Figure 8.1. The "both/and" relationship of the creative unconscious in generative trance

2. *When opposites are in harmony, life goes well.*

The either/or orientation of the conscious mind makes sense at the practical level. To create anything in the world, we must choose one value over another at any given point. To walk, we put one foot forward, then the other, then back to the first, and so on. As long as we have a rhythmic way of expressing a complementarity, there is no problem. We work hard, then we rest, then we work again; we connect with others until we need solitude, which then brings us back into connection with others; we have a stable map that eventually becomes untenable and unstable, which leads to a new stability. In this way, the conscious mind facilitates the realization of the vision of the creative unconscious (see McGilchrist, 2010).

3.   *When opposites are not in harmony, problems and symptoms develop.*

The simplest formula for developing a problem is to develop a fixed identification with one side of a complementarity, with a negative relationship on the other side. For example, Helen grew up in a family where the core rule was, "Always work hard," with the corollary injunctions "Never rest" and "Never take it easy". The family was exceptional, most members being highly successful people who also did significant community work. They resembled the old Kennedy family clan, where vacations were spent engaged in vigorous athletic competitions that everybody was required to join.

In this family, the fixed values were around the complementarity of active/rest – being active was "good" and meant *always work and be successful in the world*, while rest was "bad" and meant *sitting around and feeling guilty and worthless*. This is an example of the conscious mind preferring one side over the other, which when held in neuromuscular lock will produce a rigid imbalance.

Jung used to say that the unconscious is compensatory to (i.e., trying to balance) the imbalances of the conscious mind. That is, it is always attempting to bring creative wholeness to the system. Thus, when the conscious mind contracts around one part of the system, the unconscious will activate the complementary part which, if treated negatively, will show up as a negative symptom. Thus, it was not surprising that Helen developed a strange type of chronic fatigue that left her bedridden and unable to work. To be clear, the unconscious pattern here is *rest*, which the conscious mind filter created as *chronic fatigue*. If you want to change that negative pattern, you need to unbind the identity filter and move back into the "field of infinite possibilities" of the creative unconscious, where more positive versions of *rest* can be generated.

Helen was helped into a generative trance wherein I invited and welcomed the part of her that was experiencing chronic fatigue. (To talk to these inner parts, you need generative trance processes such as limbic resonance, open curiosity, and gentle attunement.) When I asked this part her need, the achingly beautiful response came:

I just want to surrender.

A few moments later, she added:

> But I love my work so much.

To her ego identity, these complementary needs – surrender and work – were mutually exclusive, thereby generating a conflict. In generative trance, they are *mutually inclusive*, such that their balanced integration is what allows creative living. Helen began a series of trance explorations about how she could honor both sides:

> I can do great work *and* relax deeply.

Creating a balance between the two complementary sides allowed her to replace her symptomatic version of *rest* with more positive, integrated forms.

4.   *When both sides of a complementarity are activated simultaneously in a negative context, deep splits and breakdowns occur.*

Most of the time, a given side of a complementarity is more dominant than the other. When both sides are simultaneously and equally activated, however, a strange and powerful effect occurs: the conscious mind falls apart and the quantum field of the unconscious opens. This could be something as simple and enjoyable as a good joke. One of Milton Erickson's favorites was the simple:

> Mr. and Mrs. Bigger had a baby and everybody wanted to know who was the biggest Bigger. Of course, it was the baby that was a little Bigger.

The laughter from a joke occurs when the two different frames – in this case, Bigger and bigger – are simultaneously held. The bindings of the conscious mind are popped and the creative unconscious releases with the musicality of laughter. The temporary "losing your mind" that results from laughter is but one example of what happens when opposites fire off simultaneously. A core premise of generative trance is:

> The most succinct formula for trance development is simultaneously holding contradictory positions.

This pops the single truth position upon which the conscious mind relies, thereby dropping you into the waters of the creative unconscious. The caveat is that the resulting trance can be either very negative or very positive, depending on the context. For example, Gregory Bateson (1956) proposed a "double bind" theory of schizophrenia that saw schizophrenic experience and behavior as a response to a communication system where two contradictory messages were repeatedly given – for example, *come closer* (as a verbal message) and *stay away* (as a nonverbal message) – with the unspoken rules: (1) you can't meta-comment on the bind, (2) whichever message you respond to, you're bad, and (3) you can't leave the context. According to Bateson, this *schizophrenogenic double bind* produces a structurally similar response in the recipient, namely, *schizo* (split) *phrenos* (mind).

More recently, a similar sort of double bind has been proposed by Peter Levine (2010) in his groundbreaking work on trauma. He describes a cross-species response to traumatic threat, a sort of "trauma trance" where an animal gets locked in frozen immobility or folds into helplessness. While the typical response to threat is either fight or flight, if neither of these limb-based responses is available, it sets up a sort of negative double bind that produces the trauma trance.

In a more general way, we can see most symptoms in terms of a violent clash of opposites. A simple representation of a problem is:

I want X but Y happens instead.

In such cases, X and Y can be seen as complements that, when activated in a mutually inhibitory way, overwhelm the single position of the conscious mind. If there is no positive presence to welcome and creatively hold the conflictual clash, the negative context generates a negative trance response of a symptom. A main goal of generative trance is to provide a safe and resilient context in which such conflicting parts can be untangled and then integrated into a complementary unity.

5. *When both sides of a complementarity are activated simultaneously in a positive context, good things happen.*

One of Bateson's (1955) most extraordinary contributions was his generalizing of the "double message" communication beyond schizophrenia. That is, he suggested that all distinctly human communications contain double messages. This includes humor, play, mature love (where two partners create a space that includes the different individual positions, plus a third "we" position), and trance (where there are two levels of experience, the conscious and unconscious minds). In these contexts, the "both/and" quality of the communication open a deeper dimension beyond the single frame of the conscious mind. In his later work, Bateson (1972) emphasized how any ecological map must minimally carry "double description" – that is, at least two different, even contradictory perspectives. When the different descriptions are aesthetically combined, a deeper dimension is opened, much like the process of binocular vision or stereophonic listening.

This capacity to experience seemingly contradictory realities in trance is known as "trance logic" (Orne, 1959), and is generally regarded as one of the defining phenomena of trance experience. It reflects partly the structure of hypnotic communications, where the paradoxical suggestion is given for the person to do something, but not at a conscious level (e.g., *Your hand will begin to lift all by itself, without your conscious effort*). The resulting experience is a paradoxical: I'm *both* lifting my hand *and* I'm not (consciously) lifting my hand.

This trance logic takes many different forms. For example, when I was 20 years old, I was sitting in Erickson's office with a friend of mine. Paul was also 20, and had a big mustache at the time. Erickson led Paul into a very sweet trance involving age regression. When asked, Paul reported he was 4 years old, and he really looked and sounded like it! Ever playful, Erickson asked Paul what was up on his (mustached) lip. Paul momentarily looked alarmed, then said in his best 4-year-old voice, "Nothing!"

Erickson playfully persisted, suggesting that maybe he had eaten some corn flakes for breakfast, as something sure seemed to be up on his lip. He asked Paul to reach up and touch his lip, which Paul refused. Erickson asked why not, and Paul said, "I know what's up there!"

"What?" Erickson asked.

"Hair!" Paul responded.

"What's hair doing on the lip of a 4-year-old boy?" Erickson inquired.

Paul paused, as if needing to go deeper into trance, then brightened and responded, "Oh, that's easy, that's when I was older!" Erickson laughed and agreed, "Yes, that's when you were older". He then talked about how in trance you could be both an adult and a child at the same time, in so many ways.

The value of such a possibility is hopefully self-evident. Imagine the creativity if we could experience opposite realities simultaneously – for example, having the maturity of an adult and the innocence of a child; or feeling a part of something yet also apart from it; or holding feelings of both wanting something and not needing it.

Interestingly, the capacity to enjoyably experience opposites has been found by a number of investigators to be a central characteristic of creative geniuses. Arthur Koestler, in his landmark book, *The Act of Creation* (1964), proposed that central to the creative process was the process of "bisociation," where two previously unrelated ideas integrate together. Relatedly, Frank Barron (1969) found that creative geniuses were strong in three areas: (1) the willingness/ability to sit in "not knowing" states of active curiosity; (2) a deep sense of unwavering unshakability once a conviction was developed; and (3) the appreciation of paradoxes, contradictions, and other forms of both/and logic. In another study of 91 creative geniuses, Mihály Csíkszentmihályi (1996) found that these individuals shared ten characteristics, all having to do with both/and qualities. For example, they were intensely active and energetic, but spent considerable time in restful reverie and trance-like states; they were playful but also quite disciplined; and they were both introverted and extroverted.

6.   *Generative trance is an excellent context for creatively working with the core complementarities underlying a reality or identity.*

Its positive context allows each part to experience acceptance, respect, and support. Its deconstructive nature allows the different surface forms attached to a part to be dissolved, and new possible forms to be explored. Its fluidity allows many new possible connections to be explored. In a core sense, generative trance is a creative field that carries virtually unlimited potential for new consciousness. A person shifts from identification with one position (against another) to a field that holds the interplay of all the perspectives in the field. Thus, conflicting relationships can be untangled and put back into play, allowing new connections to slowly move towards an integrative climax that gives birth to new dimensions.

Generative trance methods of complementarity

We have thus examined how complementarity is a fundamental principle of psychological reality, underlying both the constructions of problems and symptoms as well as solutions and creative consciousness. The remainder of the chapter will explore different methods for utilizing complementarity in generative trance work. Figure 8.2 lists these five methods.

Figure 8.2. Generative trance methods of complementarity

1.	The suggestion loop of complementarity
2.	Mutual trance
3.	"Good self/bad self"
4.	Reconciling opposites
5.	The somatic trance dance of integrating opposites

First method: The suggestion loop of complementarity

In Chapter 7, we examined the suggestion loop of creative acceptance, where each experiential detail is absorbed to unfold a generative trance or personal change. A second core suggestion loop for generative trance work involves inviting a person to simultaneously hold opposite experiences. This is perhaps the most succinct formula for accessing the creative unconscious. The three parts of the suggestion loop are represented in Figure 8.3.

Figure 8.3. The suggestion loop of complementarity

> 1. *X is so* (pacing a present state)
>
> 2. *Y is so* (accessing a complementary state or truth)
>
> 3. *And what a nice thing to know that you can enjoy both at the same time* (unifying opposites)

First, an invitation is offered to experience one side of a complementarity. For example:

> You can *let go* just a little bit.

After a few moments of silence (to let the inner experience develop), a complementary suggestion is presented. For example:

> And you can also *hold on* to a sense of security.

A third suggestion then encourages both experiences simultaneously:

> And what a nice thing to know that *you can experience both at the same time!*

As with all trance-related communications, the musicality of the presentation is of primary importance. Holding opposites can either feel liberating and fun – such as hearing the punchline of a good joke – or frightening and unsafe – such as when receiving double messages in a threatening context. Thus, relational rapport and limbic attunement are first developed, and the receiver is supported in developing a generative state of centering, opening to resources, and setting a positive intention. The suggestion loop exercise is emphasized as a learning experiment that belongs to the receiver. It is not a process of being tricked or overwhelmed by a hypnotist, but an opportunity for self-learning how trance-related processes can open up via playfully exploring opposites.

Figure 8.4. Complementaries for generative trance development

---

- Conscious/unconscious

- Hold on/let go

- Stay out of trance/go into trance

- Listen/don't listen

- A part of/apart from

- Left/right

- Here/there

- Remember/forget

- Then/now

Figure 8.4 shows some complementarities especially useful for developing generative trance. In workshops, the suggestion loop is usually practiced in groups of three, moving through three rounds so that each person has a chance to be Coach 1, Coach 2, and the "Trance-Former". In the training exercise, the first loop uses the first complementarity in Figure 8.4 – conscious/unconscious – and further loops progressively move through the other items listed.

When working with two coaches, the first statement of the three-part loop is spoken by Coach 1, the second by Coach 2, and then both coaches speak the third statement simultaneously and stereophonically. For example:

C1: Your conscious mind can *wonder*.

C2: And your unconscious can *wander*.

C1/C2: And what a nice thing to know you can enjoy *both* at the same time!

The process is meant to be playful and absorbing, but also gentle and respectful. The Trance-Former is invited to make the experience their own "experiment in consciousness," noticing what happens when consciousness moves from one polarity to the other, and being especially attentive to what happens when both are experienced simultaneously.

As with the first suggestion loop described in the last chapter, all parties begin with centering, letting go, setting an intention, and opening to relational connection. Once completed, the Trance-Former (who usually has eyes closed) is asked to nod when ready to receive the communications. The loops are then explored with musicality, resonance, and deep connection. Here is an excerpt of how the exercise might proceed, once the receiver is centered and has indicated readiness.

> C1: And you can enjoy listening with your *conscious mind*.

> C2: And you can also enjoy experiencing with your *unconscious mind*.

> C1/C2: And what nice thing to know you can enjoy *both* at the same time!

A few moments of silence ensure, interlaced with gentle suggestions such as: "That's it ... that's good ... just let it happen ... breathe ... open". Then another round, this time C2 beginning:

> C2: And you can *hold on* to comfort and security ...

> C1: ... and you can *let go* of tension and unnecessary thoughts.

> C1/C2: And what a nice thing to know you can enjoy *both* at the same time!

As the process unfolds, the two coaches can become more playfully interactive, weaving point and counterpoint into trance. For example (with C2 words in italics):

> And you can really enjoy *staying out* of trance ... *and going into a trance* ... staying out ... *going in* ... out ... *in* ... staying ... *going* ... *in* ... out ... And what a nice thing to know you can enjoy *both* ... both ... *both* ... both ... *at the same time* ... time ... *time* ... time ... *time*.

(To enhance the trance, words (like *time*) can be repeated with gently different tones and textures. Sometimes it's interesting and
helpful to draw out a word (like *time*) into a long wind-like sound.)

In this way, both/and experiences are woven through the mind–body fabric, with the intent of opening up interesting spaces of consciousness. This
is not doing something *to* someone but *with* someone. Thus, deep rapport is maintained within the team, and the Trance-Former's nonverbal
responses are used to adjust and guide the process. For example, any sign
of neuromuscular lock (such as eyebrow furrowing or inhibited breathing)
is a signal to slow down and be a bit more gentle, until the "green light" of
relaxed enjoyment appears in the Trance-Former's somatic state.

In generative trance, we're always feeling for the meeting place between
the conscious and unconscious worlds. If you tilt too much or too fast
towards the unconscious, you'll be greeted with tension and resistance. If
you're too far away from the quantum quivering of the unconscious, the
person will stay in their head and make it an intellectual analysis. Limbic
attunement will guide you in finding the balance point where generative
trance opens a third world that includes the conscious mind, the creative
unconscious, and much, much more.

The complementarities of Figure 8.4 are helpful for trance development.
Figure 8.5 shows complementarities useful when using generative trance
to reorganize identity. When we see fixed problems or symptoms as con-
flicts between complementary parts of self-identity, we want to notice
where these splits lie in a person's experience. The list in Figure 8.5 indicates some likely possibilities. For example, each person's life has problems and resources, a childlike side and adult parts, orientation to self and
to others, the need to say "yes" and the need to say "no," and so forth.

In creative consciousness, each side completes and supports its comple-
ment. In problems, the two sides are not in harmony or good connection.
Thus, when you experience a problem, you may forget about your resources;
you may be more comfortable saying "yes" than saying "no"; or you may
consistently orient more to others than yourself. A prolonged imbalance
between any of these complementary sides will create problems, and finding a balanced harmony between them will generate solutions.

Figure 8.5. Complementarities for creative wholeness of self

> - Problem/resource (or goal)
> - Child/adult
> - Past/future
> - Self/other
> - No/yes
> - Alone/together
> - Inside/outside
> - Don't change/change
> - Serious/playful
> - Inward/outward
> - Imagined/physical
> - Trust/don't trust

A simple way to identify core, unintegrated complementarities is to listen to where judgments are made: "I want this side, but I don't want its opposite". For example, a young man was feeling very anxious about an upcoming talk he was scheduled to give at his professional society. The goal was summarized as:

> I want to be confident in giving a speech
> *but*
> I'm too shy.

With the goal of weaving the two complements – *confidence* and *shyness* – into an integrated whole, the following trance communications were offered:

> (*Inviting both sides*) And what a nice thing to know that in trance you can experience so many different realities in a pleasurable way. You know, for example, the feeling of confidence ... and how you can feel confidence in so many ways ... different times, different places, different memories ... and as you allow those feelings to be there, it's also nice to know you can feel rather shy as well ... a sweet, delicate, almost unbearable tenderness ... that is the mark of great sensitivity and intelligence ...

(*Connecting with one side*) And you can sense that shyness in so many ways ... sweetly ... curiously ... comfortably ... where you feel it in your body ... the ages connected to it ... the breathing deepening all around it ...

(*Connecting with other side*) And then as you sense the shyness ... you can also sense the confidence ... different ages, different places in the body ... the sweet shyness ... the comfortable confidence ...

(*Integrating both sides*) And what a nice thing to know you can allow yourself to experience *both at the same time!* ... A sweet ... comfortable ... confident ... shyness ... delicately ... confidently ... integrating together ... in a very interesting ... very healing way ...

This is an abbreviated example to illuminate the steps in the sequence; in practice, each step usually needs more elaboration. As in any conflict resolution process (e.g., in business mediation or couples therapy). Each side must be differentiated and separately valued before integration is possible. The rate of shifting between sides is quite variable. Also, the way in which a negative side is framed as positive is a delicate process. (In the above example, this involved describing the shy part in terms of "delicate," "sensitive," and "intelligent".) If done too quickly, rapport will be lost; if not done, the hostile attitude towards the part will remain. Thus, while the basic process is simple – identify the conflicting parts, connect with one part and then the other, and then integrate them together – the process by which this is successfully done requires great skill. Of course, this is the rule for most generative trance work.

Second method: Mutual trance

The interconnected circles in Figure 8.1 can represent many types of relationship, including between two people. When two parts of a whole are engaged in an "I/thou" relationship, the creative unconscious unfolds as a "between state" shared by the two. It is not one person doing something to another person, or one person doing something all on their own, but two people working together to create something unique. To participate in such an experience, one must receive before giving, experience deeply before guiding, and listen carefully before speaking. In the musicality of generative trance, there must be a joint collaboration between persons, each connected to self, other, and something bigger.

Mutual trance is a process for exploring this. It is usually done with a single partner, though I've also done it in groups of three or four people as well. Each partner is both offering and receiving trance, looking to find the quantum arithmetic where

$$1 + 1 = 3$$

I have used mutual trance as a training exercise in workshops, but also with couples facing collaborative challenges (e.g., preparing for childbirth or creating a positive future together).[18]

Figure 8.6 shows the steps of the process. Once the partners settle in, they start with the preparation step. If done as a training exercise, the goal might be generally to see what kind of interesting creative trance experiences can be co-created. If done with intimate partners, the goal can be more specific – improving intimacy, preparing for a major change, and so on.

Figure 8.6. Mutual trance

1. Preparation step: center, positive intention, resources
2. Connect with partner (signal when ready)

3. Simultaneously cycle through induction loops:
   • *Now I am aware that I see* _____
   • *Now I am aware that I hear* _____
   • *Now I am aware that I feel* _____

---

18 Interestingly, this mutual trance process is usually easier for strangers (i.e., partners pairing up in a workshop setting) than for intimate partners. In fact, I have done this process a number of times with couples in therapy, as it is a metaphor for the intimacy challenge of creating a shared experiential space. I can't remember any couple getting through the exercise the first time, without some disagreement or other lack of synchrony interrupting the process. The disconnection place can be used as a good starting point to examine and repair how a couple breaks their intimacy bond.

> 4. When trance begins to develop: shift to sequential alternation of phrases (*a mountain in the distance ... the moon rising ...*)
>
> 5. Unfold and enjoy a mutually created trance field
>
> 6. When ready, gradually reorient and share

Upon completing the preparation step, partners slowly open their eyes and connect with each other. In doing so, the interest is in establishing equal connection to (1) one's center, (2) the larger field, and (3) one's partner. This is often best done by letting awareness extend far beyond the partner, and then peripherally very wide, in effect making the field the dominant awareness. One's partner is then felt within this larger field, allowing connection without merging. A head nod can indicate when this has been accomplished.

The third step is a modified version of the self-trance process outlined in the previous chapter. In this version, partners *simultaneously* speak aloud the three part statements of:

> Now I am aware that I see ...
> Now I am aware that I hear ...
> Now I am aware that I feel ...

The goal is to speak in a balanced, synchronous way, so that self and other are sensed equally. If one person is speaking faster or louder, natural adjustments are made until neither presence is more dominant than the other. This is where 1 + 1 = 3.

Of course, the content to complete each statement is usually different for each person. And as in the self-trance process, the awareness content can be actual external stimuli (e.g., *the air conditioner, the color of your shirt*) or internal imaginations (e.g., *a song, angels, a memory from childhood*). Here's a brief example:

> Robert: Now I am aware that I see ... *the eyes blinking.*
> Sandra: Now I am aware that I see ... *the wall behind you.*

Robert: Now I am aware that I hear ... *the laughter of children.*
Sandra: Now I am aware that I hear ... *silence.*

Robert: Now I am aware that I feel ... *the beginning of warmth.*
Sandra: Now I am aware that I feel ... *openness.*

After each statement, partners breathe and absorb both experiential contents, curious about how a trance can open. Partners continue to speak in limbic attunement, with musical resonance and open curiosity, reiterating the three-part statements until it feels like a good mutual trance has developed. Then the eyes can close (if they haven't already), and a deep breath allows one to sink a bit deeper into the open space of a generative trance field.

In the next step, partners *alternate* phrases to mutually unfold an interesting trance. The important thing is that each person speaks only a phrase, then the partner builds on it with another phrase, then back to the first person, and so forth. In this way, neither side can control or dominate the trance; each side takes the time to breathe in whatever has been said, notice what it creates inside, and then adds a little something to elaborate it further. Here's an example from Robert and Sandra's experiment (with Sandra's statements shown in italics):

An open field of grass ... *very wild, high grass* ... blowing in the wind ... *a beautiful wind with sparkles of magic* ... a magic that brings new surprising experiences ... *and two young children happily sitting in the field* ... just sitting, smiling, looking around ... *a boy and a girl, so curious and full of wonderment* ... and a great bird appearing in the sky ... *a bird with purple wings* ... joined by another bird ... *a bird with white wings* ... and the two birds looking down and seeing the two children ... *and the two children waving to them* ... the birds flying down into the field ... *inviting the children to take a ride on their backs* ... shall we go, then, you and I, on an evening spread against the sky? ... *Yes, let's climb on and go for a ride ...*

This mutual trance unfolded further into a wonderful trance exploration – going where no man or woman had gone before.

After perhaps 10 or 15 minutes of exploration, reorientation can occur through a mutual process of gradually returning back from trance. Experiences can be shared and processed before the exercise concludes.

Many people are deeply moved and delighted by this process. It is a simple but powerful means to step out of a separate ego-locked reality and into an experimental state of consciousness. The sequence of (1) establishing an internal generative state, (2) hooking up with another person in a generative state, and then (3) carefully balancing "giving and receiving" to unfold a mutual reality is an excellent model for a variety of types of generative collaboration work, whether it be generative trance work, an intimacy partnership, work with a business team, or a therapy or coaching relationship. In each encounter, creativity is not located in a single person; it emerges through the fabric of relational connection. To weave this fabric, giving and receiving must be in balance throughout the field.

Unfortunately, ths is too often not the case in therapy and coaching, and especially hypnotic work, where the practitioner believes he or she is primarily responsible for changing the client's behavior, while simultaneously believing it inappropriate to deeply receive from the client. This keeps experience locked inside the client, which leads to pathologizing and isolating that experience even further. When experiences enter a relational space "wherever two or more are gathered," good transformational work is possible. Seeing a therapeutic or coaching process as a form of "mutual trance" calls for the practitioner to receive deeply and be guided by the client's process at multiple levels.

For example, Karen came to see me during a transitional phase in her life. She was a psychologist who had cut way back on her work during the first eight years of her daughter's life. As her daughter settled into elementary school, Karen felt a calling to return to full-time professional work, but also felt like something was holding her back.

In the preparation phase, she set her positive intention as: "I want a positive path in my professional life". When asked to notice any resources that her unconscious brought to her, she mentioning *images of flowers blossoming, her dog Maggie*, and *a graduate school professor*. When I then invited her to center, she experienced a little difficulty, noting, "My belly feels empty and filled with pain". I asked her to breathe and notice any inner responses to my query as to what might help her with that centering process. She reported sensing the responses of *earth* and *comfort*.

I asked how much earth and comfort she presently experienced (on a 1–10 scale) and she reported 5. I asked if she would like to discover how to increase that level a bit, and she nodded. I suggested that perhaps her resources could guide her, and she smelled and saw the blooming flowers again. This relaxed her, and then the left side of her body began to tremble. I asked if she was OK, and she nodded *yes*. I suggested she go on a healing journey in which whatever positive resources needed to be remembered could be remembered, and whatever needed healing could be healed. She looked intensely absorbed but positively settled (via breathing, facial expression, muscle tonus), so I simply provided general guidance and fed back the resources she had noted, adding in a few images that came to me spontaneously in our mutual trance connection.

After about 20 minutes, I suggested she reorient. She movingly described how in trance she reconnected with a childhood polio experience that had left her left side virtually paralyzed. She described that it was intense but very positive to reconnect with this experience, as it seemed to contain much of her fear of going forward into the next step of her life. (Interestingly, she developed the polio at 8, the same present age as her daughter.) She emphasized how the connection to her resources and to the nonverbal rapport of our mutual trance made it safe and very interesting to explore these deep areas of her life. Six months later, she reported being back at work in a new job, happy and looking forward to the future.

This example illustrates how generative trance work is a dialogue between multiple levels of all members of the team. By carefully joining with another person, generative collaboration can occur at a deep level. Again, this does not mean that people merge together and lose their respective identities; rather, the mutual trance opens a larger field that holds each individual member, plus a deeper systemic intelligence. (The quantum math is 1 + 1 = 3, not 1 + 1 = 1.) Differential roles can still be held – for example, one person may be there as therapist, the other as a client – while a shared intelligence is also accessed. What mutual trance illustrates is the unfolding of a relational unconscious that emerges when skillful balancing of giving and receiving occurs across the different positions in a field.

Third method: "Good self/bad self"

The methods of complementarity are based on the premise that the wholeness of human consciousness is experienced and expressed in terms of opposites. When the dualities become fixed and antagonistic, consciousness splits into warring camps. The wholeness is lost, and with it the possibilities for authentic happiness and creativity.

A main way this split occurs is through what we might call "good self" vs. "bad self," where one side is represented as positive and the other as negative.[19] The surface forms of each side seem to confirm this judgment. In our earlier example, "active" was represented positively as *good work for others*, while "relax" was represented as *chronic fatigue*. On the surface, the case seems strong that the former really is the good side, and the latter really is the bad side.

Such appearances can be misleading, of course, as each side has many faces, some good and some not so good. For example, "fierceness" could be positive (e.g., a protection of life, challenging of injustice) or negative (e.g., a violent perpetrator, negative yelling). Its polarity of "gentleness" could equally be positive (e.g., kind tenderness, soothing compassion) or negative (e.g., placating, false sentimentality). To be generative, then, requires the appreciation that we are ultimately responsible for our experience; it is we who relationally construct them as positive or negative.

To claim this responsibility and its corresponding freedom, it is important to identify and heal our fixed divisions of self. One simple yet powerful process is the good self/bad self exercise shown in Figure 8.7. The exercise can be done in two ways. In the first, two partners alternate sharing; in the second (more appropriate when working with a client in a professional setting), the client speaks a series of good self/bad self dualities, with the practitioner each time absorbing and feeding back the four sponsorship statements. We will briefly overview the first version here.

Figure 8.7. The good self/bad self exercise

---

1. Partners nonverbally center, open to field, connect with each other

2. Partner A says:

What I want you (or the world) to see is that I am _____
What I don't want you (or the world) to see is that I am also _____

---

19 It is important to appreciate that the terms "good self" and "bad self" are used in quotation marks at all times. The idea is not that any given part is good or bad, it's that we develop these fixed evaluations of them, thereby creating a world of troubles.

---

3. Partner B listens, gives nonverbal sponsorship, then says:

I see that you are [good self]
I also see that you are [bad self]
I see that you are both [good self and bad self]
I see that you are much, much more

4. Partner B speaks two statements, A responds with the four sponsorship statements

5. Partners alternate three to five rounds, taking time to speak, touch, make visible, and release each truth

---

The first step is the setting of the generative state via centering, opening to a field awareness, and connecting with one's partner. Each partner nods when ready, then Person A speaks the two statements:

> *What I want you to know (or see) about me is that I am _____*

> *What I don't want you to know (or see) about me is that I am also _____*

For each statement, the speaker remains relationally connected and speaks slowly, opening the spaces between the words. No premeditated thought is given to the content; just notice what comes up as you get to the end of the statement. If the speaker disconnects in any way (breathing, looking away), the receiver gently and simply guides them back into connection. A main purpose is to sense whatever core identity comes up, speak it honestly and resonantly to lift its energy into the relational space, and then release. This is far from an intellectual report; it is a practice in bringing soul energies into human connection.

The receiver listens and absorbs with curiosity and openness. There is no need to analyze, change, or "do something" with what is presented. Just let it touch you and find an affectionate place in your center, while staying relationally connected. Once both presences are felt with equanimity, the receiver speaks four statements in response:

> *I see that you are [good self]*

I also see that you are [bad self]

I see that you are both [good self and bad self]

And I see that you are much, much more

Each statement is spoken authentically only when the receiver deeply senses its truth, and is said with kindness and a sort of blessing. There may be slight re-phrasings of content, especially if a "bad self" is presented in strongly negative terms. For example, if a person says, "I don't want you to see that I am a worthless idiot," this could be fed back as, "I see that there is part of you that feels you are a worthless idiot". The challenge is to stay connected with the core energy, while also gently tweaking its verbal framing.

After Person A absorbs the four reflecting statements, perhaps closing the eyes and breathing in the blessings, Person B begins with their two statements. Person A now becomes the receiver, absorbing and then reflecting back. Since it usually takes a round or two to really sink into the process, it is good to move through four or five rounds of this exchange. Here's an excerpt of two rounds:

Jim: Nick, what I want you to see are the angels in me.

And what I don't want you to see are the devils.

Nick: Jim, I can see the angels in you.

I can also see some of the devils.

I can see both dancing within you.

And I see much, much more. (smiles)

(Jim closes eyes, takes a deep breath and touches heart. Then he opens eyes and nods gently.)

Nick: Jim, what I want you to see is that I'm a loving person.

And what I don't want you to see is how desperately I'm sometimes looking for this love.

Jim: Nick, I see what a loving person you are.

And I also see how desperately you're looking for that love.

It's really great to see both. (gentle smile, a few moments of silence)

And I also see so much more at the same time. (twinkle in eye)

Jim: Nick, I want you to see my aliveness.

And I don't want you to see ... my tiredness. (looks sad)

Nick: I can see your aliveness, Jim. (pause)

And I can also see your tiredness. (pause, compassionate connection)

I can sense them both at the same time. (gentle smile)

And I can also see that there's so much, much more! (twinkle)

Nick: What I want you to see is my joy ...

And what I don't want you to see is my fear of death.

Jim: Nick, I see the joy.

And I also see the fears of death. (pause, empathic connection)

It's good to see both. (long pause, silent exchange)

> And still feel at the same time all of the other Nicks in the field …
> (smiles) Soooo many of them! (smiling)
>
> Nick: (laughing slightly) Yes, quite a lot. (both laugh)

Such statements, when shared with deep limbic resonance, can have profound impacts. The "good self" and "bad self" are like the two Greek theater masks of old, each presenting a particular dimension of life. When both are held with equanimity, powerful integrations occur. Consciousness is liberated from identifying with any mask and thus is free to rest in the quantum field of the creative unconscious, from which all forms arise and return.

The exercise also illuminates how much energy we put into "hypnotizing" ourselves and the world that we are *only this quality* and *absolutely, definitely not THAT quality*. It helps us sense that "the kingdom of God is indeed within us," that our creative unconscious contains all possible identities, so whatever I see "out there" is also in me. Then our challenge becomes how to humanize each energy that comes through us, thereby realizing its positive human value.

The four reflecting statements represent the four main foci of good transformational work: (1) attention to the problem or symptom, (2) attention to the goal or resources, (3) weaving positive connections between the two sides, and (4) always holding the space of infinite possibilities beyond any given focus. One of the major skills in such work is knowing which foci to attune to at any moment, and how to artfully switch among them.

Many people find this an extremely helpful method for connecting to core aspects of self-identity. The nonverbal attunement allows a person to sense and breathe into the somatic centers of the parts, and the shared connection allows the parts to move from an isolated internal space to a breathing relational space. And of course, having each part appreciated, especially ones thought to be "bad," sparks many good integrations.

I have used this exercise many times with clients, either at the beginning of sessions or where there is a lack of clarity about what needs to happen. In most cases, it is not a mutual exchange; rather, I am the receiver for the client. It often gets right to the heart of core identity issues, from which further work can occur. The bad self is often a hidden part for a client, so bringing it to the forefront can be very helpful.[20] For example, one woman's presenting self was typically cheerful, smiling, and attentive to others. In the exercise, her "bad self" statements included: "Sometimes I don't want to live" and "I feel resentful". These previously hidden parts, when valued and connected with her "good self" parts, generated some very helpful shifts. The next method can be very helpful in this regard.

Fourth method: Reconciling opposites

The purpose of the journey is compassion. When you have come past the pairs of opposites, you have reached compassion.

Joseph Campbell

Another way to identify and integrate conflicting parts is through a process I call *reconciling opposites*. This is an especially good method to use when a person is struggling between two sides: one side wants to do X, the other side doesn't, and the result is an impasse. The three core steps of the process are (1) identifying and finding the somatic center for the goal, (2) identifying and finding the somatic center for the problem, and (3) creating a flowing connection between them to transform the parts from enemies to allies. Figure 8.8 outlines how this might be done.

Figure 8.8. The reconciling opposites method

1. Preparation step: center, set intention, connect with resources
2. Identify goal in two-part statement: *I want X, but Y happens instead*
3. Welcome and identify somatic center for one part
4. Welcome and identify somatic center for complementary part

---

20 The complementary parts to the presenting "good self" are usually not that difficult: one need only look at the symptom, the presenting selves of the person's partner, or what a person attacks in others. These are the classic "projection" (of the unintegrated self) techniques.

> 5. Move between parts, ensuring balanced intensity levels
>
> 6. Develop connection between parts
>
> 7. Integration
>
> 8. Identify new learnings, make commitments, future orientation, gratitude, and reorientation
>
> 9. Discussion

In the first (preparation) step, the client is helped to center, identify a positive intention, and connect to resources. For this process, the goal statement has two parts:

> I would like to do X, but Y happens instead.

For example:

> I would like to be kind to my two boys, but I end up yelling at them.
>
> I would like to finish this writing project, but I end up procrastinating.
>
> I would like to have a particular conversation with my husband, but I end up feeling too shy.
>
> I would like to be confident in front of groups, but I feel scared instead.

While the two sides initially seem irreconcilable, it is suggested that they may be parts of a deeper whole. The exercise is then suggested as a way to learn how that might be possible.

In the third step, the client is asked which side (goal or problem) would be best to connect with first. Interestingly, most people select the problem side, perhaps because it often carries more energy. A positive relationship with the "negative part" is established in multiple ways: (1) it is named in human terms; (2) its somatic center is sensed and touched; (3) it is welcomed and acknowledged as "making sense" and having integrity; (4) it is given a place inside the practitioner's center (to set up a parallel tracking and relational connection); (5) any ages connected to it are noted; and (6) its intensity level is noted at different ongoing parts. Throughout the process, the client is invited to become mindful and curious about how to positively connect with that part.

This process allows the part to be welcomed in a positive light. The naming of it in the third person ("that part," "he" or "she," "the presence within you that experiences …"), the sensing of its somatic center, and the awareness of younger ages all allow it to be differentiated, so that a person can *be with the experience without becoming it*, a both/and relationship at the heart of generative consciousness. Especially central to this process is the primary connection to the *felt sense* of the experience's subtle somatic energies, which allows the release of all the negative stories, names, and other conditioned forms that may become associated with it.

The following excerpt illustrates how this was done with Jose Carlos, a man troubled by his angry outbursts with his two young boys:

> Coach: So Jose Carlos, it sounds like you're talking about two differ-
> ent things. The first is how much you love your kids and want to be
> a good father. Is that right?
>
> Jose Carlos: Yes.
>
> Coach: Great … That's good to know … And the second experience
> is that you find yourself getting really angry with them sometimes.
> Did I get that right?
>
> Jose Carlos: Yes … (looks troubled) I know I shouldn't, but it just
> seems to happen.
>
> Coach: Well, that's good to know also. And I'm sure that part makes
> a lot of sense in terms of something trying to happen deep inside of
> you. So I'd like to say to that part of you … that gets angry … I'd like
> to say to him … *Welcome* …
>
> (The coach slows down into light relational trance, becomes more
> limbically attuned, somatically sensing and gently touching his eyes
> to Jose Carlos' chest and belly area.)

Welcome! I really want to welcome that part of you, as I'm sure you are an important part of our healing team here today ... And what do you notice happening inside when I welcome him?

Jose Carlos: (looks soft) Something relaxes inside of me ... (touches solar plexus)

Coach: Well, that's good to know also. Great. And I'd to say to that part of you that just came forward ... *Thank you for joining us. Welcome* ... (pause) Now in terms of these two parts ... the one that really wants to be kind to your boys ... and the one who loses his temper ... which side would you like to begin to connect with first?

Jose Carlos: (looks stressed) Well, I don't think I should welcome that part of me that gets angry. It shouldn't exist, it's bad.

Coach: (takes breath, silent for a few moments, internally makes connection with client's "bad self") Well, I'm sure that attitude makes sense ... But I'm wondering ... when you say that, what happens in your solar plexus? (awareness attuning to that somatic center)

Jose Carlos: It gets really tight ...

Coach: It gets tight ... that's interesting to notice ... that when you talk to it in a negative way, it gets tight ... and how about when I say to that presence again ... (shifts to trance voice) *Welcome! I'm sure you've been on a long journey ... and you're an honored guest here today* ... (pauses and breathes in attunement with Jose Carlos) What do you notice there?

Jose Carlos: (tears up) It gets warm ...

Coach: (smiles) That's interesting ... So when we talk to that part in a negative way, it gets really tight. But when we talk to it in a positive way, it gets warm. Do you have a preference?

Jose Carlos: Well ... warm ... but I'm afraid of that part of me ... (looks a bit confused)

Coach: That makes sense. So do you think it might be helpful to take a little time to get to know it a bit better, and see how things just might become a little more positive for both you and that part?

Jose Carlos: OK ...

Coach: Great. So we're talking about this part that gets angry with your boys ... and if I'm hearing correctly, you said that its center is in your solar plexus ... (touches own solar plexus, points to Jose Carlos', breathes with gentle attunement, nods head gently)

Jose Carlos: Yes ...

Coach: Great, thanks for letting me know ... and I'd like to just ask you to *close your eyes for a few moments* ... (Jose Carlos closes eyes) *That's good* ... that's great ... and let yourself breathe and just become aware ... *there's some important presence deep in your belly* ... and when you connect with your boys ... it starts awakening in some way ... and so again, I'd like to just welcome that part of you ... and ask you to touch it with your hand ... (Jose Carlos places hand on solar plexus, looks deeply absorbed) *that's good ... that's good ...* and what do you notice happening now?

Jose Carlos: It feels warm, kind of like vibrating ...

Coach: It feels warm and vibrating ... great ... And by the way, I'd like to ask you to let a number come into your mind that represents an age associated with that part of you ... Don't try to think of a number, just let a number pop into your awareness ... and what do you become aware of?

Jose Carlos: The number 8 popped into my mind ...

Coach: That's interesting ... the number 8. And I'd like to say to that 8-year-old ... *Welcome! You are a valued guest here in our conversation* ... and what do you notice when I say that?

Jose Carlos: The tingling increases ... and whatever is there, feels curious ... maybe even a little happy ...

Coach: That's good to notice ... and by the way, do you remember anything meaningful happening in your life around 8?

Jose Carlos: I don't know ... well, actually ... (looks sad) well, lots of things ... but mostly, my mom and dad divorced ... and my dad left.

(This is talked about gently for a few moments, with Jose Carlos still touching his solar plexus, and the limbic attunement deepening to open a relational field.)

Coach: So far, we've talked about that something happens when you connect with your boys, something gets upset and angry ... and it's somehow connected to this feeling in your belly ... (slows down, looks gently at solar plexus) and the age of 8 is connected to that presence there ... and at 8 there was a lot of pain ... (pause, gentle breathing with Jose Carlos, compassion gently extended) ... and somehow this comes up when you're connected with your boys ... By the way, how old is your oldest son?

Jose Carlos: Well, he's 8 ... (looks startled)

Coach: Yes, "he" is 8 ... *Welcome*! I'm sure it makes sense that you're coming back into Jose Carlos' life at this point ... *Welcome*! And by the way, Jose Carlos, on a scale of 1 to 10, how much do you feel this 8-year-old presence in your belly center right now?

Jose Carlos: 10 ...

Coach: That's good ... 10 ...

This illustrates how the "bad self" of a problem can be welcomed and absorbed as a positive presence on a "solution team". As with all generative trance processes, the musicality of the exchange is of primary importance. Relational connection and resonance guide the tempo, spacing, intensity, and each subsequent response.

Once one side is sponsored, attention can shift to the complementary part. With Jose Carlos, his goal-oriented part ("I want to be kind to my children") was sensed in his heart. It was filled with love and appreciation for his two boys. He was able to feel a 10 intensity with that part as well.

As in any negotiation, once the two sides have been equally sponsored, the relationship between them can be developed. In generative trance work, *this relational connection is what activates the healing and creative properties of the unconscious*. To ensure that each part is sufficiently activated and that they are relatively balanced, intensity scaling (using the 1–10 scale) can be used. Generally, each side should be at least at level 5, and it is often good (though not essential) if the positive side is a bit higher. Then an integration can be developed. For example:

> (*Connect with one center*) And Jose Carlos, I'd like you now to shift back to your solar plexus ... placing your hand on that center ... breathing deeply into that center ... and allowing all the feelings and experiences and energies connected to that part of you that has expressed itself in anger ... and yet which you are now experiencing and understanding as having so many important needs and feelings and love ... just feel that ... (pauses)

> (*Connect with other center*) And then let yourself shift back to your heart ... touching your heart ... breathing into your heart ... feeling that part of you that is now a father ... feeling the love for the boys ... all three boys ... your son at 8 ... your other son at 6 ... yourself at 8 ... the 8-year-old ... inside and out ... breathing ... touching ... feeling ... allowing that love to spread and open in so many creative ways ...

> (*Subtle energy connecting two sides*) And then you can touch *both* centers at the same time ... the heart ... the gut ... the heart ... the gut ... that's it ... breathing ... and sending and sensing and breathing and feeling a bond of connection developing between the heart and the solar plexus ... *feeling both at the same time ... that's good ... allowing a bond to connect ... to reconnect ... to absorb ... father and son ... love and healing ... reconnection and healing ... the bond breathing its connection between the two parts ... and when you're ready you can feel that bond of connection take you even deeper into a healing trance beginning nowwwwwww ...*

> *That's good ... breathing ... allowing ... healing ... integrating ... an 8-year-old ... has come back home ... a father's connection ... a boy's healing ... that's it ... that's it ... that's it ...* (elaborated further)

Following the integration process, the final step begins the process of connecting the trance learnings into a person's life. As usual, this involves taking a few moments to identify the particular learnings or changes of most significance; make vows and commitments to realize these changes in one's life; imagine a future where the desired changes have been realized; experience and express gratitude to all those supportive of a person's journey; and then reorient.

For Jose Carlos, this was a powerful process. The complementarity shifted from "I want to be kind to my kids, but I get angry at them" to "I want to love my boys, and I need to also love my inner child". He realized that the problematic part was activated as his son neared the age when Jose Carlos lost his father to divorce. By taking the time to transform and integrate the anger, fear, and confusion associated with that part, it became a beautiful presence in his family experience.

The discovery that the problem part is an unintegrated ego state from a previous age is quite common. Also quite common is that the complementary "X but Y" parts comprise a yin/yang duality. That is, one side carries the more gentle, shy, and delicate *yin* of human spirit, while the other embodies the more active and intense *yang*. Again, the locking of a negative frame around one or both sides makes it difficult to see their positive potential. Generative trance allows each side to be deconstructed and its outer "clothing" released to allow the goodness and gifts of its inner nature to be recognized. In the fluid creative space of generative trance, this allows new, more positive forms and frames to develop.

This process of reconciling opposites can be done in a number of informal ways. It can be initiated whenever one feels an inhibition or other disturbance while engaged in a purposeful activity. Taking a few minutes, you can sense where in your body you feel the disturbance and apply the utilization mantras (*This is interesting, I'm sure this makes sense, something inside is trying to heal or awaken*; and *welcome*). Skillfully engaging with the "bad self" parts in this way, with primary attention to their subtle somatic energies, allows their positive nature to be sensed and experienced. The sensing of the goal can then be added, and a connection between the two parts developed to allow a natural integration that restores wholeness.

Fifth method: The somatic trance dance of integrating opposites

If I could say it, I wouldn't have to dance it.

Isadora Duncan

The *somatic modeling* of problems explored in the last chapter can be elaborated so that both a goal ("I want X") *and* its interfering problem ("but Y happens instead") are somatically modeled and then integrated. This process, which I call *the somatic trance dance of opposites*, is similar to the *reconciling opposites* method we've just covered, the main difference being in how the complementary sides are represented. (In *reconciling opposites*, somatic centers are used; in *trance dance*, somatic modeling is used.) The structure for the process is outlined in Figure 8.9.

Figure 8.9. The trance dance of integrating opposites

Step 1: Preparation

    1.   Center

    2.   Intention: *I want X, but Y happens instead*

    3.   Resources

Step 2: Unfolding a generative trance

    1.   Develop somatic models of problem/goal

    2.   First (light) trance: slowly and repetitively move from one somatic pattern to the other, with positive curiosity

    3.   Reorient and process a bit

Second (deeper) trance: repeat trance dance at a deeper level, adding generative trance dimensions:

- Centering
- Slow, rhythmic, repetitive movements
- Sensuality and resonance
- Grace
- Relational mantras

Step 3: Trance-forming identity states

1. Allow the trance dance to explore the basic needs and resources of each side

2. Find connections between sides

3. Integration

Step 4: Integrating back into ordinary reality

1. Future orientation, seeing changes in action in future

2. Vows and commitments

3. Gratitude

4. Review experiences for important learnings

5. Reorientation

As before, the preparation step is done, including the two-part expression of the goal:

> I want X but Y happens instead.

One person's statement was:

> I want to finish my dissertation *but* I end up procrastinating.

To somatically model one side, gently repeat the core statement (e.g. "I want to finish my dissertation"), then breathe and ask your body to find a movement expressing this side. For example, with the above fellow, *finishing the dissertation* was represented as a narrow focus, hands pointed intently towards a future. The somatic model should feel intuitively right (to both the person and any observer), and adjustments are often needed.

Once one side is somatically modeled, the same can be done for the opposite side. In the above case, *procrastination* was represented with eyes and body moving around in all directions. As is usually the case, the models for the conflicting sides were complementary to each other – e.g., the scattered wide-body attentions vs. the narrow focus. Other examples illustrate this complementarity:

1. *I want to feel confident* (hands extends outwards in an opening movement) BUT *I end up feeling insecure* (arms and shoulders fold inwards).

2. *I want to be clean and sober* (sits up straight, extends right hand into the world) BUT *I end up drinking every night* (slumped posture, eyes down, hands moving to mouth in drinking motion).

3. *I want to be at peace with myself* (eyes closing and hands gently touching heart) BUT *I can't stop worrying* (hands pull hair out).

In this way, the somatic modeling often shows a sort of yin yang dance between conflicting parts: one side moves inwards, the other outwards. The *trance dance* method allows them to be realized as allies, not enemies; two sides of a deeper wholeness.

The exploration of the "trance dance" can be done in two rounds. The first is a brief (about five minute) light trance exploration to get a feel for the process and begin to sense the positive value of each part. The person centers and attunes, then very gently somatically moves back and forth between the parts. No words are used, the movement is very slow and graceful (about five or six times slower than normal), and a curiosity is held regarding the deeper longing and intention of each side. Various versions of the relational mantras can be gently and resonantly offered by the coach and/or used silently by the client. For example:

My unconscious is trying to bring me an important experience. What is it? …

My body is showing me a deep need. What is it? …

It's OK to open to this learning …

Relax and let go …

Listen to the body.

Any signs of neuromuscular lock are noted and released during the process.

The process is concluded after five minutes or so, and a brief discussion ensues. A second round is undertaken, this one involving a deeper, more sustained generative trance involving sensuality and aesthetic resonance, slow and graceful movements, repetitive rhythms, and the relational mantras. I sometimes suggest that clients imagine themselves as Balinese trance dancers, dancing a world into being. *Special emphasis is placed on staying centered while making each movement;*[21] this sometimes requires a person to adjust the movement slightly.

The trance dance is explored for 10 to 15 minutes, with suggestions to sense the deeper positive intentions of the movements and how they can be experienced and expressed in many new ways. An integration process then allows the person to create new, more positive identity maps of the relational parts.

I have used this process in numerous ways to sense the positive intention and needs underlying a repetitive negative pattern. Bringing musicality to a negative pattern illuminates its positive potential, revealing why the pattern has so insistently repeated itself: the creative unconscious is trying to bring healing and wholeness. The trance dances allow human presence to join that process and thereby allow the positive value to be realized.

Rhythmically exploring the patterns reveals their archetypal nature.[22] For example, when we represent the experience of feeling insecure in terms of a somatic movement of pulling inward, it becomes apparent that the movement itself – returning inside – is central to human experience. If performed with neuromuscular lock, it will be experienced as anxiety or insecurity. But when performed with grace, musicality, and centeredness, the very same archetypal movement can be experienced as gentle inward attunement. When we then look at this positive value (of gentle inner attunement) relative to the goal – for example, "I want to be confident" (expressed as opening outward) – we see that it completes the goal and brings it to a deeper level. Again, *the problem is an attempt by the creative*

---

21   Somatic modeling will reveal that when a person does the problem movement, it invariably disconnects them from their center. A basic equation of generative trance work is: *symptom plus centering equals resource.* That is, if we can keep our center as we move through an experience, it will be realized as a resource. So the important adjustment is made in this exercise to modify the movement in order to maintain the center.

22   For fascinating research on the attunement of archetypal experiences via body postures and movements, see Hopton (2005) and Gore (2009).

unconscious to balance and complete the one-sided view of the conscious mind.
The trance dance of opposites beautifully illustrates this point, while also allowing the pattern to be experienced and expressed in many new positive ways.

Summary

In generative trance, we are interested in activating the creative unconscious whenever new learning and identity is needed. At such times, the set maps of the conscious mind are a liability, allowing only "more of the same" patterning. The principle of complementarity is central to opening a generative state. Holding opposites – whether it be through a good joke, play, a negative double bind, or a paradoxical riddle – temporarily dissolves the fixed frames of the conscious mind, thereby allowing the unconscious to generate a non-dualistic space of creative consciousness. We have examined various methods by which this can be done: (1) the complementarity suggestion loops, (2) mutual trance, (3) good self/ bad self, (4) reconciling opposites, and (5) the trance dance of opposites. When used in a generative space marked by centering, positive intention, limbic resonance, musicality, and resources, generative trance and amazing transformational experiences can result.

Chapter 9
The Principle of Infinite Possibilities

Nothing is more dangerous than an idea when it is the only one you have.

Émile Chartier

All life is an experiment. The more experiments you make, the better.

Ralph Waldo Emerson

If you wish to advance into the infinite, explore the finite in all directions.

Johann Wolfgang von Goethe

To live generatively, we need many ways to understand and experience life. When we rigidly get locked into just one way, problems are sure to develop. Keeping many possibilities open is thus crucial to creative success. Helpful in this regard is what I call *the principle of infinite possibilities*, which states than any core human pattern can be experienced and expressed in a virtually infinite number of different ways.

The two levels underlying the principle are represented in Figure 9.1. The figure shows how a general goal can be expressed in many ways, an example of the "divergent thinking" process that is characteristic of many creative thinkers (Runco, 1991; Kaufman & Sternberg, 2010). Of course, this two-level idea of reality construction has been emphasized throughout the book. Figure 9.2 shows the five specific methods we will focus upon in this chapter for implementing this generative principle.

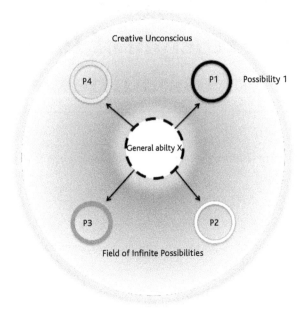

Figure 9.1. The principle of infinite possibilities

Figure 9.2. Methods for generating multiple possibilities

1.	Suggestion loop of multiple possibilities
2.	Generating new choices
3.	The tetralemma
4.	Metaphorical stories
5.	The council of resources

First method: Suggestion loop of multiple possibilities

In the previous two chapters we explored the suggestion loops of creative acceptance and complementarity. The third basic suggestion loop for generative trance is shown in Figure 9.3. It is used to suggest all the different ways an experience (e.g., trance) might unfold. This gives the creative unconscious choice, while also presupposing that the experience or goal will be realized.

Figure 9.3. Suggestion loop of multiple possibilities

1. Statement of core ability (*You can experience X in many ways*)

2. Possibility 1 (*Maybe it will happen in this way*)

3. Possibility 2 (*or perhaps it will happen in this way*)

4. Possibility 3 (*or maybe this way*)

5. Suggestion: discover which way is best for you

6. Feedback: what happened?

7. Incorporate and return to Step 1

In the first step, a general skill or ability is identified in simple terms:

You can experience X in many ways.

Where "X" could be many things:

You can experience *trance* in so many ways.

You can experience *safety* in many ways.

You can experience your *relationship with food* in many ways.

You can experience your *relationship to pain* in many ways.

As before, the goal should be succinct (five words or less), positive, and resonant. To use it within the suggestion loop, the preparation step is first done. A person is invited to center, set an intention, and connect with resources. They are then invited to experience how suggestions of different possible experiences can help them in the process.

When ready, the person can signal with a head nod. The first general suggestion is offered:

> You can experience trance in so many ways ... (*general suggestion*)

Then the next three or four statements suggest different possible ways that it might occur:

> Perhaps you will notice a shift in your body awareness ... (*specific possible way*)
>
> Or perhaps the beginning of a visual change ... (*second possible way*)
>
> Or perhaps the beginning of a shift in your listening ... (*third possible way*)

The general suggestion is repeated:

> And just take a breath and sense how trance can begin now to develop for you ...

And then feedback is requested:

> And what are you aware of now?

Whatever the person feeds back is used to begin the next round of statements:

> Client: I feel some warmth in my chest.
>
> Coach: That's good to know ... And just let yourself take a nice slow breath and become curious about how *that feeling of warmth can continue to open a very interesting, comfortable trance* ... (*general suggestion*)
>
> Perhaps it will gently spread out across your body ... (*specific possibility*)
>
> Or perhaps it will be joined by interesting visual shifts ... (*specific possibility*)

Or perhaps it will allow you to let your breath take you deeper ... (*specific possibility*)

Because you really can enjoy discovering your best way to let a trance unfold from the inside out ... (*general suggestion*)

And what are you aware of now? (*request for feedback*)

Even experiential responses that seemingly interfere with trance can be similarly joined and unfolded in positive ways:

Client: I feel a bit of fear ...

Coach: That's good to know. Thanks for bringing that experiential part of you into our conversation. And where do you feel that fear?

(Here the coach slows down and becomes more gentle, adapting a nonverbal resonance that soothes the fear.)

Client: I don't know ... all over.

Coach: And would it be alright to see how to best be with that fear?

Client: I think so ...

Coach: You think so ... that's good to know ... So let's take a breath and at the very least honor that fear by slowing down and not going too fast ...

(Both client and coach breathe, coach limbically attunes and gently relaxes a bit more.)

And as you sense that bit of fear, I wonder what else would be helpful to sense? (*general suggestion*)

Perhaps gently touching wherever you feel the fear with your hand and your breath ... (*specific possibility*)

Or perhaps remembering a happy memory from your life ... (*specific possibility*)

Or perhaps remembering what your favorite color is ... (*specific possibility*)

Or perhaps by feeling the sweet warmth of your chest revive and gently touch the fear ... (*specific possibility*)

And what are you aware of now? (*request for feedback*)

For such communications, whether done with one's self or another person, the words are secondary to the relational connection and nonverbal musicality of the communications.

The general attitude in using this principle is that each moment of experience can open in any number of positive directions. This allows the trance and experiential changes to open from the inside outwards.

The micro-level unfolding of multiple possibilities can be applied in many different ways. For example, Milton Erickson would often use it with himself and his patients as a pain control technique. The suggestion would be to become deeply mindful and curious about the exact nature of the pain – its precise location and boundaries in the body, its different colors and textures, its pulse and intensity, and so on. Then the curiosity would orient to the different ways it naturally changed, at the most subtle levels. For example:

Coach: I'd like to just suggest you close your eyes for a few moments ... and let yourself take a breath ... and notice exactly where in your body you feel that pain.

Bill: I feel it in my shoulders ...

Coach: You feel a pain in the shoulders. And where exactly does the pain end ... Is it at the shoulder cuff? Just breathe and notice and let yourself become very curious ...

Bill: About here ... (points to top of shoulder)

Coach: About there ... And what kind of sensation is it? Is it sharp ... or burning like a fire ... or perhaps a deep ache? ... Please just become curious about witnessing ... noting ... the exact, always changing nature of the pain ...

Bill: It's like my whole shoulder is on fire ...

Coach: Like your whole shoulder is on fire ... that's interesting ... And do you think you'd like to begin to learn how your creative unconscious can change that experience in different ways?

Bill: Yes.

Coach: That's good ... So as you listen to the sound of my voice ... and really, deeply absorb ... at the right level of trance ... at the right distance ... to become curious about the smallest beginning of the change ... Maybe the fire will have a color that changes ... Maybe it will spread a little further and begin to lessen as it does ... Maybe it will shift ever so slightly to a different location ... You really can deeply absorb and become curious about the exact way that your creative unconscious is already changing that pain in interesting ways ... And what are you aware of now?

Bill: I'm really drawn to the color of the flame, and it's turning blue ...

Coach: That's interesting. And do you find that interesting?

Bill: Yes ...

Coach: That's good ... and so why not just let yourself really take a breath that moves through your whole body ... so you can really begin to focus even deeper on the color of that flame. And as you really focus on the color of the flame ... it can shift in so many interesting ways ... breathing ... blue ... it could be orange ... colors can change into healing images ... so many ways the flame can change ...

In this way, Bill's pain shifted from a general pain to a fire in the shoulders, to a blue flame, to an image of a volcano, to lava flowing down his arms, to an open breathing space in his shoulders, to a release in his body that allowed a healing trance on the volcanic island of Hawaii.

Such a process allows the creative unconscious to unfold interesting positive responses at each moment in time. The conscious mind is there to develop and maintain a generative state (centering, positive intention, and resources), establish limbic attunement, then let attention open peripherally to many possible paths emanating from each experiential point in time. This stands in marked contrast to the traditional mode of the controlling conscious mind that tries to impose one possible path. By reorganizing in this way, a generative trance unfolds in natural, forever interesting ways.

Second method: Generating new choices

Another way to open multiple possibilities is called the *generating new choices method*. It operates on our core premise that when we get stuck, we can use trance to (1) release the negative pattern, (2) connect deeply with the quantum deep structure of the pattern, which holds many possible forms, and (3) then generate new forms that will more positively express the need or intention of the deeper core.

Figure 9.4 shows a general way to make this shift.

Figure 9.4. Generating new choices

1. Preparation step: center, intention, resources
2. Light trance: review previous attempts to realize goal
3. Deeper trance: ask creative unconscious to generate new solutions
4. Integrate to create new identity map
5. Future orientation: review, future orient, vows, gratitude
6. Reorientation
7. Further work

Once the preparation step has been completed, the second step uses trance to review the ways that a person has attempted to realize the intention in the past. The purpose here is not primarily intellectual understanding, but mindful contemplation of the different paths so far used. For example:

> And in sensing the center ... and your resources ... let yourself
> attune to the important positive intention that you hold in your
> work here today ... (pause) Over the next five minutes, let your cre-
> ative unconscious lead you on a review of the different ways that
> you have sought to achieve this intention over time. Perhaps you
> will notice experiences all the way back in childhood ... perhaps a
> number of experiential awarenesses having to do with recent years.
> What a nice thing to know that this important intention of [name
> positive intention] has been motivating and organizing your behav-
> ior in so many ways over time ... and so just let yourself relax and
> center deeper and go on a five minute review of the different ways
> that you have tried to achieve the goal of that intention.

After the person reorients, a brief discussion occurs, and then a second
trance is used to invite the creative unconscious to develop new possible ways to realize the goal. One way to do this is having the person very
slowly move through a repetitive trance dance of opening their arms outwards, like a budding flower, and then returning back to resting position.
Similar to the somatic modeling trances discussed in previous chapters, it
works nicely as a guiding metaphor for the process of bringing something
new into the world. Here's a brief example of how it might be guided:

> Let yourself take a few moments now to settle in and settle down
> again into a generative resting place ... You can close your eyes ...
> take a deep breath ... and return back to center ... and let me know
> when you have done that by nodding your head ... (elaborate if
> needed, until head nods)

> And in sensing that core center, you can attune to the core inten-
> tion you are honoring here today: *What I most want to create in my
> life is* [name positive intention]. Just let yourself silently speak that
> intention ... *What I most want to create in my life is* ... feeling it reso-
> nate deep through and beyond your body ... *What I most want to cre-
> ate in my life is* ... a beautiful coherence of purpose and curiosity ...
> *What I most want to create in my life is* ... And you can nod your head
> when you feel connected and committed to that positive intention
> ... (elaborate if needed, until head nods)

> And then let yourself open to any and all resources your creative
> unconscious brings into your field of awareness over the next few
> minutes ... to enjoy all the connections ... all the support ... all the
> community of positive resources to aid you in this journey here

today ... and when you feel you have sufficient resources, you can nod your head ... (elaborate until head nods)

That's good ... thank you ... and then when you're ready, I'm going to ask you very, very slowly to let your arms lift ... like a flower opening into the world ... the movements can be slow and so gentle ... like something being born into the world ... coming from a place deep within ... about four or five times slower than a normal conscious movement ... and you can help that process a little bit consciously ... letting the arms *lift* ever so slightly, so slightly that it may seem like they're not lifting at all, even though they are lifting ever so slightly now ... and only lift them consciously for one second ... then let your unconscious *lift* them ever so slightly for the second second ... *that's good* ... and then you can shift back to a conscious lifting ... so that every other moment your conscious mind is *lifting* in the smallest possible movement ... and every other *other* moment your creative unconscious is lifting and opening into the world ... so the hands ever so slowly lift and open, *like a flower opening to the sun* ... *like a person offering a prayer* ... like a person opening to a new solution from the creative unconscious ... so as your hands lift to that open position, your unconscious can create a new, more satisfying way to realize that intention ... as you watch, witness, weave and watch your unconscious opening new patterns ... new maps ... new pathways ... to experience and express the goal of [name positive intention].

These communications are elaborated until the hands reach their full opening, whereupon integration of the new map is suggested:

And as your hands and your deepest self fully open to that new way of being ... when you're ready you can let the hands begin to reverse their movement ... and very, very slowly ... as slowly as they have been moving ... very, very slowly moving back down to the original resting position ... and as the hands reverse their journey, you can let the new learnings integrate and find a place deep inside of you, becoming a helpful map for the future ... breathing ... integrating ... shifting ... all the way back to the resting position.

Once the hands return to the resting position, several more cycles can be explored, each allowing a new positive map to be developed. Using the somatic trance movements to guide the process provides good feedback for all involved about the optimal rate for the creative unconscious.

Consonant with many trance induction methods, slow and repetitive patterning also entrains and absorbs attention in ways that lessen conscious control and increase creative processing.

Once the new choices have been generated, an integration step is used to deepen and consolidate them. The general process here has been previously described, in which a gradually intensifying weaving of the different parts culminates in a creative climax that gives birth to a new core identity map.

The final step of connecting the changes to the external world is then completed. Significant changes are duly noted, an orientation is made to a future in which the new choices are utilized, vows to achieve the future are made, and some moments of gratitude are encouraged. Reorientation then occurs, and some processing is done.

Post-trance work is often needed. Integrating the new choices into daily life can bring interesting challenges. A friend of mine used this process to help end his 20 year relationship with cigarettes. He discovered that a positive intention of his smoking was to take time for himself and breathe deeply into his heart. (Yes, I know, smoking is not the best way to do that.) He was happy to discover in trance some spiritual practices, especially breathing practices, as new choices for realizing this intention. However, he also discovered that he was missing the cigarettes, almost like an old friend who could be counted on for comfort. Only when he expressed compassion for this old choice, and undertook a ritual of saying goodbye to the "old friend," did the path fully open to the new choices.

I often encourage people to see their old negative patterns as representing the best they could do earlier in their lives, and as now constituting "default values" or "automatic programs" that could easily activate if other, more positive ways to satisfy the underlying need are not being practiced. If the old pattern reappears, this signals that a positive need is being neglected. By returning to a mindful recognition, the new positive maps can be exercised again. Thus, relapses become an integral, positive part of the process of growth and transformation. When regarded positively – for example, with the relational mantras – they can actually contribute to the development of the new, more helpful choices.

Third method: The tetralemma

The *tetralemma* is a logic system that emphasizes four truth values for a given statement:

1. X is true.

2. Not-X is true (*or* X is not true).

3. Both X and not-X are true (*or* both X is true and X is not true).

4. Neither X nor not-X is true (*or* neither X is true nor X is not true).

This system was developed in the Western Greek tradition as well in the Hindu traditions, especially by Nagarjuna (see Jones, 2010). Buddhism, especially in Tibet, took Nagarjuna's system as a basic training practice.

In the Buddhist traditions, the tetralemma is used to sense the deeper levels of multiple truth. It is an excellent practice for moving from the ego identification with a single truth, to the creative consciousness of multiple truths. For example, say a person is stuck in a problem identity of *I am a trauma survivor*. Operating at the ego level, this becomes the only truth available, thereby creating enormous problems. By shifting to the genera- tive level that holds multiple other truths (e.g., *I love good jokes, I feel whole when I'm in nature, I am my daughter's loving father*), the trauma survivor identity can be absorbed and transformed in this larger creative space.

Figure 9.5 shows an outline for the *tetralemma* process. In the first step, a limiting belief or truth is identified and expressed succinctly. It could be a belief about one's self (e.g., *I don't know what I'm doing*), the world (e.g., *life is unfair, people are untrustworthy*), or another person (e.g., *my client doesn't want to change, my wife is critical*).

To explore this in the tetralemma, you first create a place where you can move one step in each of four directions: right, left, forward, and back. Standing in the middle, you center, sense the four directions, and release everything else. You then will be moving in the four directions, each time stepping into a different truth regarding that statement: it's true, it's not true (or its opposite is true), it's both true and not true (or both it and its opposite are true), and it's neither true nor not true. This is not an intellectual exercise, but a deeper sensing of quantum truth. Thus, all the trance attunement skills we have covered are brought into play to open this deeper space.

Figure 9.5. The tetralemma of multiple truths

1. Identify a limiting truth or belief

2. Trace and step into the middle of a four-directional circle. Center and open to the four directions

3a. Step to the right, center and attune to the truth: *X is true.*
3b. Step back to the center, release and open

4a. Step to the left, center and attune to the truth: *Not-X is true* (or *X is not true*).
4b. Step back to the center, release and open

5a. Step forward, attune to the truth: *Both X and not-X are true* (or *X is both true and not true*).
5b. Step back to the center, release and open

6a. Take one step back and attune to the truth: *Neither X nor not-X is true* (or *X is neither true nor not true*)
6b. Step back to the center, release and open to all truths simultaneously

7. Integrate, sensing "center of centers"

8. Reorientation

After each direction, there is a return to center, where release and openness is renewed. Following the four directions, the movement back to center opens a sort of "truth of truths," where the multiple contradictory truths are all experienced simultaneously. This opens a meta-space in which to sense how the different truths can be used wisely and integratively in each moment of time.

The following is a transcript excerpt from a group process where the tetralemma was explored.

Introduction

We have been talking about how problems and limitations develop around what I have called the tyranny of the single description. This is where two of my main teachers, Gregory Bateson and Milton Erickson, most deeply overlapped. Bateson said that to have any systemic or intelligent understanding of a living system, you minimally need what he called *double description*, or at least two different maps of that system. Similarly, Erickson would say that problems develop when understanding becomes too rigid. In that regard, one of the main methods we have been exploring for dissolving problematic states and opening creative states is the process of holding opposite truths simultaneously. It will give you a bit of a spiritual orgasm and open you to deeper consciousness. We've touched upon how one way of doing this is through the venerable old tradition of the *tetralemma*, which is still very actively used in Buddhism, especially in Tibet. So let's explore how to do that.

To begin, please stand and find your own space in the room. You need enough room to take one step forward, one back, one to the left, and one to the right. So claim a little niche where you can do that. This is a process that you can do by yourself when you are looking to change a conflict into a complementarity. While it can be done with many different beliefs, for the group process I'm going to suggest we work with a particular complementarity central to generative trance work. Namely, each of us is both wounded (and incomplete, and not whole) *and* at the same time unwounded (and complete, and whole). Each truth completes the other and if we sense only one side, we get into trouble. So we're going to explore how to tune into one side, then the other, then both at the same time, then neither, then in a generative space where all truths sing in a choir of consciousness.

Center

So let's start with where you are now ... Take a few moments to center ... to align ... to relax ... to breathe ... to open ... and just sense as you breathe a sense of light moving through your body ... from the heavens above ... to the earth below ... and then opening outwards into the world ... You will know you have found the rhythm because it is pleasurable ... Settle down, settle in, drop into center, and then open into the living field of the world. You can do this with the movement of your hands if you like. Let it be a very slow movement, four or five times slower than an ordinary movement. Opening your arms, dropping your arms, letting your hands move to center, then as you exhale, lift your arms out into the world. In aikido we call this ... *drop into center, open into field* ... drop into center, open into field ... like a very slow *tai chi, qigong* movement. Slow, gentle, graceful repetitive movements. Drop into center, open into field ... letting your mind–body find its own subtle movements, your verbal mind in your head becoming secondary.

And from that place, you can begin to sense yourself at the threshold of a journey ... a journey of exploration of your deepest identity ... a journey of opening to the many different facets of the diamond truth of your deep self ... letting yourself relax, drop into center, open into field ... relax, drop into center ... open into field ... and the journey here today will be around the many facets of your identity regarding woundedness and unwoundedness ... letting yourself develop a loving, curious, relationship with each side of your human being ... How on the one hand you are always whole, always complete ... how the light of the human spirit cannot be broken ... how can you damage light? ... And how on the other hand, to be human is to be broken, wounded, not complete ... isn't that good to know? (twinkle) So in the musical rhythms of your deepest creative self, let us do the dance of the tetralemma ...

You might sense it with the words, *I am ... I am ... I am here.*

First truth: *I am unwounded and unwoundable*

When you are ready, take one step to the right ... into the space of this is true: *I am unwounded ... and unwoundable* ... I am whole ... I am unbroken ... Don't think it in your head. Let your body attune to it ... let yourself use the statement to find it ... let your body be a musical instrument, gently feeling for the resonances of *I am unwounded and unwoundable* ... *My spirit cannot be damaged* ... *I am whole and of light* ... Breathe with that ... move with that ... find in the resonances the truth ... the words ... the images ... the symbols ... the feelings ... all the subtle dimensions ... as when you feel love ... you are love ... love is unwounded and unwoundable ... you are whole ... breathe ... sense that ... sense your connection to others from this place of unwoundedness, wholeness, body of pure light ... (moments of silence)

And then when you are ready, take a breath ... and take a step back to the left ... back into the center place ... and as you step into the space of the center, take a deep breath and let go of that first position ... and just feel the sense of a deeper openness ... empty of form ... simply ... *I am* ... *I am* ... *I am* ... you can release from that first position, just feel that sense of open luminescence ... original mind ... empty of form ... radiant ... silent ... awareness ... (moments of silence)

Second truth: *I am wounded and woundable*

And when you are ready, take a step to the left ... and as you take a step to the left, step into the complementary truth – *I am wounded ... There is a brokenness within me ... There is a place in which I am not whole.* No need to approach this negatively ... just be curious about the places that are not whole ... use the statement as a tuning fork ... as a resonator to find those parts of you that are wounded ... breathe ... open ... sense ... *I am wounded ... I am unwhole ... I have been hurt.* And just breathe with that truth ... feel it in an open way ... a loving way ... opening the space for those parts ... feel that truth ... stay present with it ... be with it. And notice from that place how you walk in the world, how you relate to others, how you create your reality when you are in that place ... Just witness ... just be aware ... just be a space of awareness ... (moments of silence)

And then when you are ready, take a step back to the right ... to the center ... Breathe, release ... let go ... breathe ... no form, just being ... dropping into center ... opening into field. And you may want to move your hands slowly a few times, to open the center once again, freely into the world ... and then just sense ... *I am* ... *I am* ... *I am here* ...

Third truth: *I am both unwounded and wounded*

And then when you are ready, take one step forward ... and as you step one step forward, step into the third truth ... *I am unwounded and whole ... I am unbroken ... and ... I am also wounded and broken ... I am also wounded ...* And in the gentle music of your mind–body, feel both of those truths simultaneously ... let them be there equally ... let them come together ... at the same time ... *I am unwounded and I am wounded ...* Just feel and tune and find the subtle frequencies attuned to that both/and truth ... let your creative self help you feel the resonances where you can sense both – wholeness and woundedness at the same time ... body of light, body of pain ... Feel the space to breathe with both ... loving ... with curiosity ... welcoming ... weaving ... Each absorbing ... completing ... deepening the other ... Feel both at the same time ... and something even deeper emerging from that wholeness ... both/and ... and much, much more ... enjoy and sense the strength, the power, even the beauty of that. (moments of silence)

And then when you are ready, take a step back into the center ... feel yourself return to center ... return to the breathing ... letting go ... releasing from any position ... coming back home to an open space ... centered ... breathing ... *I am ... I am ... I am ...* Like the sky ... like the trees ... like the ocean ... just presence ... *I am ... I am ... I am ...* Open to every season, open to every element of your nature, present ...

Fourth truth: *I am neither unwounded nor wounded*

And then when you are ready, take a step backwards into the fourth truth ... I am neither broken nor whole. *I am neither ... nor ... Neither unwounded ... nor wounded ...* Who are you now? Breathe, open, attune with that truth value ... letting creative wisdom teach you ... reach you ... with the awareness ... *I am neither ... one side nor the other side.* Let your unconscious wisdom teach you that place ... that space ... that face ... Experience who ... what ... emerges from the truth of that truth. I am neither broken nor whole. Connect with the mind of your center. Let all the images, the feelings come from the mind of the center. Neither nor ... (moments of silence)

Return to center: integration

And then finally, when you are ready ... take a step forward again
... back to the center ... and let yourself release again ... breathe ...
center ... open ... releasing any attachment to any particular form ...
just breathing ... sensing whatever is flowing through ... And when
you feel that open channel, you can allow yourself to open to the
integration ... of standing in the center ... opening your mind ...
your heart ... your body ... your whole being ... to feel all four directions ... to the one side ... to the other side ... to in front ... to in
back ... begin to feel each direction, and the truths associated with
them ... *unwounded* ... *wounded* ... *both unwounded and wounded* ...
unwounded ... *neither nor* ... *both and* ... *wounded* ... *unwounded* ... all
flowing through center ... winds of change, rivers of truth ... move
with the nature of it all ... like a beautiful piece of music being created within you ... through you ... for you ... of you ... as all the
truths ... wholeness ... brokenness ... both ... neither nor ... a mosaic
... a mandala ... so many different experiences in your life ... so many
different truths ... so many different dimensions ... to be breathed
... integrated ... threads of different truths weaving a new garment
... open to the four directions ... the energies ... colors ... feelings ...
of the four directions ... integrating through the center ... into the
fifth dimension ... the direction of your whole self opening to it all
...

Breathe ... into and through and as ... the center where each direction ... every truth ... has its own note ... minor ... major ... chords
... accords ... discords ... weaving into an aesthetic wonder ... music
to behold ... a pattern of different threads ... woundedness ... so
much there ... unwounded spirit ... so much deeper ... both and ...
neither nor ... every truth weaving together, a truth even deeper
emerging and being born ... different threads of truth ... threads of
silk weaving ... a beautiful kimono of the soul ... a beautiful garment
expressing the patterns of your deepest wholeness ... breathing ...
weaving ... integrating ... where each has its own music, where each
is its own thread. An integrated pattern of wholeness to guide you
on this great journey you are on. Sensing at different points in time
... the woundedness ... with love, with understanding, with curiosity ... and the unwoundedness ... the shining light of the spirit, the
sense of unbroken love ... the infinite space of wholeness of life ...

and you are both ... and you are neither ... and you are much, much more! (twinkle)

The return home

And then take a few moments to feel into your center. If you'd like, take one or both of your hands ... and touch your center ... and sense what you have experienced here ... what you want to bring forward into your life ... take a few moments to sense any vows ... any commitments ... any promises you want to make to yourself ... about how you want to live ... with the truth of your woundedness ... with the truth of your unwoundedness ... with the truth that you are each ... you are both ... you are neither ... you are ... *you are much, much more* ... you are ... Take a few moments to complete that, sensing that wherever you go, there are the four directions to draw from ... to play with ... to live from ... And then when you are ready, you can slowly return back into the room ... (moments of reorientation)

Welcome back!

Discussion and processing can follow the exercise. In a group situation, participants are usually invited to get into groups of three or four and share for ten minutes or so, followed by a general group discussion.

Many interesting experiences occur in the tetralemma process. In the above group, a woman shared how the trance rhythms of the process created a feeling within and around her of a "great song that was being sung". It opened a healing space for her to sense "a great thorn that was stuck deep in her heart," connected to tremendous pain. She was able to be with it lovingly, and then was amazed that during the both/and process it transformed in many ways, connecting many early experiences of hurt to a healing field.

Another participant described his surprise in discovering that his initial experience of the unwounded self was a sort of "new age" position of an "all light" being who insisted "I have no problems at all," while simultaneously feeing insecure and afraid. While initially frightened about the prospect of having that "good self" connect with the wounded part, he found that shifting among the different truth positions let him touch the spaces without being overwhelmed. The integration process at the end was especially powerful for him, giving rise to a sense of himself as a vulnerable, grounded, and open man.

For many people, the neither/nor position is especially interesting. A sense of curiosity often arises regarding an identity that is not defined in terms of being for or against some position. A space beyond opposites is often the result, which opens many new learnings.

The tetralemma can be an extremely helpful process. It allows each side of a truth to be positively held and sponsored, and then integrated into a deeper mandala of self-identity that is not located in any particular place or form. It is a generative space or context that holds multiple forms, thereby allowing many new creative patterns to develop.

Fourth method: Metaphorical stories

The principle of infinite possibilities can also be realized through metaphorical stories. This was a central method in Milton Erickson's therapeutic trance work, especially in his later years. In the basic process, a problem or goal is expressed as an example of a core (or archetypal) human process. For example, a problem with food is identified:

> A relationship to food can be experienced in so many different ways.

Then multiple stories about different relationships to food are developed and offered to a person in trance. The goal is to invite a person to let go of a fixed (negative) map of how to realize a core need, move into the quantum field of the creative unconscious, and explore alternate maps. A general structure for this approach is shown in Figure 9.6.

Figure 9.6. Using metaphorical stories in generative trance work

---

1. Identify problem/goal

2. Develop at least three metaphorical stories about achieving goal

3. Preparation step: center, intention, resources

4. Tell stories with trance rhythms

5. Integration: new patterns are developed

6. Future orientation

7. Reorientation

8. Further work

Step 1: Identify problem/goal

In the first step, careful attention is paid to developing the goal. We've seen how in generative trance work this can be done in two ways:

> I want X.
>
> *or*
>
> I want X but Y interferes.

A well-formed goal should be positive, succinct (five words or less), and resonant.

Step 2: Develop metaphorical stories

The goal is then used to develop transformational stories. Figure 9.7 lists a six-step process for doing this effectively.

Figure 9.7. Steps in developing stories

1.	Centering and opening
2.	Attuning to the person in question
3.	Using the goal as a creative mantra
4.	Writing down stories and symbols
5.	Selecting relevant stories
6.	Refining the stories

In the first step, an open and curious generative trance is developed, since the symbolic/metaphorical nature of stories comes from the creative unconscious. The second step involves attuning to the person in question, since helpful stories need to properly fit a given person and situation. This might be done through somatic modeling of that person or through visually imagining them orienting to the goal.

Once attuned, the goal can be used as a "creative mantra"; that is, one can silently repeat it in a gentle way with a curiosity about what images or stories arise from the creative unconscious. All the stories are written down, without any critical editing or judgment. For example, some stories that arose while contemplating Frank, a shy man wanting to "be more confident in social relationships" included the following:

- A puppy learning to be more bold.

- Albert Einstein not talking until he was 3 or 4 and not doing well in grade school.

- A client overcoming shyness through a series of trance sessions.

- The slow emergence of blooming flowers after a long winter that seemed to go on forever.

- Story of how Joe Louis, the great boxing champion, successfully dealt with anxiety by attending deeply to the present moment.

Once possible stories are generated, they are sensed in terms of which would be the best fit for the person and situation in question. Some considerations include whether the content of the story would be interesting to the client, and whether the changes involved would be fit for the person's desired changes. For example, if the story describes a drastic immediate change that seems far outside of a person's capabilities or beliefs, it would probably not be helpful.

For Frank, I selected the Albert Einstein story, given his interest in science and Einstein; the Joe Louis story, because it involved a process of becoming so absorbed in a task that anxiety disappeared; and the story about a man in trance who realized his shyness as a resource. Once the stories are selected, further thought is given regarding which details might be most relevant to the person in question and how the story might be elaborated. If a person's goal has a strong obstacle to it, consideration is given to how to include the obstacles in the story. For Frank, he was worried about being tongue-tied, so that feature was duly noted as being important to somehow include in the story.

For example, the story about reframed shyness involved a long series of discoveries and experiences by a man. Early parts of his journey involved being afraid to meet people; finding deep absorption in reading, especially science; trying but failing to find the courage to ask girls out; being afraid to speak out in class (even though he was an excellent student); and self-loathing. Subsequent parts included finding his life calling as a scientist; continued social insecurity; developing hiking and outdoors activities as hobbies; and cultivating a few nerdy friends. Then a mid-life crisis led him to find a more positive relationship with his shyness, which he came to appreciate as his sensitive curiosity that allowed him to connect deeply with the world, as long as he had resources to protect the "delicate presence within".

In unpacking such a story, it becomes apparent that there are infinite versions that can be told. One version could be quite brief, while another might be extremely long. Any detail can be elaborated or diminished according to the learning needs of the moment. In short, a story is an extremely flexible pattern for creating new learnings in the creative unconscious. Thus, preliminary thought is given regarding which processes to feature, which core themes to mark out, and how else the given situation of the person might be joined and expanded via the story. And of course, there is much adaption of the story during the actual telling, to stay with the trance music parameters of limbic resonance, repetition of key themes, rhythmic patterning, and so on.

Step 3: Preparation

First of all, establish the proper conditions for a transformative story through centering, creating a positive intention, and eliciting the appropriate resources. Frank found that he could center by being deeply absorbed in the physical heartbeat in his chest, then opening his attention infinitely outwards from that center point. Interestingly, his field of resources included R2-D2 (the sweet *Star Wars* robot) and a smiling Albert Einstein. His goal was: "I want to be more comfortable about including my shyness".

Step 4: Tell stories with trance rhythms

Once a person has developed a generative state, a general orientation to the story-telling process can be offered:

> And you've come here today with that general intention of [name goal]. It's good to know that your creative unconscious can help make the necessary changes to achieve that goal. To help in that process, I'd like to tell you a few stories that may be relevant. And of course, as in any trance process, you don't need to consciously analyze or intellectually understand the stories. Rather, let yourself receive the stories in a trance, and let your creative unconscious translate the stories into those meanings that will allow you to best realize your goal. For example, you might find that as I tell a story about a particular topic, you might be experiencing a process involving a very different topic.

> And so take some time to move to the right depth and the proper quality of trance to best absorb the stories in a helpful way. And when you've done that and you're ready to receive the stories, you can signal with a head nod.

(Gently elaborate until signal is given.)

The stories can be told, following the structure of the suggestion loop of multiple possibilities (see Figure 9.3), in which a general statement is offered and then elaborated with multiple possible paths for realizing it:

You can experience X in so many ways. I'll give you an example ...

In offering the story, primary attention is given to developing and maintaining a generative trance, since it is precisely this enhanced state of consciousness that will allow the stories to have a transformational effect. Thus, limbic attunement and resonance is the base connection that guides all communications, since this is a primary means for knowing that a generative field is open. All the trance music patterns – rhythms, nonverbal resonance, repetitions, tempo, sensual imagery and feeling, and so on – are integral to the process. Like in any performance art, the story-teller is adjusting the process to enhance the trance field.

Thus, resources are emphasized within the story and the pace lessened if it feels too intense for the person; or absorption is deepened and emotional challenges heightened if the story seems not sufficiently engaging. At any point if it feels like a person is having difficulties, simple verbal inquiry about what's going on may be used. Again, stories are extremely flexible vehicles for experiential learning that can and should be adjusted within the forever changing patterns of the relationship.

For example, Frank's responses to the story about reframed shyness were instructive. As I began to mention a curiosity about the value of the shyness, his absorption seemed to deepen. As I continued by describing how the story character deepened his positive connection to the shyness by physically touching its somatic center, Frank gently touched his own heart and tears began to develop. I took this as feedback that this dimension was helpful, and thus elaborated upon it.

In telling multiple stories, bridges between them may be simply accomplished with the general statement (as in the suggestion loop of Figure 9.3):

> And so you really can experience X in so many interesting and helpful ways. I'll give you another example ...[23]

When presented under the proper conditions, the stories typically dissolve the neuromuscular lock of fixed maps and open the quantum field of the creative unconscious. Each story and its elements float within this oceanic field, with the generative state allowing different positive meanings and applications to develop.

Steps 5–7: Integration, future orientation, and reorientation

The different possibilities implicit in each story may be integrated into a new identity map, followed by a future orientation and reorientation process. These steps can be done in any of the ways already detailed in earlier chapters.

When Frank reoriented, he shared a very interesting process. As he listened to the story about a shy person, something began to resonate in his chest. A dark film dissipated around his heart and some younger version of him began to emerge. At first he was afraid, but as the story continued he began to connect with the "younger Frank," a shy, almost mute boy who was deathly afraid of the anger in his home. When he opened to the presence, a great feeling of relief and love filled him. The content of the story and the trance rhythms of the story-telling seemed to provide a safe place and deep permission to make this reconnection.

---

23   In working with his students, Milton Erickson would often start the day with a simple question: "What do you want to learn today?" It was good to have a goal prepared since Erickson was remarkably responsive to specific requests. But often he would answer with stories or other symbolic (e.g., trance phenomena) responses. He might tell five or six stories, connecting each with the statement, "I'll give you another example ..." After an extended period (sometimes hours) of such entrancing presentations, he would stop and say, "Any other questions?" We would usually laugh, as the original question could not be remembered in the wake of the entrancing answer.

Step 8: Further work

Trance changes typically need to be further developed. For Frank, his shyness became a tender part of him that needed both recognition and protection. We explored how to bring a stronger "yang" part of him to shield this shy and gentle "yin" part, especially appreciating how the gentle part was really the more sensitive and subtle consciousness of the two. This led to a variety of explorations on how to integrate the two sides in a creative partnership.

Stories are of course one of the oldest teaching methods the world over. They absorb attention and speak directly to the symbolic language of the creative unconscious, thereby allowing deep learning to occur. As with all generative trance processes, the key to using them successfully is to establish and be guided by deep relational connections at many levels. They are not techniques to do *to* someone, but creative processes to explore *with* someone.

Fifth method: The council of resources

The creative unconscious is guided by ongoing feedback at many levels. As Csíkszentmihályi (1991) noted, an optimal flow state requires the setting of general goals, along with testable sub-goals that can indicate whether one is properly on track. One major type of feedback is through the mentors and guides that support us on our journey. Each represents a viewpoint that can indicate different possible ways to proceed. One way to make use of them in generative trance is through what I call the *council of resources* method, represented in Figure 9.8.

Figure 9.8. The council of resources method

1. Identify goal

2. Develop (and spatially locate) council of resources

3. Preparation step

4. Attune to goal: self-contemplation of direction

5. Attune to each council member and receive their advice

6. Reorient to goal, integrate all positions

7. Future orientation

8. Reorientation

Step 1: Identify goal

The process begins with the setting of a goal. This simple but not always easy step should be done carefully to ensure that the goal is positive, succinct (five words or less), and resonant.

Step 2: Develop (and spatially locate) the council of resources

The second step involves developing a trance field of resource guides to support the goal journey. A general way to introduce the process is as follows:

> So you've identified this very important goal of [name goal]. To achieve it, generative trance can be helpful in many ways. One way is to ask your creative unconscious to help you develop a positive resource team that can guide and support you on this journey. We

all "get by with a little help from our friends," and all rely upon the loving and wise feedback of beings who deeply support us on the journey. Carl Jung used to say that we each need to find our "community of saints"; that is, those beings who really support and love us on our life path. What Jung called the "community of saints" I would like to refer to as the council of resources that can be used to consult and guide and support the journey.

To develop your council of resources, it's good to start by sensing who might be a really good positive resource or guide for you on this particular journey of [state goal]. There are many types of guides who can support you in different ways. They might give you encouragement, provide safety, make specific suggestions, answer questions, provide a listening ground, be good models, motivate you, and so forth. In terms of who might constitute a guide, it could be someone you know in real life – a teacher, a family member, a friend. It could be a historical figure, a spiritual being, or a mythical character. It might even be something like the river or the forest. The important thing is that you find those guides that will be most helpful for you on this journey. Does that make sense?

(Answer any questions.)

To develop the council, a person first centers and attunes to their goal, then asks their creative unconscious to bring forward whatever guides might be most helpful. Generally, two or three guides are optimal for the process.

For each guide identified, a few moments are taken to sense their optimal spatial location (in the surrounding field). This spatializing helps to sense the guide as a distinct experiential presence (rather than merely as an intellectual concept), and also expands the field of awareness beyond the body. Both shifts contribute to generative trance.

As with all generative trance processes, encouragement is given to just let the images and awarenesses come. Any signs of neuromuscular lock are met with relaxation suggestions. For example:

Relax your forehead, relax your shoulders ... that's good ... just let it happen ... that's good ... just be curious as to which image your creative unconscious brings forward.

In this way, a council of resources is opened in a person's field, providing a protective circle as well as a base for sound feedback and guidance.

Step 3: Preparation

Once the council has been developed, the trance work proper can proceed. This starts with the preparation step for generative trance work, involving centering, attunement to positive intention, and resources. In this process, the council members are used as the resources. A person can give a signal – a simple head nod or a finger signal – to indicate completion of this step.

Step 4: Attune to goal: self-contemplation of direction

Once in a generative state, a person can take five minutes to contemplate how they might achieve the goal or realize the intention:

> And in that state of attunement, let yourself take some time ... about five minutes or so ... to begin to contemplate different ways ... different solutions for achieving the goal of [name goal]. Just let any images, thoughts, ideas ... flow into your awareness ... in terms of how to achieve the goal. No need at this point to consciously analyze or force ... just let different possibilities flow from your creative unconscious ...

After five minutes, the person may reorient and share what happened, or move right into the next step.[24]

---

24   As discussed, the "chunking" of a session can vary considerably. If a person needs more structure and smaller pieces of work (for safety purposes), then trance work can be a series of short pieces. Other people need less structure and can flow through a longer session.

Step 5: Receive feedback from each council member

In this next step, feedback is received (in trance) from each council member about a person's plans or ideas. This can be done in different ways. One is to sense the council member in the field, silently ask for their feedback, and then absorb it. Another is to become the council member, either by physically stepping into their position or imagining doing so. From this position, a person senses and witnesses the views and feedback of that council member.

After each council member expresses their feedback, the person moves back into their own position, takes some moments to receive and contemplate the feedback, expresses gratitude, then repeats the process with the next council member. In this shifting through multiple points of reference, primary care is given to maintaining the underlying generative trance through limbic resonance and trance musicality considerations. The whole process takes 15–20 minutes.

Step 6: Reorient to goal: integrate all positions

In the next step, the different perspectives offered by the council of resources, along with a person's own views, are blended into an integration process. Figure 9.9 shows this as a classic example of generative trance integration. The person is represented in the center, surrounded by a "quaterno" of resources. When woven together, they form an integrated "mandala of self".

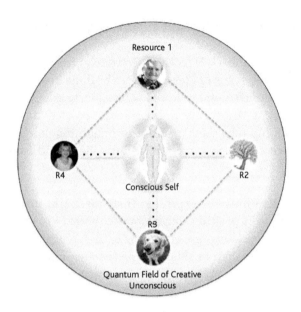

Figure 9.9. Joining with a field of resources to create a generative self

Here is an example of how the integration might be invited:

> And in returning back to center ... taking a breath ... settling in, settling down ... opening up again to a wide field in which you can sense your center ... your positive goal of [name goal] ... and some of the many positions and perspectives about that goal ... your own perspectives ... the feedback offered by [name Guide 1] ... the feedback offered by [name Guide 2] ... and the feedback offered by [name Guide 3] ... and breathing, ... going a little bit deeper ... deep enough to sense all the different presences working in cooperation to achieve that goal ... your own presence ... and the presence of each of the guides in the space around you ... And as you can begin to sense all four presences simultaneously ... like they were members of a symphony orchestra ... all playing together ... members of an intimate team ... each having his or her own wisdom ... each having a unique perspective ... you can begin to sense each part playing harmonies with the other parts ... colors ... images ... sounds ... feelings ... representing the different positions ... harmonizing into an integration ... a patterning ... blending ... harmonizing ... building ... deepening ... quickening ... new patterns emerging from the harmonies ... moving towards an integration ... pulsating ... breathing ... moving towards an integration ... in which all the different

parts come together to form a deeper whole ... and deeper map ... a deeper way of realizing the goal ... feeling that integration come all the way together *noww!*

(Winds of change can be added to "blow the mind" into new spaces.)

(Some moments of silence, then gentle supporting statements.)

That's it ... that's it ... That's good ... a deeper communion ... a beautiful sense of realizing your deepest dreams ... (elaborate for several more minutes)

Steps 7–8: Future orientation and reorientation

These last steps in the work have been covered at length, and of course involve attending to how the reorganizations made in trance can make their way into the ordinary realities of a person's everyday life.

Summary

The *principle of infinite possibilities* is a core element of generative cognitive consciousness. It is a way of guiding our awareness to open to multiple possibilities, especially when what we're doing isn't working. The principle encourages the "divergent thinking" process that is characteristic of creative thinkers and is integral to generative trance.

Of the many ways that this principle can be applied, we have examined five:

1. The suggestion loop of multiple possibilities

2. The generating new choices process

3. The tetralemma process

4. Metaphorical stories

5. The council of resources

Each provides a way to new possibilities at every step of a creative process. Taken together, they illustrate the value and importance of a radiant awareness that is forever extending beyond its present state.

Epilogue

Over the course of the book, we have seen that generative trance work is distinguished by a constellation of inter-related ideas:

1. Life can be lived as a great journey of consciousness.

2. Reality and identity are constructed. This creative process moves through 3 worlds: the original consciousness of content-free luminescence, the quantum field of infinite possibilities, and the classical world of specific actualities.

3. The gateways between these worlds are *filters* that transduce one world into another, like light passing through a stained glass window.

4. The movement through filters allows us to see two levels of reality construction. At the first (quantum) level, a pattern has many different possible forms and values. As it passes through the filter of an observing consciousness (e.g., a nervous system, a social field, a psychological mood), it assumes a specific actual form.

5. These filters may be translucent and open, such that information/ energy *creatively flows* between the worlds – for example, the quantum world of infinite possibility and the classical world of specific actuality – resulting in creative consciousness. Or they may be opaque and closed through the *neuromuscular lock* patterns of fight, flight, freeze, or fold, resulting in a static, isolated consciousness.

6. Trance is a process of creative flow in which reality filters are temporarily loosened, such that old maps and conditioned patterns are relaxed and a creative quantum field is opened. This allows the typically fixed submodalities of identity – body image, memory, beliefs about the future, perception, space and time – to become variable, thereby allowing new identities and realities to be formed.

7. There are many types of trance – some positive, some not.

8. Generative trance is a unique type of positive trance in which mindful self-awareness reciprocally engages with the creative unconscious to birth new identities and realities, especially through the transformation of the underlying reality filters.

9. Generative trance is developed by upgrading three general types of mind filters – somatic, cognitive, and field – to a higher level of consciousness. This higher level adds a new dimension of subtle mindfulness, awakening a "body of bodies," "field of fields," and "mind of minds".

10. Generative trance is distinguished by COSMIC consciousness: centered, open (to mindfulness), subtle awareness, musicality, positive intention, and creative engagement.

11. The sustained presence of this generative consciousness can transform lives in many positive ways, with noticeable increases in happiness, health, helpfulness to others, and healing of self and the world.

Taken together, these ideas suggest a creative life path in which consciousness more deeply participates in the construction, deconstruction, and reconstruction of identity and reality – both at personal and collective levels. What we have covered in these pages is intended as a beginning, not an end.

It's a bit like in martial arts, where being awarded your first black belt means that now you are a beginner, that you now have the basics needed to really train. The principles and processes in the book are intended similarly, to be a basic framework for cultivating generative consciousness.

We can thus say at best:

These are only hints and guesses,

Hints followed by guesses; and the rest

Is prayer, observance, discipline, thought and action.

T. S. Eliot, "The Dry Salvages" from *Four Quartets*

My fervent hope is that you continue to work with whatever has touched or encouraged you in these pages, guided especially by the practical principles of (1) living from a center, (2) opening to a generative field, and (3) creatively engaging whatever comes your way.

To do so, there is no substitute for daily practices. I often emphasize to clients that our life quality is as good as our practices. We usually live our lives around the two pillars of work and love. As important as they are, they involve a lot of responsibility to others. We need a third base, the mind–body practices that cultivate self-awareness. There are many possible practices – walking, meditating, gardening, music, reading, to name a few. The important thing is to find a handful that are really resonant and helpful, and practice them regularly. That will help train the generative state needed for both everyday living and meeting the extraordinary challenges along the way.

Of course, the overwhelming excuse is, *I don't have time.* It's important to realize that *you never will be given the time, you must take it.* Even (or especially) in a very busy life, the inclusion of practices actually creates more time to be and perform in higher quality ways.

These practices will help you better deal with the failures and unexpected experiences of daily life. Most of what we try doesn't work, so it's crucial to develop a skillful relationship to failure, being positively informed and motivated by it, rather than discouraged and defeated.

One helpful practice is to keep coming back to positive intention. It is easy to get lost in problems, giving primary attention to what isn't working or what isn't happening. Joseph Chilton Pearce (1981) calls this the *error-correction error.* He notes that as humans we are guided by various "primary injunctions" such as *walk,* each of which carries a set of secondary processes – e.g,. in learning to walk, we must *crawl, stand, balance, imbalance* (one foot forward), and that old family favorite, *fall.*

Of course, toddlers don't experience falling as a problem or failure. They fall, they get up, they walk again. There comes a time, however, when we learn that we shouldn't fall, that we shouldn't do something, that we shouldn't be a certain way. At that moment, Pearce says, our consciousness shifts from the primary (positive intention) to the secondary "don't fall". We become ensnared in the "error-correction error" of trying to get rid of the problem, and lose track of the deeper positive vision. In practicing the three steps of *drop into center, open into field, attune to positive intention*, we can move forward once again.

This forward path can be supported immensely by *vows of nonviolence.* We too often respond negatively to our failures and mistakes – with self-criticism, going on a binge of some sort, lashing out at others, giving up, etc. *It's this negative response that creates most of the damage, not the mistake itself.* I consider them all forms of self-violence, and deeply encourage clients to make vows that no matter what they do or don't do, they don't deserve to be treated violently, by themselves or others. One of the most helpful findings in learning theory is that punishment doesn't help learning, it just temporarily suppresses behavior. (So as soon as you relax, the old pattern comes back.) Identifying and releasing these conditioned responses of self-violence allows more positive forms of creative engagement with one's experience.

Creative acceptance also allows one to skillfully make use of the many surprises in life. The old adage rings true, *Man plans and God laughs.* While our isolated ego cannot precisely control what happens, it *can* creatively engage with whatever shows up. This, of course, is a core premise of generative trance work: creativity is a conversation between the conscious mind (and its intentions, expectations, desires, etc) and the creative unconscious.

If you look back at the last ten years of your life, it's likely that you didn't predict many, if not most, of the positive developments. So realistically, your ego can't control the future. But you *can* train yourself to stay centered and mindful, set goals and make plans, and develop the inner and outer connections needed for success. Then you can skillfully accept and make positive use of whatever happens, be willing to be forever pleasantly surprised, and learn anew how to best connect with the present moment. It's the combination of the *yin* and the *yang*, the receptive and the active, that allows you to creatively live the great journey of consciousness.

This is what I've tried to convey in the previous pages: that in addition to our individual self-awareness, we are part of a greater wholeness and intelligence that is trying to realize itself. Arthur Koestler (1964) coined the term *holon* to describe a living consciousness that is whole at one level, yet part of a greater whole at the next higher level. This is an excellent description of human beings: we are whole within ourselves, but part of a much greater evolving intelligence. Living this dual-level consciousness is at the heart of the generative self.

There is a story of an old rabbi who walks around town for some time wearing a long black overcoat, his hands stuck in its pockets. When someone finally asks what he's up to, he pulls out his hands to show each holding a strip of paper. The one says, *I am the Divine, I am everything, I am love itself.* The other says, *I am but a speck of dust, here but for a few moments.* As we say in generative trance, *And what a nice thing to know that you can enjoy BOTH at the same time!* This is what we're looking to realize in this work.

Rumi speaks supportively about this crossing between the worlds:

> The breezes at dawn have secrets to tell
>
> Don't go back to sleep.
>
> You must ask for what you really want
>
> Don't go back to sleep.
>
>
> People are going back and forth
>
> Across the threshold
>
> Where the two worlds meet
>
> The door is round and open
>
> Don't go back to sleep.

May you awaken each day more fully into your deepest life path.

References

Barron, F. (1969). *Creative Person, Creative Process*. New York: Holt, Rinehart & Winston.

Bateson, G. (1955). A theory of play and fantasy: a report on the theoretical aspects of the project for study of the role of paradoxes of abstraction in communication. *Psychiatr Res Rep Am Psychiatr Assoc*. 2: 39–51. (Reprinted in Bateson, *Steps to an Ecology of Mind*, pp. 177–193.)

Bateson, G., Jackson, D. D., Haley, J., and Weakland, J. (1956). Toward a theory of schizophrenia. *Behavioral Science* 1: 251–264. (Reprinted in Bateson, *Steps to an Ecology of Mind*, pp. 201–227.)

Bateson, G. (1972). *Steps to an Ecology of Mind: Collected Essays in Anthropology, Psychiatry, Evolution, and Epistemology*. New York: Ballantine Books.

Buber, M. (1923/1958). *I and Thou*, tr. R. G. Smith. New York: Scriber & Sons.

Campbell, J. (1949). *The Hero with a Thousand Faces*. Princeton, NJ: Princeton University Press.

Csíkszentmihályi, M. (1991). *Flow: The Psychology of Optimal Experience*. New York: Harper Collins.

Csíkszentmihályi, M. (1996). *Creativity: Flow and the Psychology of Discovery and Invention*. New York: Harper Perennial.

Dale, C. (2009). *The Subtle Body: An Encyclopedia of Your Energetic Anatomy*. Boulder, CO: Sounds True.

de Mille, A. (1991). *Martha: The Life and Work of Martha Graham*. New York: Knopf Doubleday.

Dunbar, R. (2004). *The Human Story: A New History of Mankind's Evolution*. London: Faber.

Eliade, M. (1963/1998). *Myth and Reality*. Prospects Heights, IL: Waveland Press.

Gendlin, E. (1978). *Focusing*. New York: Bantam.

Gilligan, S. G. (1983). Effects of emotional intensity on learning. Unpublished doctoral dissertation, Stanford University.

Gilligan, S. G. (1987). *Therapeutic Trances: The Cooperation Principle in Ericksonian Hypnotherapy*. New York: Brunner/Mazel.

Gilligan, S. G. (1997). *The Courage to Love: Principles and Practices of Self-Relations Psychotherapy*. New York: Norton Professional Books.

Gilligan, S. G. and Bower, G. H. (1984). Cognitive consequences of emotional arousal. In C. E. Izard, J. Kagan and R. Zajonc (eds.), *Emotions, Cognitions, and Behavior*. New York: Cambridge Press.

Gilligan, S. G. and Dilts, R. (2009). *The Hero's Journey: A Voyage of Self-Discovery*. Carmarthen, Wales: Crown House Publishing.

Gore, B. (2009). *The Ecstatic Experience: Healing Postures for Spirit Journeys*. Rochester, VT: Bear & Co.

Goswami, A. (1993). *The Self-Aware Universe: How Consciousness Creates the World*. New York: Tarcher/Putnam.

Hilgard, E. R. (1965). *Hypnotic Susceptibility*. New York: Harcourt, Brace, Jovanovich.

Holmes T. H. and Rahe R. H. (1967). The social readjustment rating scale. *Journal of Psychosomatic Research* 11(2): 213–218.

Hopton, I. (2005). *Archetypal Postures in the Process of Creativity*. La Fontbelle, France: La Fontbelle Press.

Horowitz, M. J., Duff, D. F., and Stratton, L. O. (1964). Body buffer zone. *Archives of General Psychology* 1(6): 651–656.

Jones, R. (2010). *Nagarjuna: Buddhism's Most Important Philosopher*. New York: Jackson Square Books.

Kaufman, J. C., and Sternberg, R. J. (eds.) (2010). *The Cambridge Handbook of Creativity*. New York: Cambridge University Press.

King, M. L. (1986). *A Testament of Hope: The Essential Writings and Speeches*. New York: Harper Collins.

Koestler, A. (1964). *The Act of Creation: A Study of the Conscious and Unconscious in Science and Art*. New York: Macmillan.

Levine, P. (1997). *Waking the Tiger: Healing Trauma*. Berkeley, CA: North Atlantic Books.

Levine, P. (2010). *In An Unspoken Voice: How the Body Releases Trauma and Restores Goodness*. Berkeley, CA: North Atlantic Books.

McGilchrist, I. (2009). *The Master and His Emissary: The Divided Brain and the Making of the Western World*. New Haven, CT: Yale University Press.

McGilchrist, I. (2010). The divided brain and the making of the Western world (video). Available from http://www.thersa.org/events/video/vision-videos/iain-mcgilchrist (accessed January 26, 2011).

Malloch, S. and Trevarthen, C. (eds.) (2009). *Communicative Musicality: Exploring the Basis of Human Companionship*. Oxford: Oxford University Press.

O'Donohue, J. (1997). *Anam Cara: A Book of Celtic Wisdom*. New York: HarperCollins.

Orne, M. T. (1959). The nature of hypnosis artifact and essence. *Journal of Abnormal and Social Psychology* 58: 277–299.

Osbon, D. (1991). *Reflections on the Art of Living: A Joseph Campbell Companion*. New York: HarperCollins.

Pearce, J. C. (1981). *The Bond of Power*. New York: Dutton.

Pribram, K. (1971). *Languages of the Brain: Experimental Paradoxes and Principles in Neuropsychology*. Englewood Cliffs, NJ: Prentice Hall.

Rahe, R. H. and Arthur, R. J. (1978). Life change and illness studies: past history and future directions. *Journal of Human Stress* 4(1): 3–15.

Ramachandran, V. S. (2011). *The Tell-Tale Brain: A Neuroscientist's Quest for What Makes Us Human*. New York: Norton.

Ramachandran, V. S. and Blakeslee, S. (1999). *Phantoms in the Brain: Probing the Mysteries of the Human Mind*. New York: Harper.

Roberts, M. (1996). *The Man Who Listens to Horses*. New York: Ballantine Books.

Ross, L. (1977). The intuitive psychologist and his shortcomings: distortions in the attribution process. In L. Berkowitz (ed.), *Advances in Experimental Social Psychology*, Vol. 10. New York: Academic Press, pp. 173–220.

Rossi, E. L. (ed.) (1980a). *The Collected Papers of Milton Erickson on Hypnosis*, Vol. 1: The *Nature of Hypnosis and Suggestion*. New York: Irvington.

Rossi, E. L. (ed.) (1980b). *The Collected Papers of Milton Erickson on Hypnosis*, Vol. 4: *Innovative Psychotherapy*. New York: Irvington.

Runco, M. A. (1991). *Divergent Thinking*. Norwood, NJ: Ablex Publishing.

Sachs, O. (2006). The power of music. *Brain* 129(10): 2528–2532.

Sapolsky, R. M. (1988). *Why Zebras Don't Get Ulcers: An Updated Guide to Stress, Stress Related Diseases, and Coping*. New York: W.H. Freeman.

Selye, H. (1956). *The Stress of Life*. New York: McGraw Hill.

Shapiro, F. (2001). *Eye Movement Desensitization and Reprocessing (EMDR): Basic Principles, Protocols, and Procedures*, 2nd edn. New York: Guilford.

Shapiro, F. (ed.) (2002). *EMDR as an Integrative Psychotherapy Approach: Experts of Diverse Orientations Explore the Paradigm Prism*. Washington, DC: APA Books.

Wallas, G. (1926). *The Art of Thought*. New York: Harcourt, Brace and Co.

Wangyal, T. (2002) *Healing with Form, Energy, and Light: The Five Elements in Tibetan Shamanism, Tantra, and Dzogchen*. Ithaca, NY: Snow Lion Publications.

Watzlawick, P., Weakland, J., and Fisch, R. (1974). *Change: Principles of Problem Formation and Problem Resolution*. New York: Norton.

Wilber, K. (2001). *A Brief History of Everything*. Boston, MA: Shambhala.

Yeshe, T. (1987). *Introduction to Tantra: The Transformation of Desire*. Boston, MA: Wisdom Publications.